Learn Chinese

Without

WRITING 2

The Chinese Alphabets Book

Declutter Your Mind to Learn Chinese

W.Q. BLOSH

Learn Chinese Without Writing 2
The Chinese Alphabets Book
W.Q. BLOSH

FIRST EDITION

Written and designed by W.Q. BLOSH

Email: wqblosh@gmail.com

ISBN: 978-981-09-8641-4 (Paperback)

Printed by IngramSparks

PREFACE

Introduction

This book is a continuation of the first book *Learn Chinese Without Writing (LCWW1)*. It shares the same goal of helping you to develop the ability to extract critical information—*structures, patterns and relationships between strokes*—from Chinese characters.

If you have read *LCWW1*, this book will be easy for you. If you have not read it, there are two revision exercises for the 35 strokes and a recap of the key idea 'Triple ABCs Concept' and geometry concepts.

As we are introducing new concepts and terminologies on how to analyse Chinese characters—never taught elsewhere—we recommend that you start from *LCWW1* even if you already know Chinese. Concepts you learnt in *LCWW1* will be applied in this and subsequent books.

Challenges

Chinese language is not an exact science. It was never a practice to explain every single detail (*e.g. how long a stroke should be, how close or far apart the strokes should be, where do they intersect exactly*). It is always at the discretion of the learner after he/she has observed, practiced, reflected and internalised his/her learning. This tacit learning habit is something many native learners do instinctively without realising. For foreign learners, some form of coaching is definitely required but there is hardly any resource available at the point of creating these books.

It was a challenge to create this book, describing the characteristics of Chinese characters and getting them organised. It was difficult because there was no precedent and we have to think differently beyond what was taught.

A Sample of qTRAIL

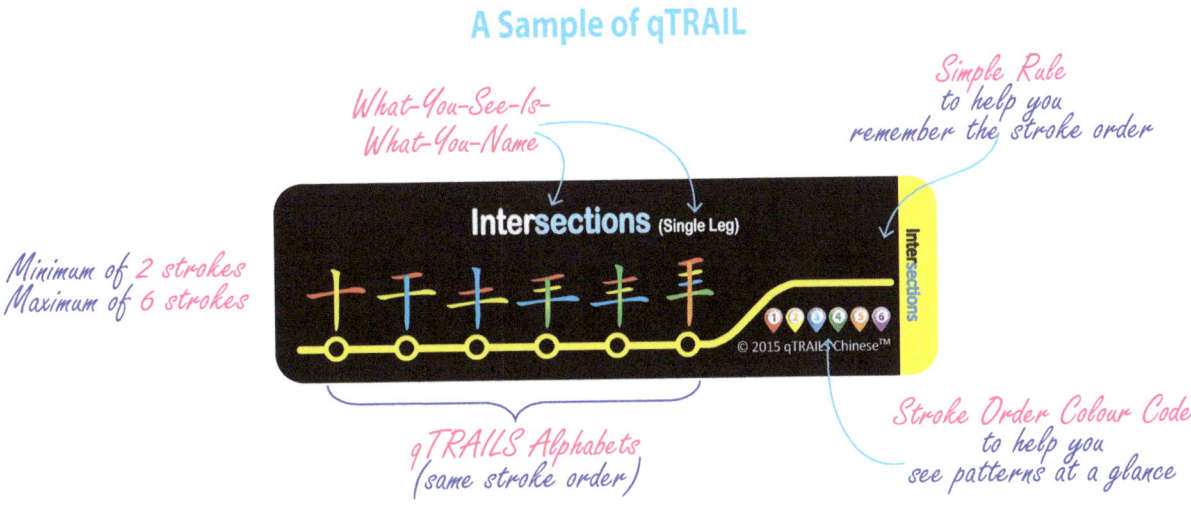

What-You-See-Is-What-You-Name

Simple Rule to help you remember the stroke order

Minimum of 2 strokes
Maximum of 6 strokes

qTRAILS Alphabets (same stroke order)

Stroke Order Colour Code to help you see patterns at a glance

Behind-the-Scene

Understanding the daunting tasks all beginners have to go through that require full capacity of their brains, we figure out that we have to find some patterns in Chinese characters and work out the mechanisms on how to 'construct' these characters. If learners have clear guidance, then they could decipher, configure, extrapolate ... on their own. They will feel empowered to possess the ability to 'see' Chinese characters in a different light.

Hence, we decided to work backwards...starting with 5,000 plus *(now more are included)* **frequently-used simplified Chinese characters** and dissected each of them in unconventional ways. The old way of dividing characters is not good enough to analyse and classify them by appearance. We analysed how the parts and strokes of each character were put together ...this would be the way we will take them apart for scrutiny.

Then we classified the **qTRAILS Alphabets**—parts with the same stroke pattern—as a group and got 32 stroke patterns for *basic alphabets*. *Variations* can be derived from these 32 stroke patterns by modifying or adding a stroke to the basic alphabets. There are a few *exceptions*. The maximum number of strokes for these Chinese alphabets is six (6) and the minimum number is two (2).

Overview of 3 Books

In *LCWW1*, you 'see' through the lenses of Geometry ... you see shapes, curves, lines, angles. In this book *LCWW2*, you will see patterns through the **stroke order** of Chinese characters. To help you remember them better, we lined up parts with the same stroke pattern on a trail. We call it **qTRAIL** *(pronounced as 'q-TRAIL') (quick trail)*. The parts on the trails are called **qTRAILS Alphabets** *(see diagram on previous page)*. Like what we did in LCWW1, we hope to develop your ability to 'see' patterns at a glance—this time with the use of colours. Six colours will be used to show you the sequence the strokes of each alphabet have to be written.

In the upcoming book *LCWW3*, you will learn to see patterns through structures . If *LCWW2* is the '**Chinese Alphabets Book**', then *LCWW3* will be the '**Chinese Spelling Book**', that is it shows you how to 'spell' (construct) Chinese characters. In contrast to English words which are always spelt from left to right, Chinese characters have more than a dozen types of basic structures. When these structures are combined to form complex structures, there is a myriad of possibilities. *LCWW2* shows you the stroke order, *LCWW3* will show you the part order of characters.

Chinese Strokes Book

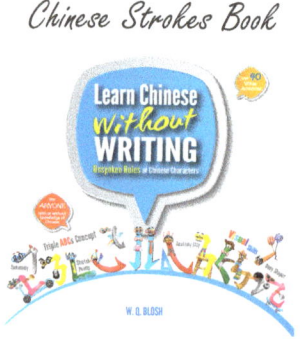

Chinese Alphabets Book

Chinese Spelling Book

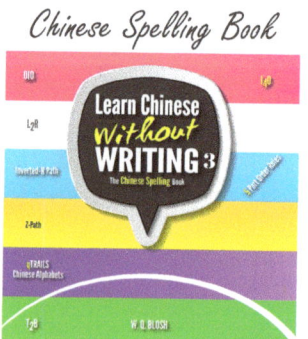

Overview of 3 Books

Book 1
35 Strokes

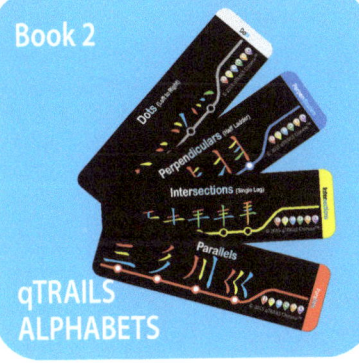

Book 2
32 Stroke Patterns
240 qTRAILS Alphabets

Book 3
Structures of
Chinese Characters

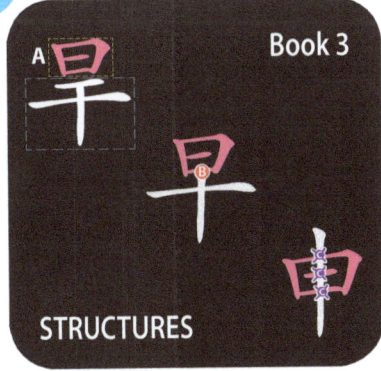

Learn Through Colours

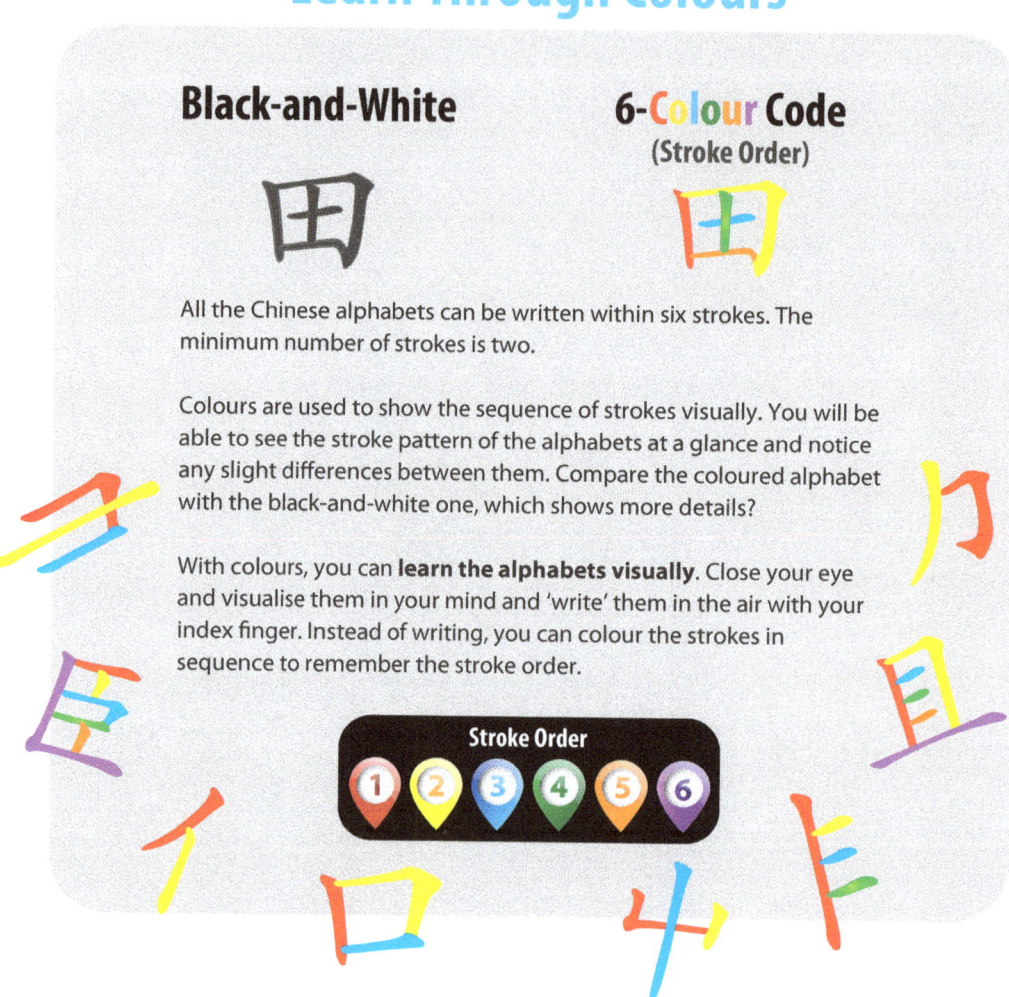

Black-and-White

6-Colour Code
(Stroke Order)

All the Chinese alphabets can be written within six strokes. The minimum number of strokes is two.

Colours are used to show the sequence of strokes visually. You will be able to see the stroke pattern of the alphabets at a glance and notice any slight differences between them. Compare the coloured alphabet with the black-and-white one, which shows more details?

With colours, you can **learn the alphabets visually**. Close your eye and visualise them in your mind and 'write' them in the air with your index finger. Instead of writing, you can colour the strokes in sequence to remember the stroke order.

Stroke Order
1 2 3 4 5 6

Why...

Since the invention of writing, the world has been transformed and our minds have been extended. Our ability to write help us to pass on our knowledge and inspiration and enhance our appreciation of the world and our capacities for learning and communication.

Quick Characters Recognition

Like in other languages, the need to write by hand has greatly diminished but the need to recognise words or characters is as important. Even with the aid of electronic devices that limit the range of words to choose from when inputting text, our grasp of the language still depends on our ability to recognise and use words. Our books focus on building the ability to *learn visually* by seeing patterns and colours in characters which will increase the accuracy and speed of character recognition.

Play Chinese Word Games

Another reason for doing this is it is difficult to 'play' Chinese characters. You can name so many English word games (*crossword puzzles, scrabble, boggle, word search*) that help you learn and remember words through fun but you can hardly find any Chinese word games, mainly due the complexities and lack of common elements of Chinese characters (*due to the way it has been taught till now*). Hence, you can see that the fun of playing Chinese characters is still yet to be explored. Discovering the Chinese Alphabets of Chinese characters laid the foundation for such possibilities to materialise some day.

When Chinese language can be made easier for all people, more people will be exposed to another world of thinking, hence extending another of our capability.

Why do we include so many activities in a book?

The 32 stroke patterns could be presented in a sheet of paper, why a 300-page book?

By going through the different ways of learning you give the new learning multiple layers of meaning. You will be engaging with the content in different ways.

We believe that when learning is easy, it is often superficial and soon forgotten. When learning is effortful, it changes the brain, makes new connections and creates stronger memory.

So you will need to Interact with the book. This is NOT a book to be read from start to end. There are plenty of activities to do.

Learn visually through guided observation

Learn physically by writing in the air with your finger or colouring

Learn analytically by analysing the components (*e.g. ATH, AOB, similarities and differences*)

Learn aurally by hearing yourself read out the rules (*e.g. "Horizontals first, Vertical last"*)

Reflect more
Do more analysis on your own to differentiate the Chinese alphabets.

It's Easy! It's Intuitive!

Look at these symbols. Make a good guess and match each group to a suitable name based on their appearance.

Enclosure / Frame

Perpendiculars

Dots

Intersections

Flag

Split & Cross

Complete this activity before continuing.

How to remember this character?

How would you remember this character? Divide this character to show
how you would attempt to remember this character.

Suggestion:
You can try to break it down into strokes or parts to help you remember the character.

Complete this activity before continuing.

Write this word

1. Write this word:

1 2 3 4 5 6 7 8 9 10 11 12
extravaganza

2. Write the same word but in this order:

a) Write the the 11th, 7th, 4th, 3rd, 1st alphabets first and leave space for the remaining alphabets

b) Then fill in the 12th, 10th, 9th, 8th, 6th, 5th, 2nd alphabets.

Note: Do not use any other tool, just a pen/pencil.

Complete this activity before continuing.

Content

List of Activities

Introduction

'PILE' OF CHARACTERS

For many new learners, the more characters they 'collect', the higher the pile of characters become—unorganised and unreachable.

To declutter, there must be a 'clutter' in the first place. As many people would have experienced ... the more possessions they own, the more time and effort is required to organise and maintain them. From time to time, they have to throw out stuff they do not need—part of the process of decluttering.

There are thousands of Chinese characters. Unlike English, which can be organised alphabetically, there is no easy way to organise characters for easy memory. When you acquire Chinese characters without a systematic way to 'store' them in your memory, you will have trouble retrieving them when you need them. It is like piling up your physical possessions without an organised storage and retrieval system. This book helps you to DECLUTTER and get organised!

What is a clutter?

CLUTTER is
- A confusing or disorderly state or collection and a possible symptom of compulsive hoarding.

- To fill or cover with scattered things

- To jumble

- To fill or litter with things in a disorderly manner

Why does your mind get 'cluttered' when learning Chinese?

Poorly Defined Scope of Learning

In some books, websites and forums, writers provided advice without differentiating between simplified and traditional Chinese characters. Worse still some even provided advice spanning across several East Asian languages (e.g. Japanese, Korean, Vietnamese and Cantonese). Even though there are many common characters in these languages, they are very different languages in terms of pronunciation and the range of characters used. Some of the characters in one language could appear to be very alien to speakers of another language.

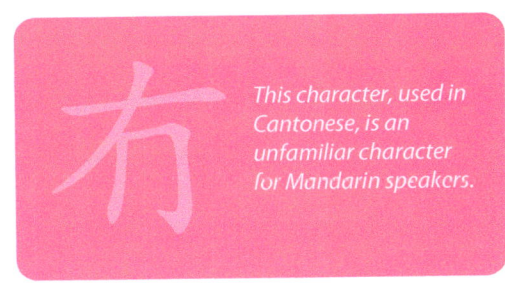

This character, used in Cantonese, is an unfamiliar character for Mandarin speakers.

Chinese
forced, reluctantly

Japanese
studying, studies

Simplified

Book

Traditional

Simplified

Painting

Traditional

Sometimes, even when the same characters are used, the meaning could be very different. For example. these characters are used in Chinese and Japanese but they have different meanings and pronunciation.

You also need to differentiate between simplified and traditional Chinese characters, the former are derived from the latter. Characters sharing the same meaning could be written very differently.

Poor Storage and Retrieval System

A good storage and retrieval system for anything —physical or mental—requires well-thought designs that take into consideration all the possibilities. It needs to have a clear framework and easy-to-understand guidelines so that everyone stores and retrieves things the same way.

Sadly, it has always been difficult to classify Chinese characters. The common classification methods are by sound or parts (radicals) or stroke count. Chinese characters were not classified by appearance. Hence, when you encounter a new character that you do not know its meaning and pronunciation, it is difficult to look up this character in a paper dictionary or to key it into an electronic device. You have to know how to pronounce the character or break it down into its components, which can be difficult for beginners.

When learning gets messy, your mind becomes cluttered, as a result you may lose confidence in learning and get really frustrated. You may find that learning Chinese is difficult because there is no order or systematic learning. The more characters you acquire, the higher the stack of characters piled up. They take up a lot of your memory space, like a computer that has not done defragmentation for a long time. Even though you know these characters, you will find it difficult to recall them when you need them.

Why you need to 'declutter your mind to learn Chinese'?

MENTAL CLUTTER gets in the way of being able to think clearly and focus on what really matters.

Without a mental map of Chinese characters, it is difficult to see the similarities and differences between characters. The brain gets cluttered when more characters are added.

Decluttering the mind requires us to become intentional on where we place our attention and how we spend our time and energy.

Get Organised to Free Up Mental Space

Here are the ways we help you to declutter your mind to learn Chinese

1. Identify What is Essential to Learn and Prioritise

Determine if you are learning simplifed or traditional Chinese characters. This series of books focus on *simplified* Chinese characters only.

Focus on one task at a time and clear away everything else. Learn to 'see' before learning how to speak, read and write. Focusing on appearance is easier to start and master and this will give you confidence to continue. Pronunciation requires more time as you need to train the muscles in your tongue and attune your ears to the new sounds.

3. Make it Manageable

When you know that what you need to learn is finite, that is there is a fixed number of alphabets that you need to learn, you will have more confidence to manage your learning. For instance, in English there are only 26 alphabets and all words must be formed with them and they are always arranged from left to right.

For Chinese language, if you know that there is a fixed number parts that you are going to encounter, you will find that each new character you learn are made up of parts you are familiar and it is not a totally new encounter. You know where the boundaries are, as there will not be new encounters that will surprise or stress you.

2. See Patterns and Build Easy Storage and Retrieval

If you are able to notice patterns in characters, you can develop a way to classify and store them. Learn a systematic way of storing and retrieving characters by their appearance.

4. Apply 80/20 Rule

Instead of learning a few thousands characters, learn 200 over alphabets which can be classified into 32 stroke patterns!

Instead of learning every possible structures of Chinese characters, learn only the basic structures and how they can be applied to decipher characters with more complex structures in subsequent books.

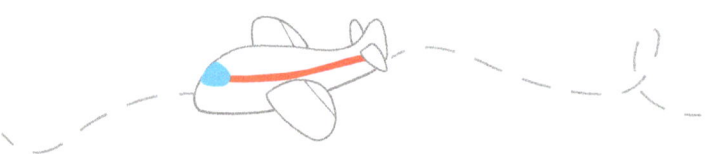

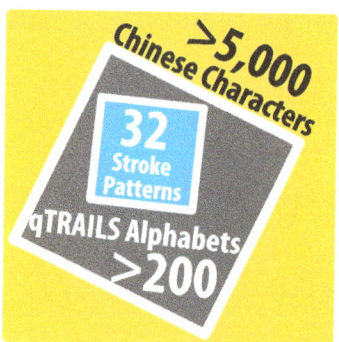

5. Put Routine Work on Auto-Pilot Mode

If you know that there are standard ways to decipher characters and write them, you can build routines that train you to work on an auto-pilot mode without much effort. Efforts can be diverted for other learning.

6. Break Old Habits

Turn unmindful writing practices into purposeful learning activities. Engage yourself through other modes of learning *(e.g. hands-on activities; colorful visual graphics)*. Discard old memories that hinder your learning.

7. Reflection

Reflecting on what you have just learnt help you to consolidate the knowledge you have just picked up. Relating what you have learnt to the languages you know and your own experiences could help you gain different perspectives.

Reflection work could also become good summary of what you have learnt and can be used for easy quick reference later. Do not skip this. Answers not provided though.

What-You-See-Is-What-You-Name

Check answers here.

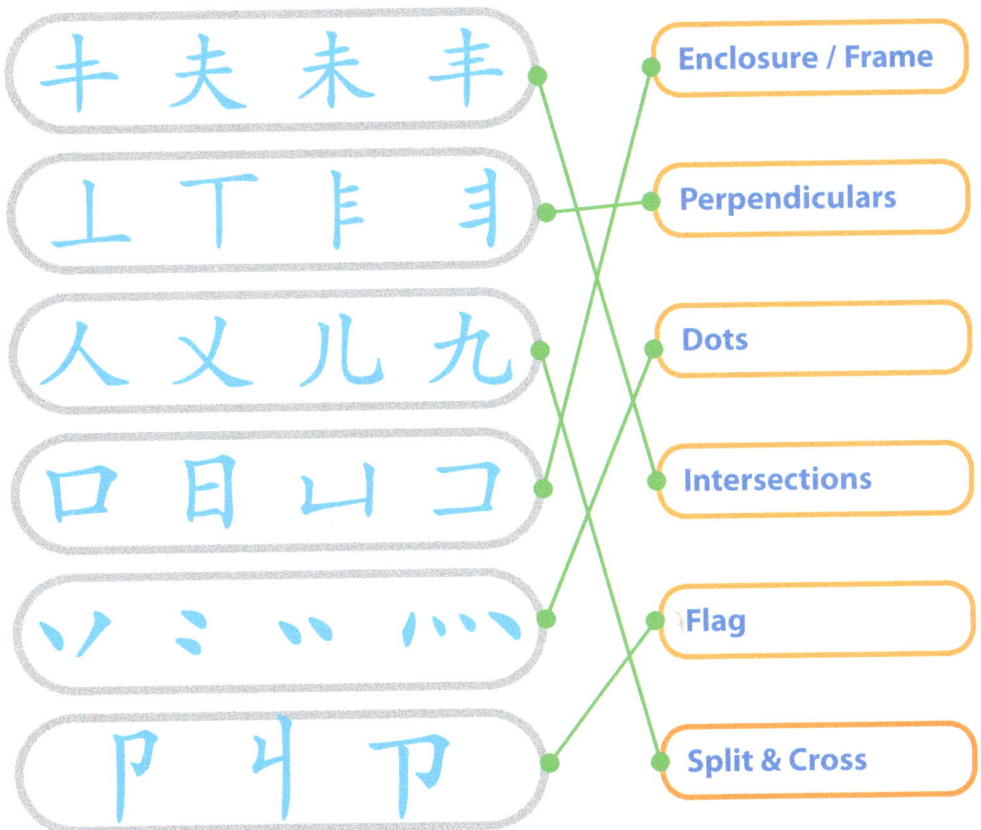

Did you get them correct? Like in the first book, the qTRAILS Alphabets are also named according to their appearance.

Stroke-by-Stroke vs Part-by-Part

Which of these two methods did you use?

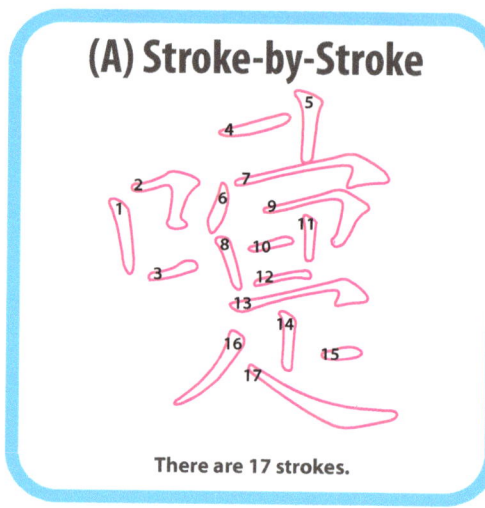

(A) Stroke-by-Stroke

There are 17 strokes.

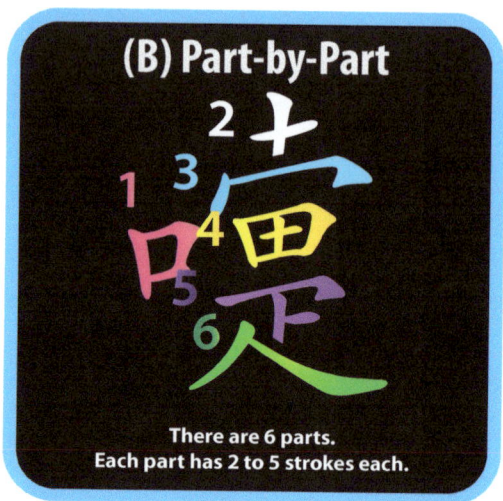

(B) Part-by-Part

There are 6 parts.
Each part has 2 to 5 strokes each.

Compare 17 strokes with 6 parts, which is easier to remember?

It is obvious that learning a character Part-by-Part (PBP) is easier. These parts function like English alphabets—they are repeatedly used to create different Chinese characters.

Many learners will counter that they are already using the PBP method, as they can recognise the same components in different characters.

The value-added contribution that we make here is to identify and organise these 200 over alphabets systematically in 32 stroke patterns. This further reduce the mental demand required to remember the alphabets and their stroke order.

Redefining Composition of Characters

Through this series of books, we are seeking to redefine our understanding on the composition of Chinese characters. Chinese characters are composed by parts which consist of **qTRAILS Alphabet(s)** and/or **stroke(s)**.

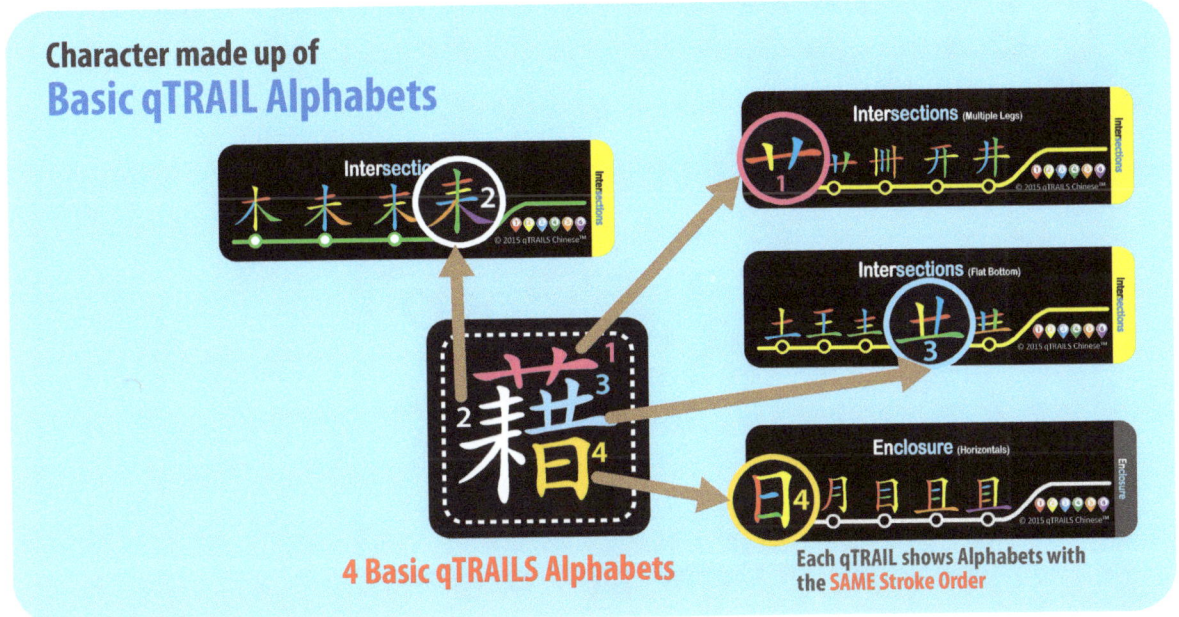

Character made up of
Basic qTRAIL Alphabets

4 Basic qTRAILS Alphabets

Each qTRAIL shows Alphabets with the SAME Stroke Order

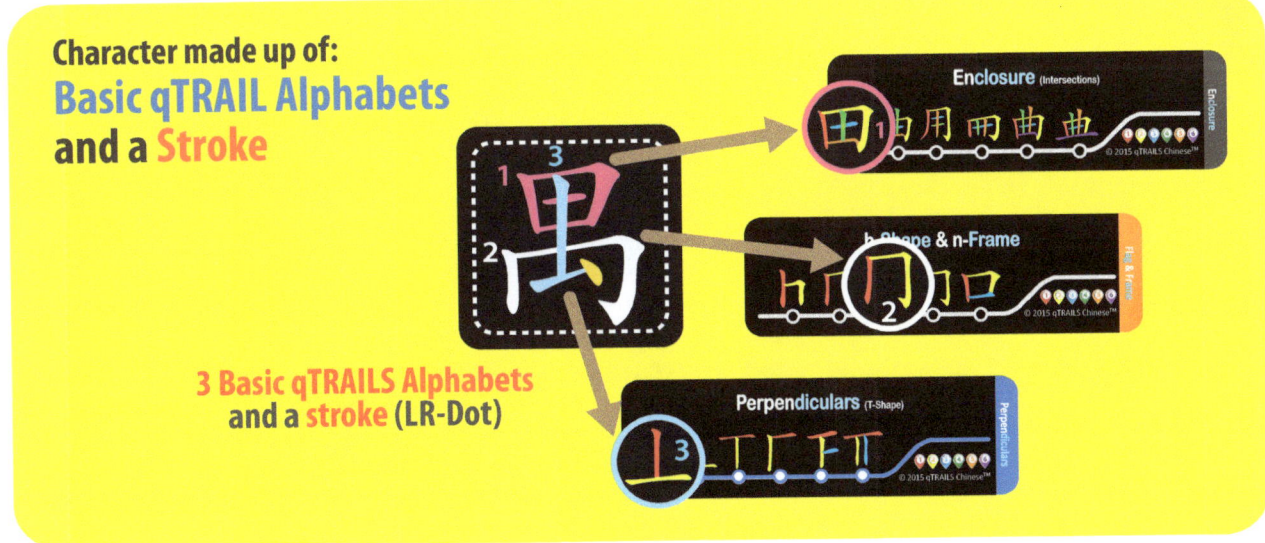

Character made up of:
Basic qTRAIL Alphabets
and a Stroke

3 Basic qTRAILS Alphabets
and a stroke (LR-Dot)

What You'll Learn

1 *Chinese Alphabets*

Write Chinese Alphabets in correct stroke order

Differentiate between similar-looking alphabets

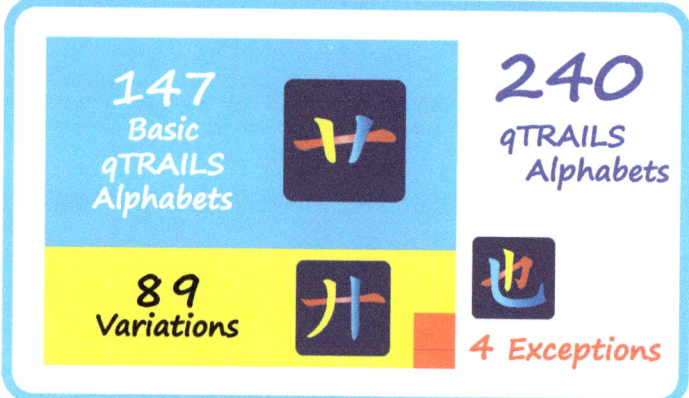

147 Basic qTRAILS Alphabets

240 qTRAILS Alphabets

89 Variations

4 Exceptions

2 *Stroke Order*

Learn 32 Stroke Patterns

NOTE: In LCWW3 you will learn how to combine them to form frequently-used simplified Chinese characters easily.

Target audiences

Anyone, with or without any knowledge of Chinese. Whether you are a beginner or an advanced learner, the content here will be new to you. Everyone will benefit from the content as it was never published elsewhere.

Is it Necessary to Write Chinese Characters in a Certain Order?

Is it really necessary to write the strokes of Chinese characters
in a certain order?
Can't I just start from any stroke?
Can I change the stroke order?

Why Write in a Certain Order?

Refer to the activity 'Write this word' on page _x_.

For people who are used to writing words in a left to right orientation, that activity could be disorientating. It requires you to gauge the space that each alphabet takes up and the spaces between alphabets. Was your writing slower when you did not write in the usual left to right order? In the second activity, were the alphabets of different sizes and not as neat and organised?

Only 'One Order'

In many languages, there is only one way to write, that is from left to right, no alphabet is skipped. Hence, there is really no need to teach the order of alphabets or strokes.

Many Possible Orders

In Chinese, there are so many possible starting points within the box and so many possible combinations of alphabets and strokes. Hence, it is easier and faster to write if there is a standard order to write. When the same character is always written in a particular order, it becomes auto-pilot and you develop your muscle memory. It is a procedural memory that helps you to become very good at writing Chinese characters without really thinking.

Who determined the stroke order of these characters?

The stroke order we introduced in this book is based on the recommended stroke order stipulated by China authorities for simplified Chinese characters. There are a few exceptions that we recommended a different order after due consideration and for easier memory. We will explain further in LCWW3 when we will discuss how to decode Chinese characters.

Can I vary the stroke order?

At the beginning, it is easier to start with the given order as it will help you to remember characters and distinguish between similar ones. Slowly, you will develop your own style of writing after learning 'tonnes' of characters.

The Story II ...
Going to the Boot Camps

To get ready for actual performances, the Performers are going to boot camps . . .

They'll be trained on how to make **Chinese APLHABETS (Partial Formations)** (Each alphabet is formed by 2 to 6 perfomers)

3 to 6 alphabets with the **same stroke order** are grouped on a **qTRAIL**

In each Boot Camp, they'll learn to create alphabets from **similar qTRAILS**

In actual performances, they will combine these alphabets quickly to create **characters (full formations)**.

Use Your Imagination

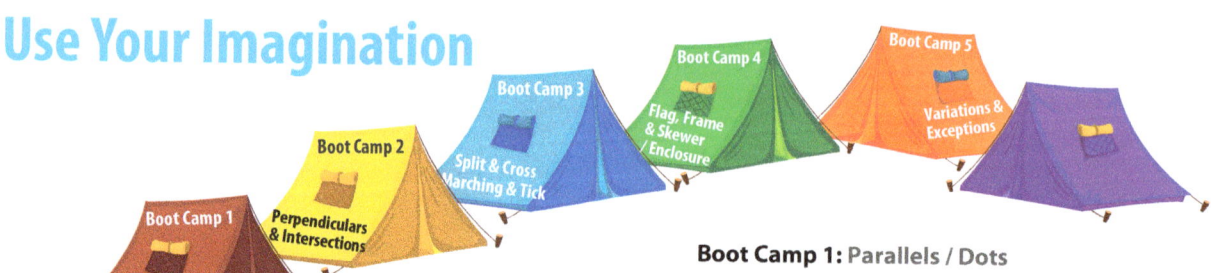

In LCWW1, we imagined strokes as PERFORMERS whose jobs are to create a FORMATION (character) within a BOX STAGE during actual performance.

Boot Camps

To help the performers remember the routines and perform to excellence during actual performances, they have to go through boot camps. During the camps, they will learn to create PARTIAL FORMATIONS (qTRAILS Alphabets) and each of them has to get into position in the correct order (stroke order).

qTRAILS

The training during boot camps is made more effective by organising parts that have the same stroke order on the same trail. It is called a *qTRAIL* (quick trail). Performers will learn similiar qTRAILS in a boot camp. There are five boot camps:

Boot Camp 1: Parallels / Dots

Boot Camp 2: Perpendiculars / Intersections

Boot Camp 3: Split and Cross / Marching & Tick

Boot Camp 4: Flag, Frame & Skewer / Enclosure

Boot Camp 5: Variations / Exceptions

In the first four camps, they will learn basic alphabets and in the last camp they will learn how to vary the basic alphabets to create varied alphabets and exceptions.

Participants in Each Boot Camp

30 out of 35 performers will participate in the boot camps. Only Vertical, Horizontal, RL-Slash and LR-Slash will participate in all the camps.

> ## Terms Used in the Story
> * Strokes = Performers
> * Chinese Alphabets = Partial Formations
> * Characters = Formations

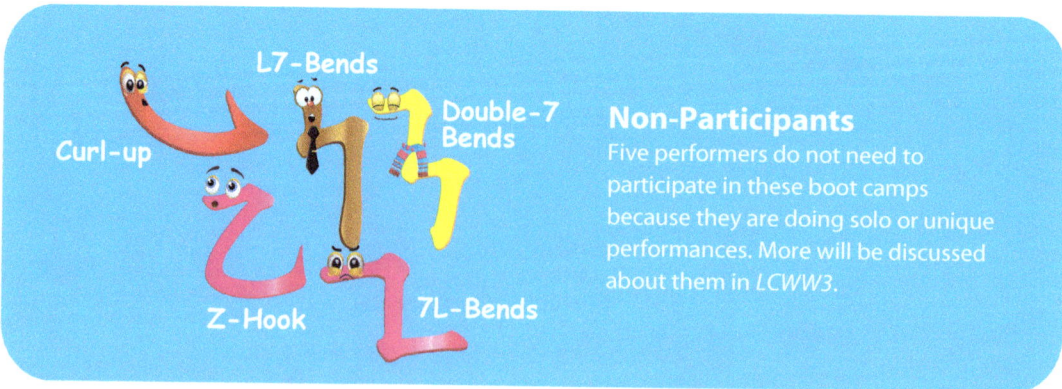

Non-Participants

Five performers do not need to participate in these boot camps because they are doing solo or unique performances. More will be discussed about them in *LCWW3*.

Recap

Do these two activities to learn about the 35 strokes before continuing

Go to Page 16

Revision 1: 35 Strokes Poster

If you have not read *LCWW1*, check the answers at the back of the book for this activity, remember their names.

1. Recall the name of each stroke and write the name beside the stroke.

2. Colour the strokes to make them more attractive.

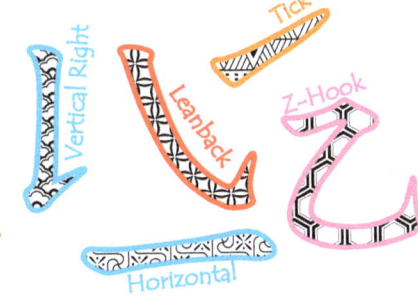

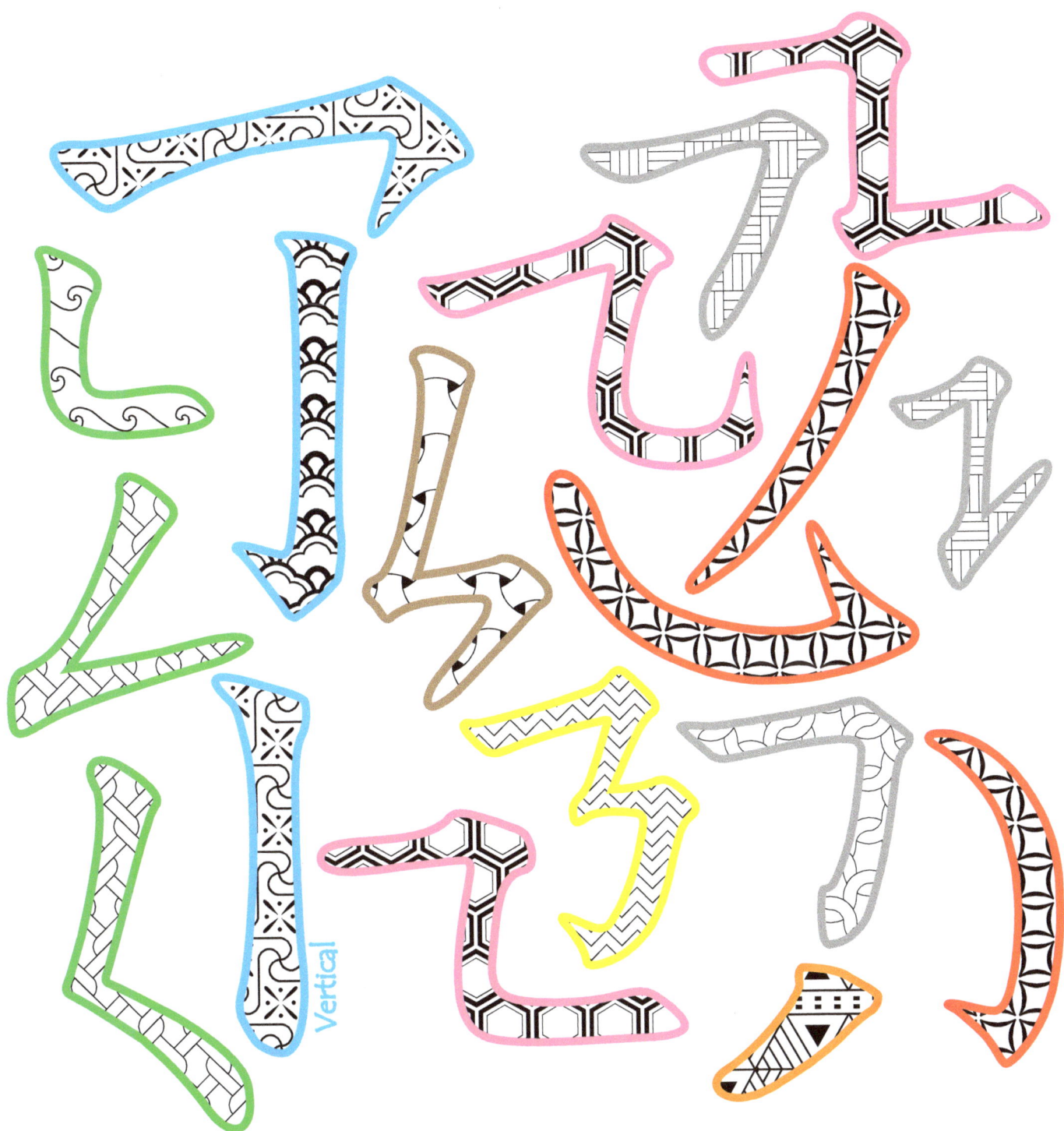

Vertical

Revision on 35 Strokes

Revision 2: Strokes Flash Cards

Go to Page 285

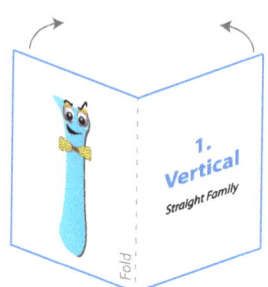

Flash Cards Creation

Create flash cards to revise the 35 strokes taught in (*LCWW1*).

1. Draw the stroke in the box next to its name. See examples given.

2. Check the answers for Revision 1 to make sure that the strokes drawn are correct.

3. Colour the strokes and 'decorate' the cards to create colourful learning cards

4. Cut out the cards along the given lines. Note each card is made up of <u>two</u> boxes.

5. Fold along the dotted line on each card and your flash cards are done.

Strokes Revisions

Revise the strokes using these flash cards.

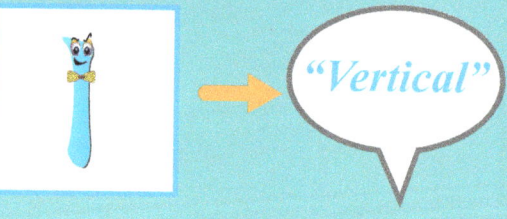

Revision Exercise A

1. Put all the cards into a stack with the **strokes** facing up.

2. Pick a random card.

3. **Look at the stroke and call out its name.**

"*Vertical*"

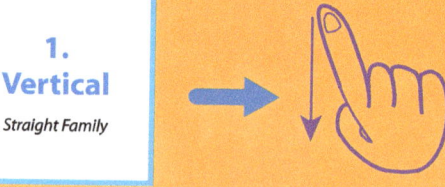

Revision Exercise B

1. Put all the cards into a stack with the **names** facing up.

2. Pick a random card.

3. **Look at the stroke name and 'draw' the stroke in the air or on paper.**

1.
Vertical

Straight Family

Recap on Triple ABCs Concepts

1st Set of ABC (ABC1)
FEATURES OF STROKES

Angles

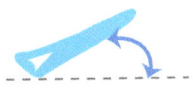

Angle to Horizontal (ATH):
The angle a stroke makes with the horizontal.

Bends

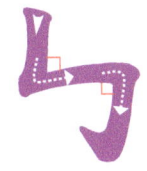

Angle of **B**end (AOB):
This applies to strokes from the Bends Families only. The angle is broadly classified as '**Acute**' (zero to 90 degrees) or '**Right-angled**' (90 degrees).

Curves

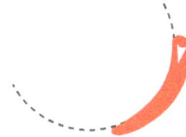

Curvature
It is about the curviness of strokes. It can be shown by drawing a circle with arc that has the same curvature as a stroke.

2nd Set of ABC (ABC2)
WAYS OF COMBINING THE STROKES

Apart

Apart
Strokes not touching one another.

Bonding

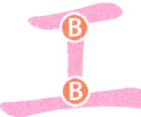

Bonding
One point of a stroke touches another stroke.
The point of contact is a **B**ond Point (BP).

Crossing

Crossing
Two strokes intersecting each other.
The point of contact is a **C**ross Point (CP).

Observe the distance of a BP/CP from the head or tail of a stroke.

The third set of ABC (Adaptation, Balance and Centre) will be discussed in LCWW3.

Geometry Concepts

The Geometry and Triple ABCs Concepts will be applied to analyse qTRAILS Alphabets in the 'Anatomy of Chinese Alphabets'. You will be guided to do the analysis gradually.

For more detailed information on these concepts, please read LCWW1.

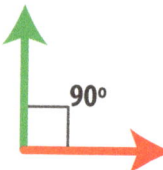

Angle of Joint (AOJ):
The angle two strokes make at the Bond Point or Cross Point.

1. Angles

a) Right angle

90°

b) Acute angle

> 0°
< 90°

2. Slopes

a) Positive gradient

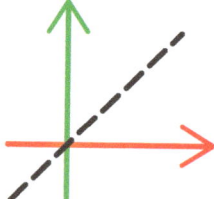

b) Negative gradient

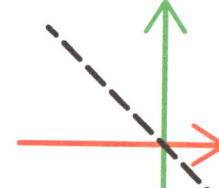

What You Need to Do

To remember the 32 qTRAILS better, you can go through these 5 ways of interacting with each qTRAIL.

 **1** *(1) Close your eyes and visualise these Chinese alphabets in your mind.*

 **2** *(2) Analyse these Chinese alphabets*

 **3** *(3) Read the rules aloud.*

 **4** *(4) Trace the strokes with a finger or colour them according to the given stroke order.*

 **5** *(5) Colour the alphabets in the given stroke order.*

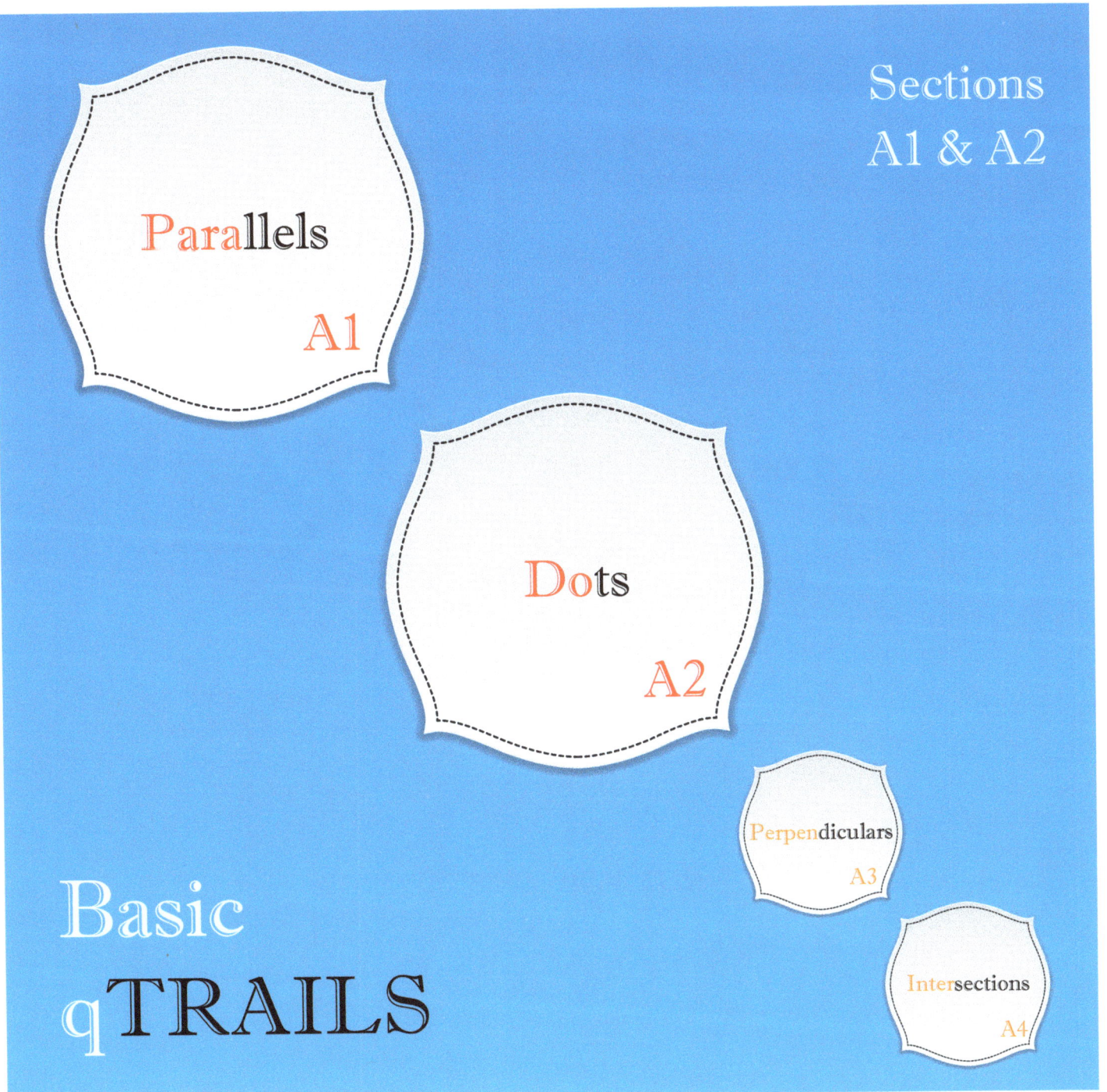

Parallels

A1

Dots

A2

Perpendiculars

A3

Intersections

A4

Basic
qTRAILS

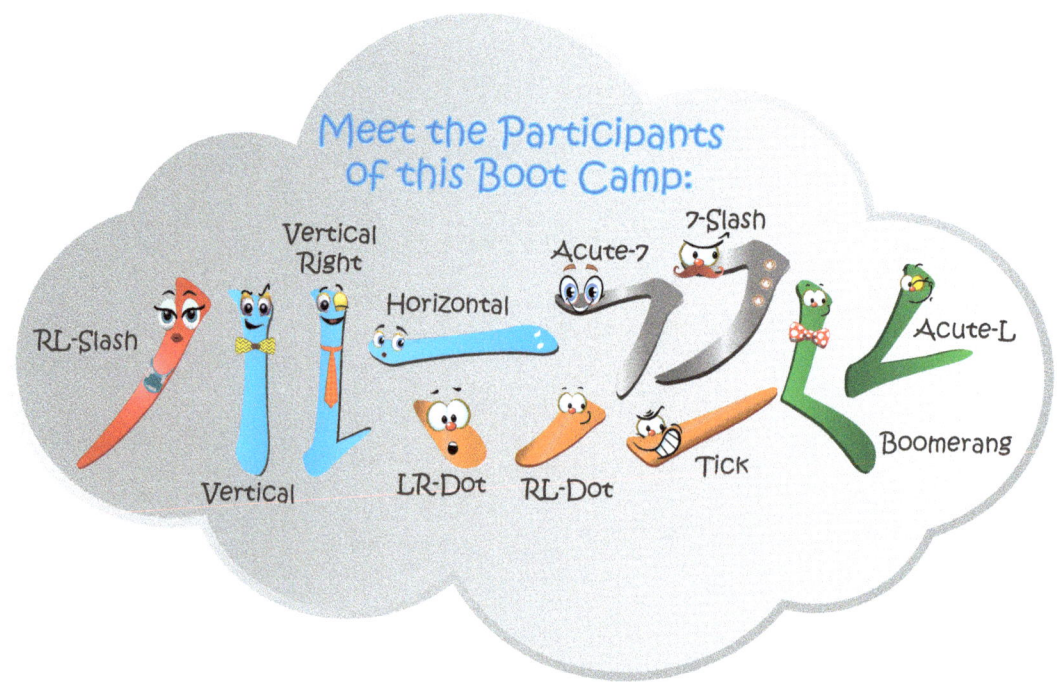

Boot Camp 1
Parallels and Dots
These 11 performers come from 5 families.

Parallels

1

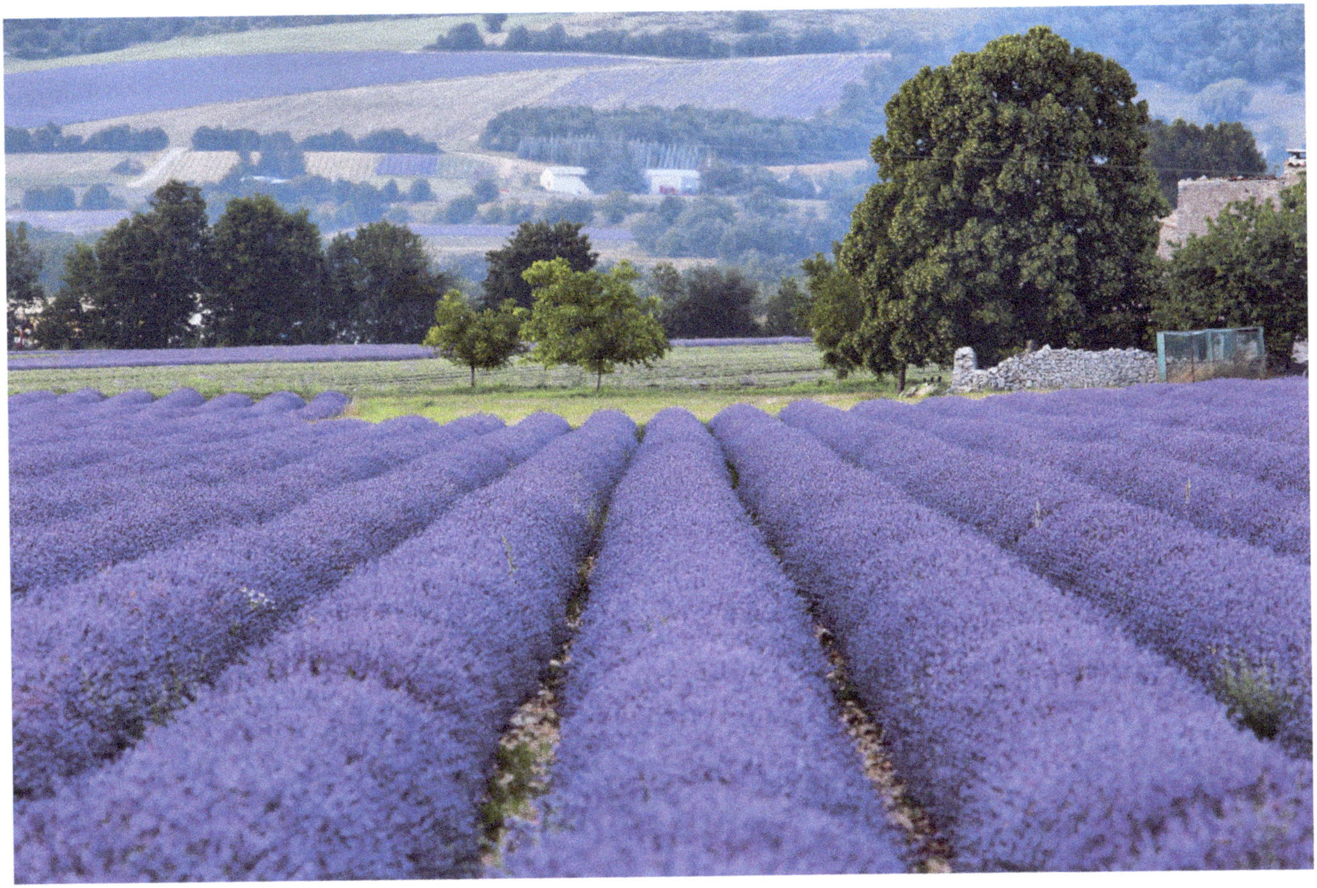

Parallels
(1) Parallels

① Parallels

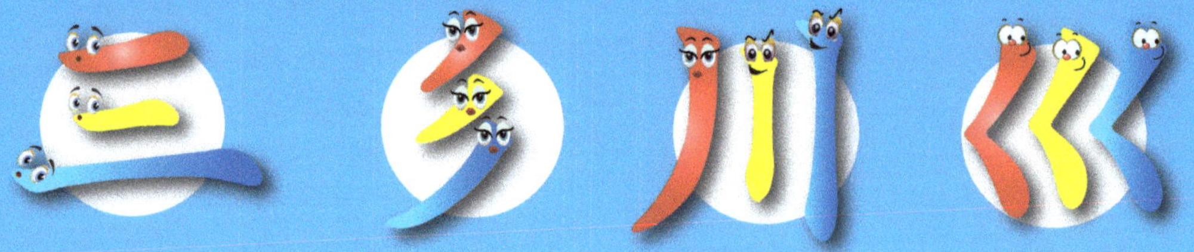

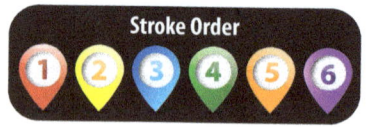

Stroke Order
① ② ③ ④ ⑤ ⑥

(1) Close your eyes and visualise these Chinese alphabets in your mind.

Anatomy of Chinese Alphabets
Applying Triple ABCs Concept

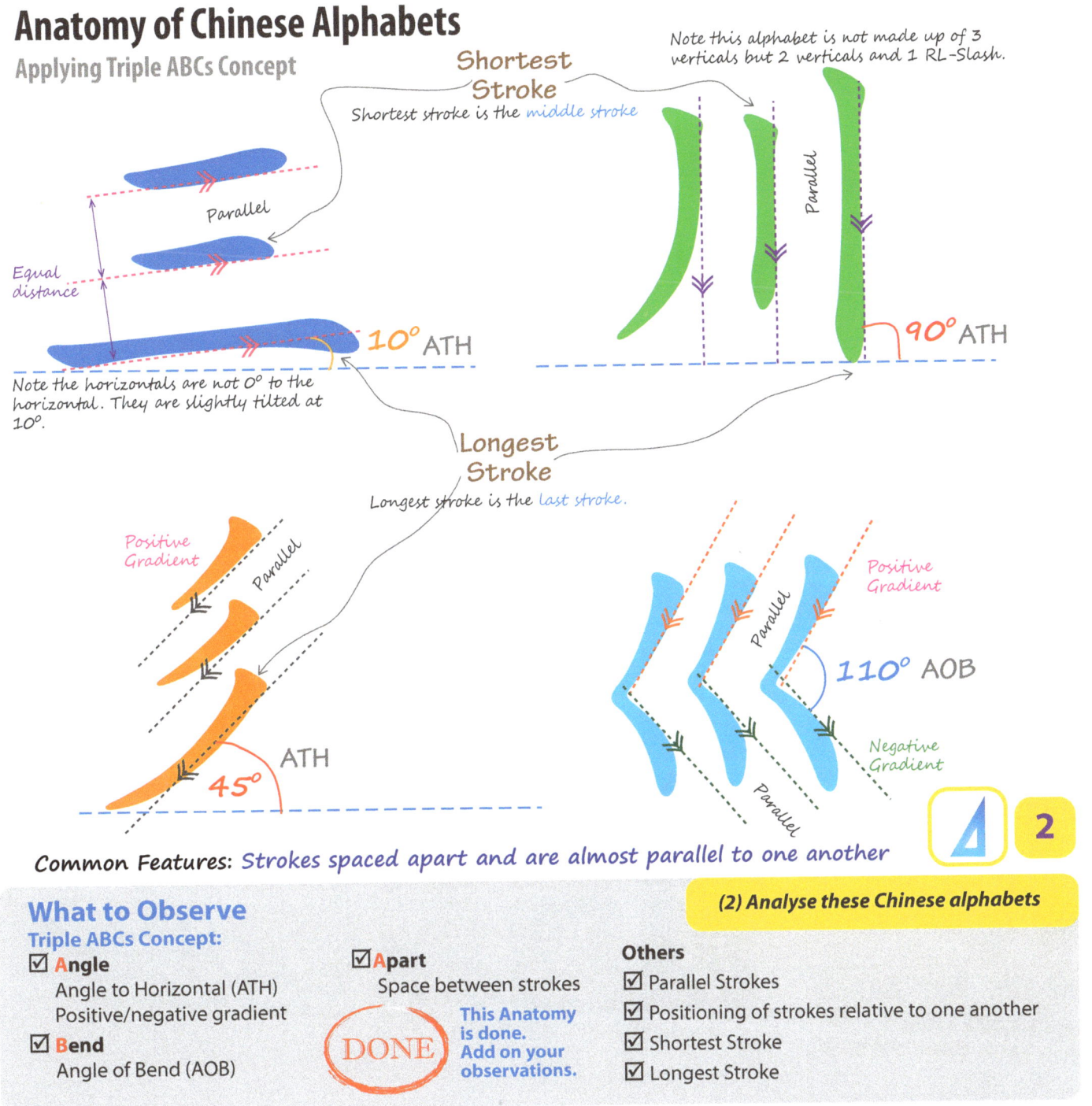

Shortest Stroke
Shortest stroke is the *middle stroke*

Note this alphabet is not made up of 3 verticals but 2 verticals and 1 RL-Slash.

Parallel

Equal distance

Parallel

10° ATH

90° ATH

Note the horizontals are not 0° to the horizontal. They are slightly tilted at 10°.

Longest Stroke
Longest stroke is the *last stroke*.

Positive Gradient

Parallel

ATH

45°

Positive Gradient

Parallel

110° AOB

Negative Gradient

Parallel

2

Common Features: Strokes spaced apart and are almost parallel to one another

What to Observe
Triple ABCs Concept:

☑ **A**ngle
Angle to Horizontal (ATH)
Positive/negative gradient

☑ **B**end
Angle of Bend (AOB)

☑ **A**part
Space between strokes

DONE — This Anatomy is done. Add on your observations.

Others
☑ Parallel Strokes
☑ Positioning of strokes relative to one another
☑ Shortest Stroke
☑ Longest Stroke

(2) Analyse these Chinese alphabets

3  **(3) Read the rules aloud.**

4  **(4) Trace the strokes with a finger or colour them according to the given stroke order.**

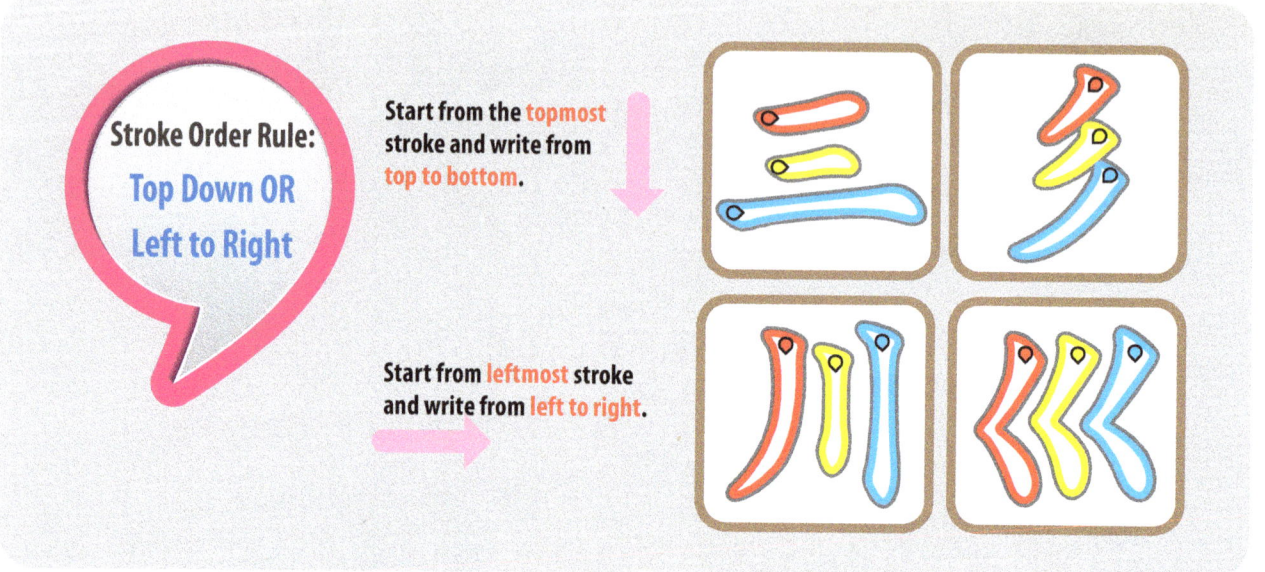

Stroke Order Rule:

Top Down OR

Left to Right

Start from the topmost stroke and write from top to bottom.

Start from leftmost stroke and write from left to right.

The Chinese alphabets you have just learnt appear in these characters.

5

(5) Colour the alphabets in the given stroke order.

Activity 1

Dots

Dots
(2) Dots (Left to Right)
(3) Dots (Top Down)
(4) Final Dot

2 Dots (Left to Right)

Stroke Order
1
2
3
4
5
6

1

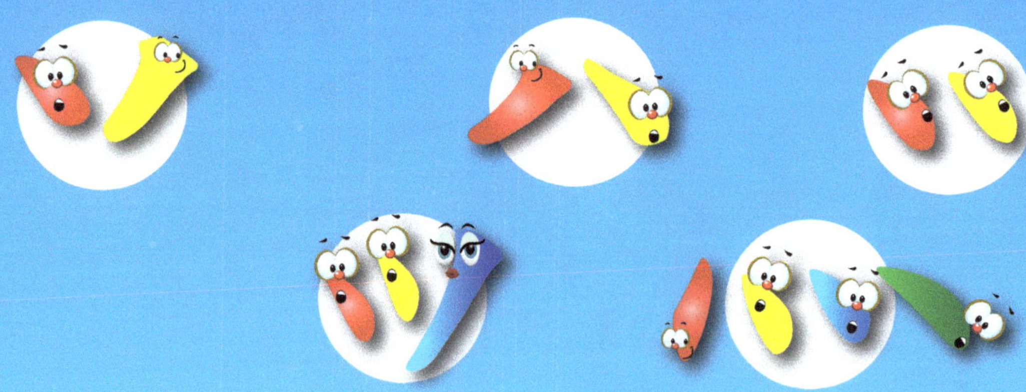

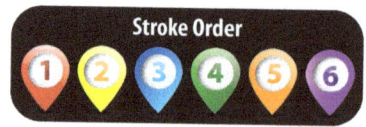

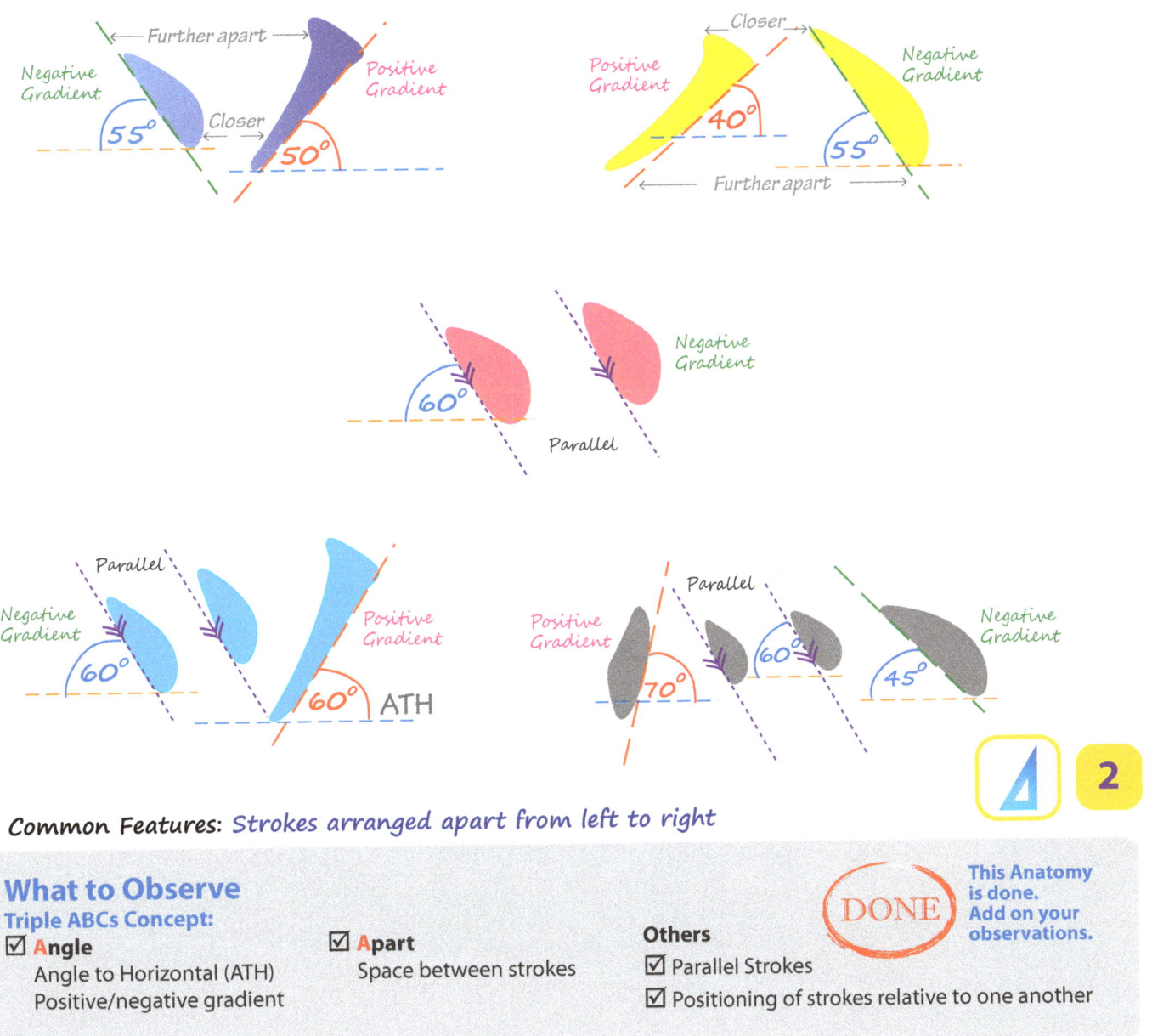

Common Features: *Strokes arranged apart from left to right*

3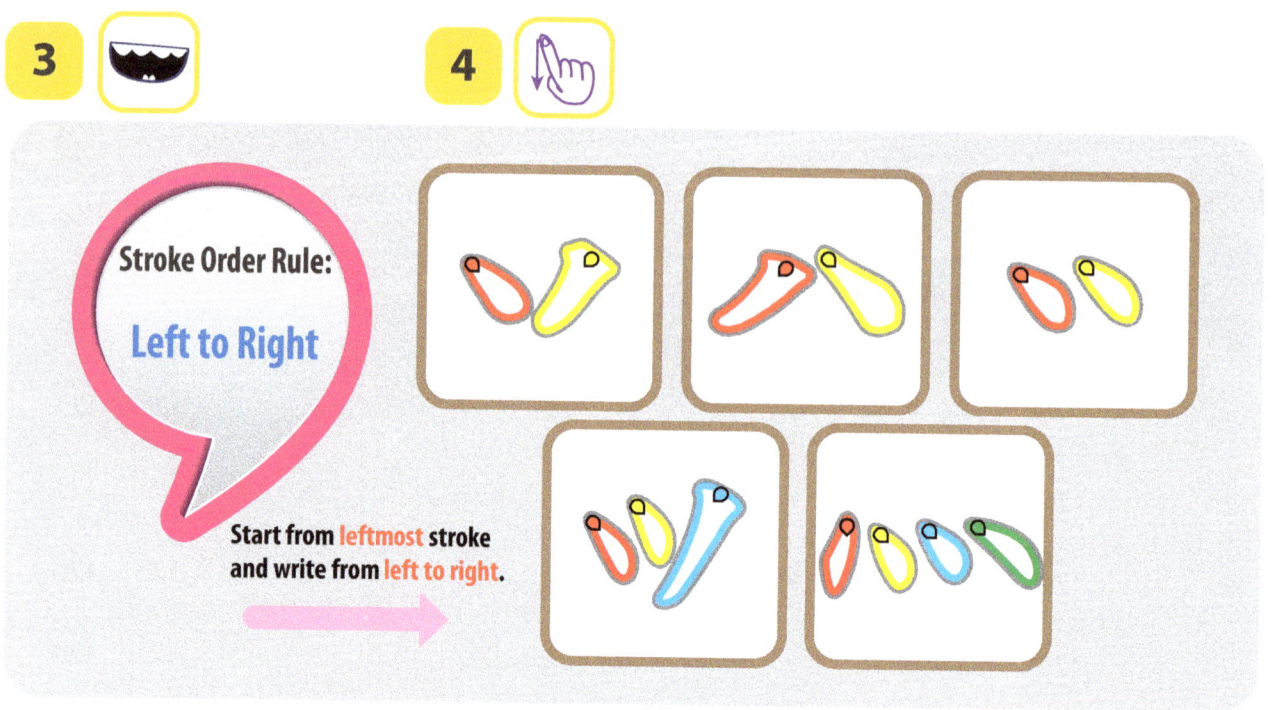

4

Stroke Order Rule:

Left to Right

Start from **leftmost** stroke and write from **left to right**.

5

羔 兴 总 忝
交 光 金 学
豆 黑 乐 办

Activity 2

3 Dots (Top Down)

Stroke Order
1 2 3 4 5 6

1

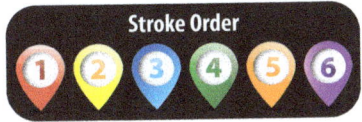

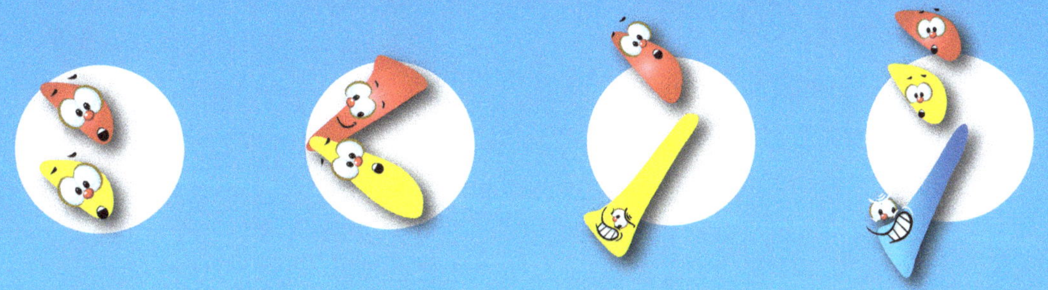

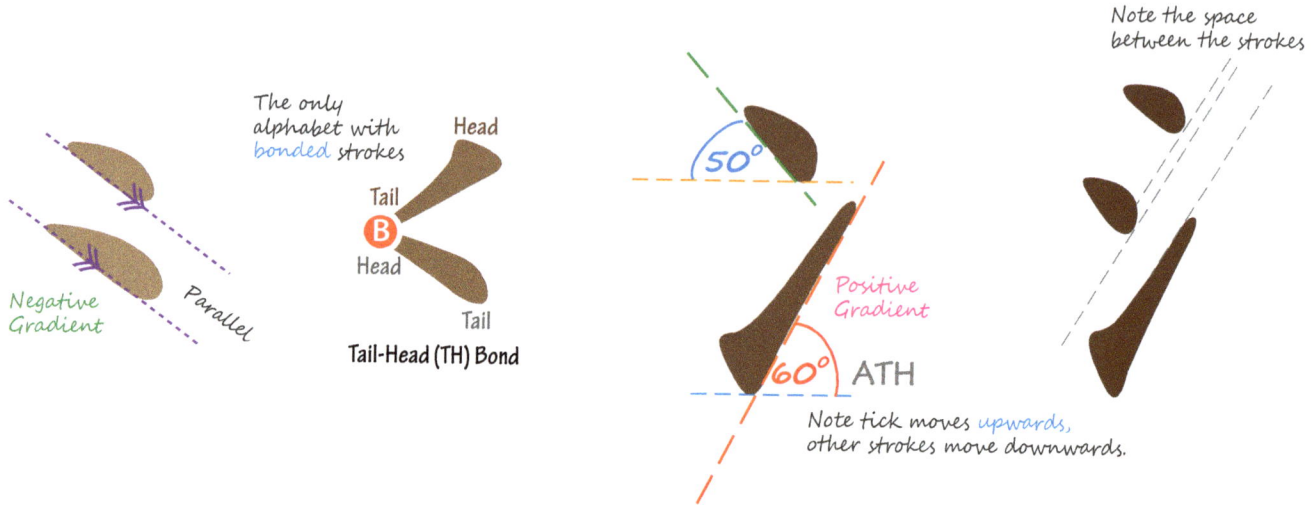

The only alphabet with *bonded* strokes

Head

Tail

B

Head

Tail

Tail-Head (TH) Bond

Negative Gradient

Parallel

50°

Positive Gradient

60° ATH

Note tick moves *upwards*, other strokes move downwards.

Note the space between the strokes

Common Features: Strokes arranged from top to bottom

 2

What to Observe
Triple ABCs Concept:

☑ **A**ngle
  Angle to Horizontal (ATH)
  Positive/negative gradient

☑ **A**part
  Space between strokes

☑ **B**onding
  Bond Point / Bond Type
  Distance from Head/Tail

Others
☑ Parallel Strokes
☑ Positioning of strokes relative to one another
☑ Direction of stroke

DONE

This Anatomy is done. Add on your observations.

3

Stroke Order Rule:

Top Down

Start from the **topmost** stroke and write from **top to bottom**.

4

5

江　头　衫　冬
衬　河　病　飞
尽　球　洗　妆　Activity 3

④ Final Dot

1

Anatomy of Chinese Alphabets

Applying Triple ABCs Concept

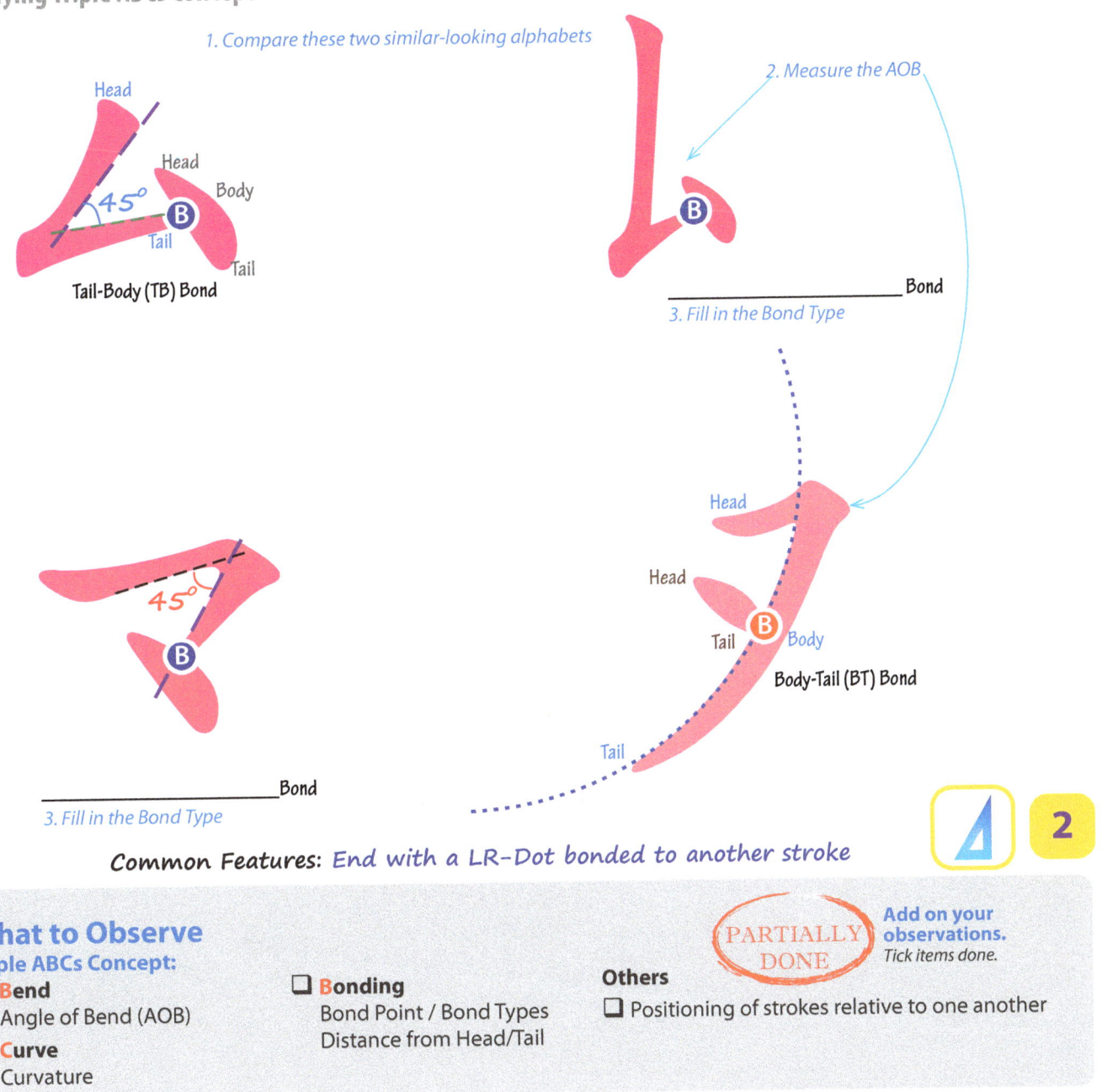

1. Compare these two similar-looking alphabets

Head

Head

Body

45°

(B)

Tail

Tail

Tail-Body (TB) Bond

2. Measure the AOB

(B)

_____ Bond

3. Fill in the Bond Type

Head

Head

Tail (B) Body

Body-Tail (BT) Bond

Tail

45°

(B)

_____ Bond

3. Fill in the Bond Type

Common Features: *End with a LR-Dot bonded to another stroke*

2

What to Observe
Triple ABCs Concept:

☐ **B**end
   Angle of Bend (AOB)

☐ **C**urve
   Curvature

☐ **B**onding
   Bond Point / Bond Types
   Distance from Head/Tail

Others
☐ Positioning of strokes relative to one another

PARTIALLY DONE

Add on your observations.
Tick items done.

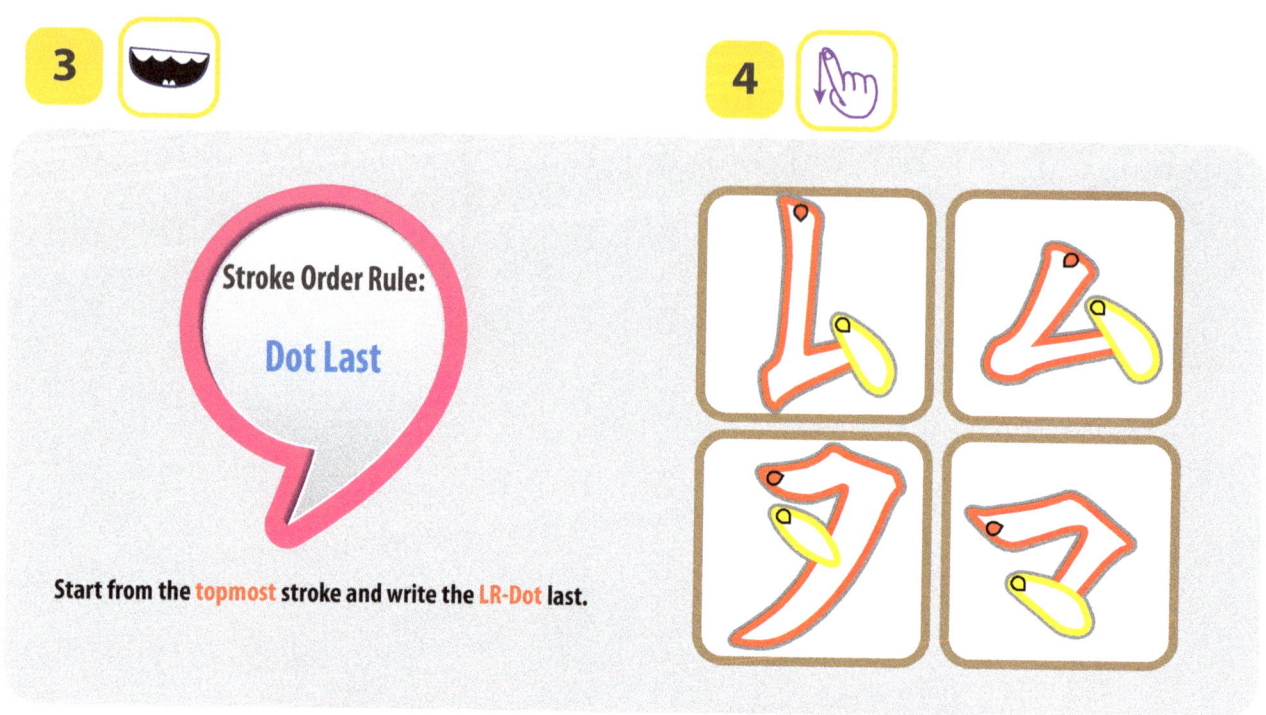

Stroke Order Rule:

Dot Last

Start from the **topmost** stroke and write the **LR-Dot** last.

5

公 予 去 瓜
柔 令 么 癸
登 至 孤 郎

Activity 4

Comparison across qTRAILS 1 - 4

Sections A1 & A2

(1) In these 3 qTRAILS, 12 alphabets have strokes that are apart, only 1 alphabet is bonded.

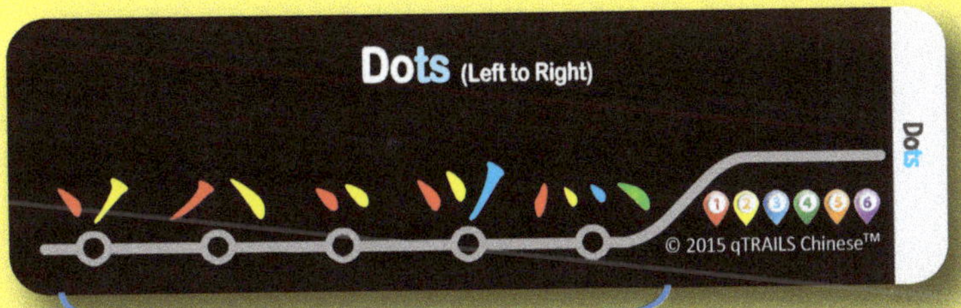

Dots (Left to Right)
Dots
© 2015 qTRAILS Chinese™

Strokes of these 7 alphabets are arranged from left to right (2)

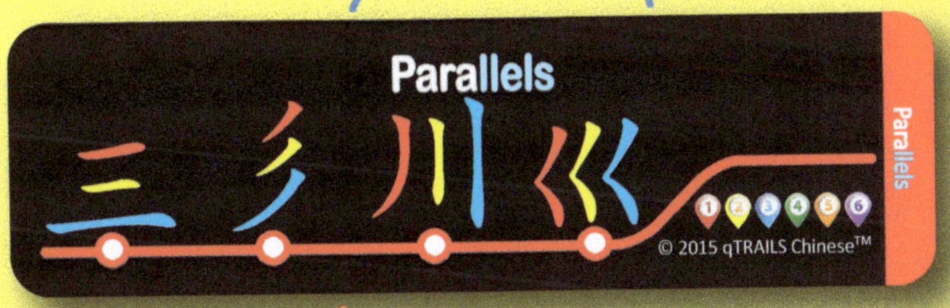

Parallels
Parallels
© 2015 qTRAILS Chinese™

Strokes of these 6 alphabets are arranged top down (3)

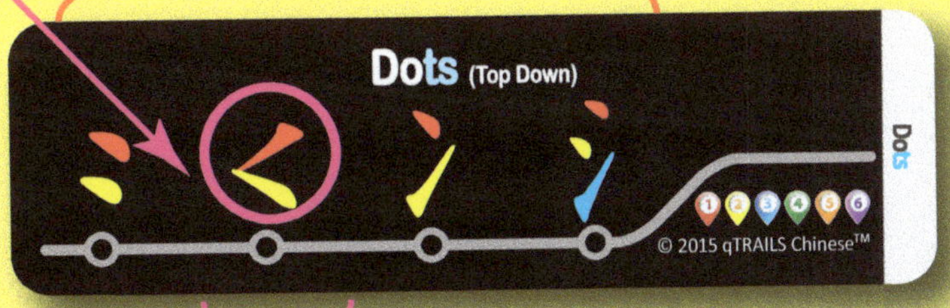

Dots (Top Down)
Dots
© 2015 qTRAILS Chinese™

Strokes of these 5 alphabets are bonded (4)

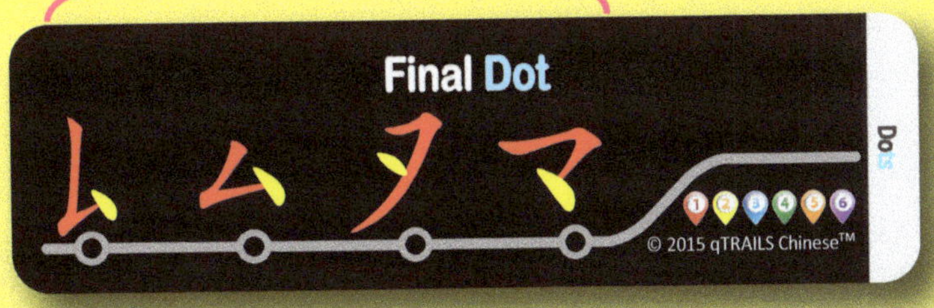

Final Dot
Dots
© 2015 qTRAILS Chinese™

qTRAILS 1 to 4

1. List **qTRAILS Alphabets** with strokes that are written:
   a) From Top to Bottom
   b) From Left to Right

2. List **qTRAILS Alphabets** with strokes that are
   a) Apart
   b) Bonded

3. List the **qTRAILS Alphabets** with the stroke order ending with a
   a) Tick
   b) LR-Dot

4. List the **qTRAILS Alphabets** with at least one pair of parallel strokes.

My
Reflection

My Questions:
Write down your own questions.

Reflection

If you have read LCWW1, you would have experienced how to analyse on what you have learnt. In this book, there will be more reflection to be done.

What to ponder

* What did I learn?
* How can I relate it to what I already know?
     ("It looks like the English alphabet …", "It looks like the object …")
* How can I remember the Chinese alphabets better?

… Pose your own questions (some questions are provided to help you re-organise the content

What to do

* Summarise what you gathered from the 'Anatomy of Chinese Alphabets' of each qTRAIL and 'Comparison acoss qTRAILS'.
* On the Reflection pages, create a 2-page summary for easy reference.
* Reproduce what you have just learnt without going back to the pages.

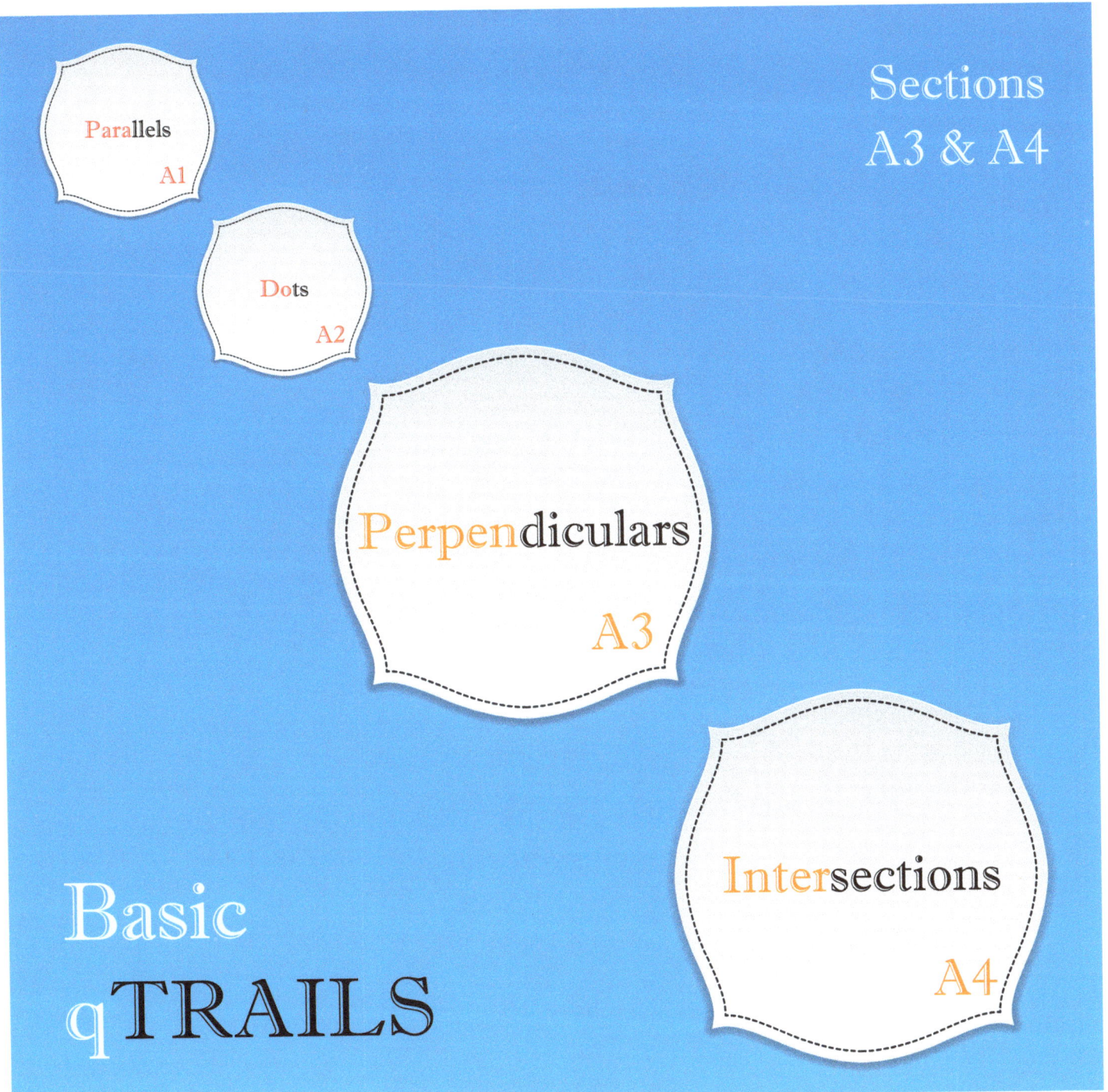

Parallels

A1

Dots

A2

Perpendiculars

A3

Intersections

A4

Basic
qTRAILS

Meet the Participants of this Boot Camp:

LR-Slash

RL-Slash

Horizontal

Vertical

Boot Camp 2
Perpendiculars and Intersections

In Boot Camp 2, LR-Slash joins the other 3 performers from Boot Camp 1.

Perpendiculars

Perpendiculars
(5) Perpendiculars (Half Ladder)
(6) Perpendisculars (T-Shape)

⑤ Perpendiculars (Half Ladder)

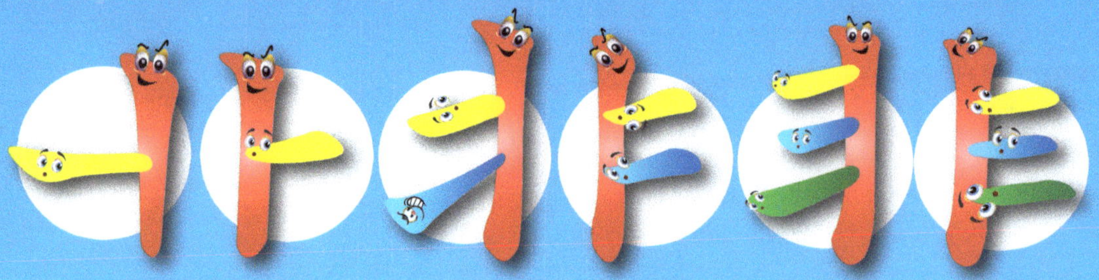

Stroke Order
1 2 3 4 5 6

Anatomy of Chinese Alphabets

Applying Triple ABCs Concept

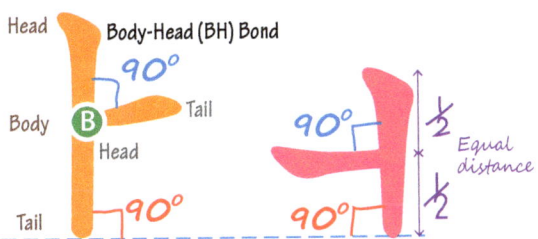

Head

Body-Head (BH) Bond

Body **B**

Head

90°

Tail

90°

Tail

90°

90°

90°

½

½

Equal distance

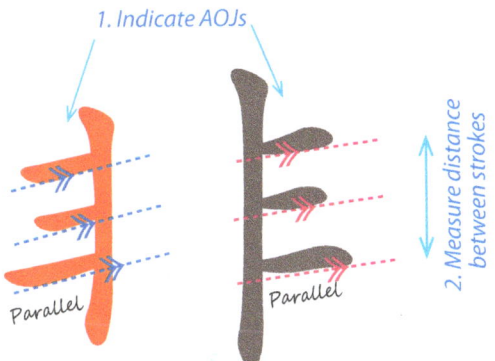

1. Indicate AOJs

2. Measure distance between strokes

Parallel

Parallel

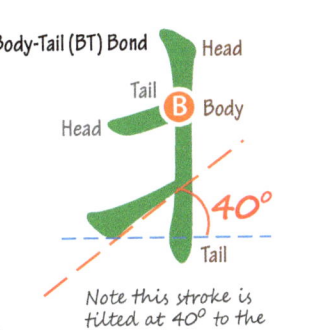

Body-Tail (BT) Bond

Tail

Head

B

Head

Body

Tail

40°

Note this stroke is tilted at 40° to the horizontal

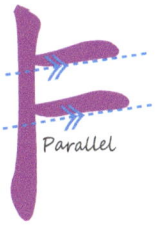

Parallel

Common Features:

Stand on one 'leg' with Horizontals / Tick perpendicularly bonded to a Vertical

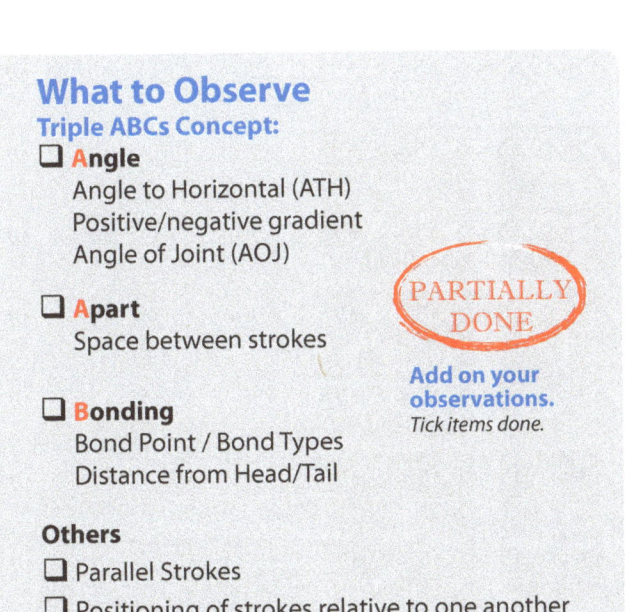

What to Observe
Triple ABCs Concept:

☐ **A**ngle
Angle to Horizontal (ATH)
Positive/negative gradient
Angle of Joint (AOJ)

☐ **A**part
Space between strokes

☐ **B**onding
Bond Point / Bond Types
Distance from Head/Tail

Others
☐ Parallel Strokes
☐ Positioning of strokes relative to one another

PARTIALLY DONE

Add on your observations.
Tick items done.

2

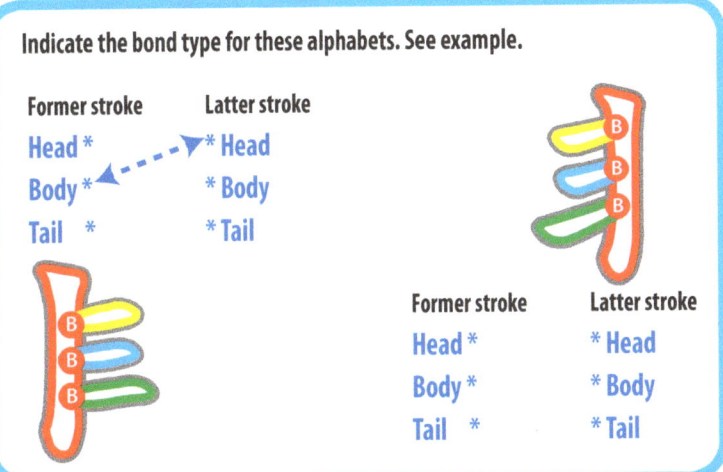

Indicate the bond type for these alphabets. See example.

Former stroke | Latter stroke
Head * → * Head
Body * ← * Body
Tail * * Tail

Former stroke | Latter stroke
Head * * Head
Body * * Body
Tail * * Tail

3

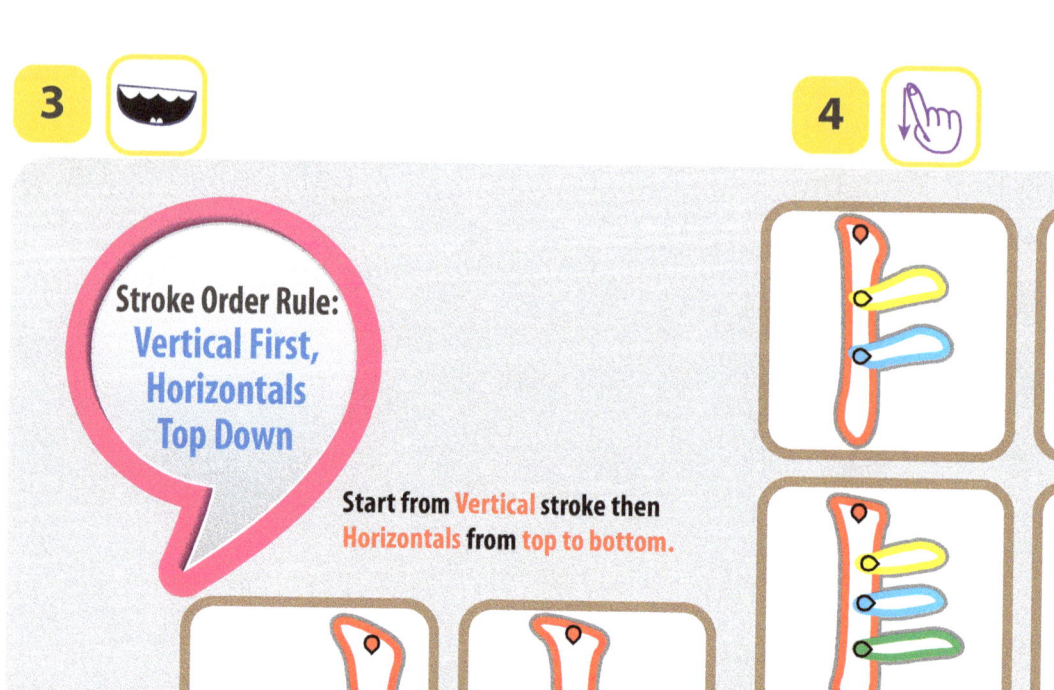

Stroke Order Rule:
**Vertical First,
Horizontals
Top Down**

Start from **Vertical** stroke then
Horizontals from **top to bottom.**

4

5

Activity 5

6 Perpendiculars (T-Shape)

Stroke Order
1
2
3
4
5
6

1

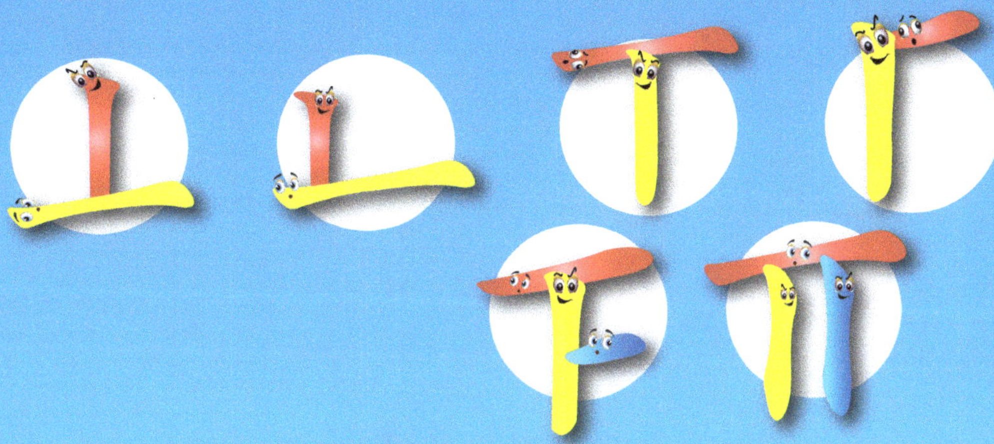

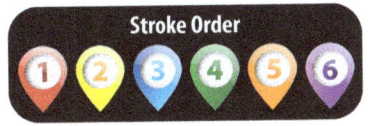

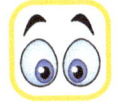

Anatomy of Chinese Alphabets
Applying Triple ABCs Concept

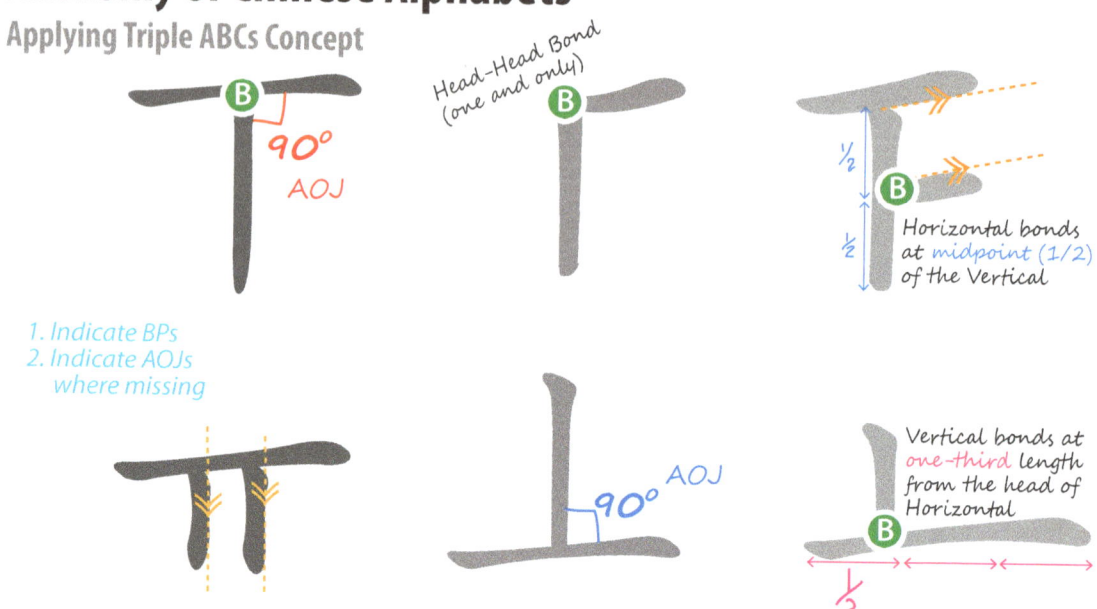

Head-Head Bond
(one and only)

90°
AOJ

½
½
Horizontal bonds
at *midpoint (1/2)*
of the Vertical

1. Indicate BPs
2. Indicate AOJs
   where missing

90° AOJ

Vertical bonds at
one-third length
from the head of
Horizontal

⅓

2

Common Features:
Horizontal(s) perpendicularly bonded to Vertical(s), forming different T-shape formations

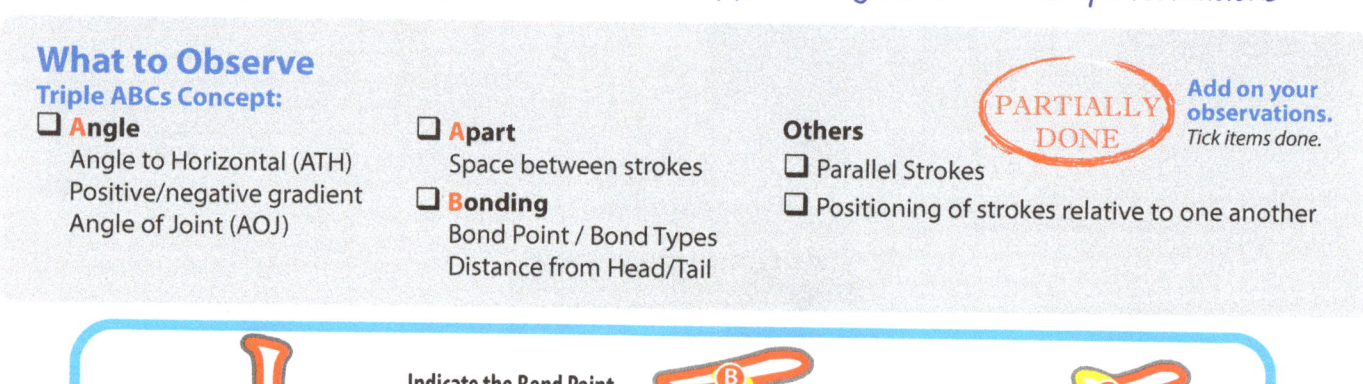

What to Observe
Triple ABCs Concept:

☐ **Angle**
Angle to Horizontal (ATH)
Positive/negative gradient
Angle of Joint (AOJ)

☐ **Apart**
Space between strokes

☐ **Bonding**
Bond Point / Bond Types
Distance from Head/Tail

Others

☐ Parallel Strokes

☐ Positioning of strokes relative to one another

PARTIALLY DONE

Add on your observations.
Tick items done.

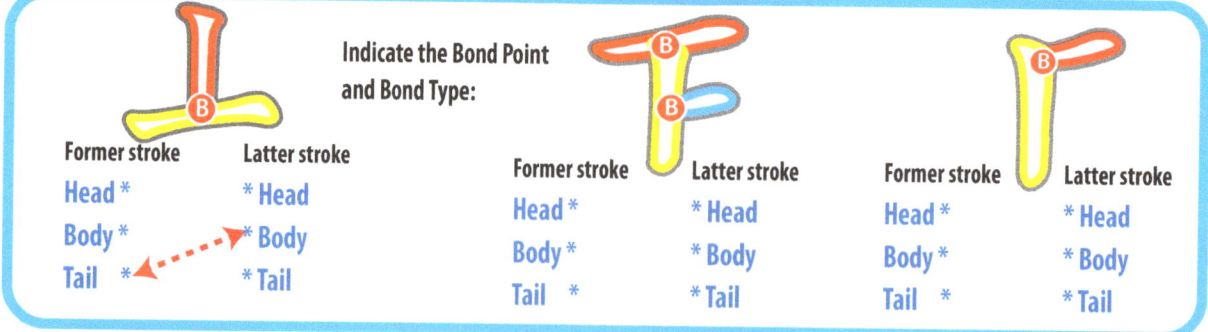

Indicate the Bond Point
and Bond Type:

Former stroke	Latter stroke
Head *	* Head
Body *	* Body
Tail *	* Tail

Former stroke	Latter stroke
Head *	* Head
Body *	* Body
Tail *	* Tail

Former stroke	Latter stroke
Head *	* Head
Body *	* Body
Tail *	* Tail

Stroke Order Rule:
Top Down
Left to Right

Start top down from Vertical then Horizontal.

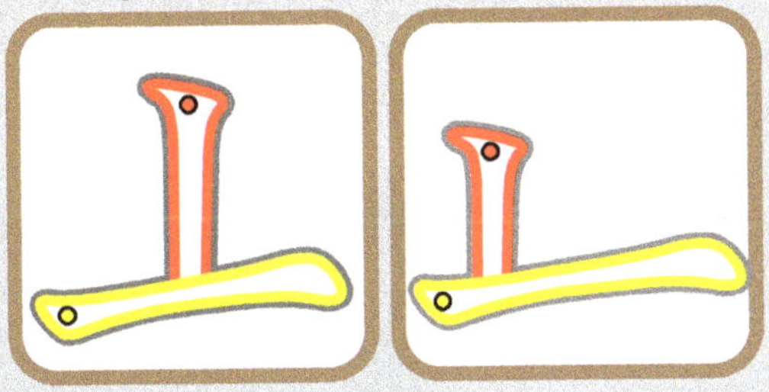

Start top down from Horizontal then Vertical(s) (left to right) and Horizontal (if any) last.

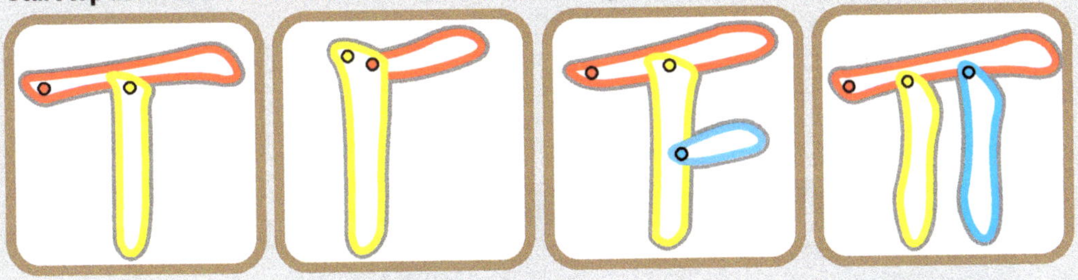

Comparison across qTRAILS 5 - 6

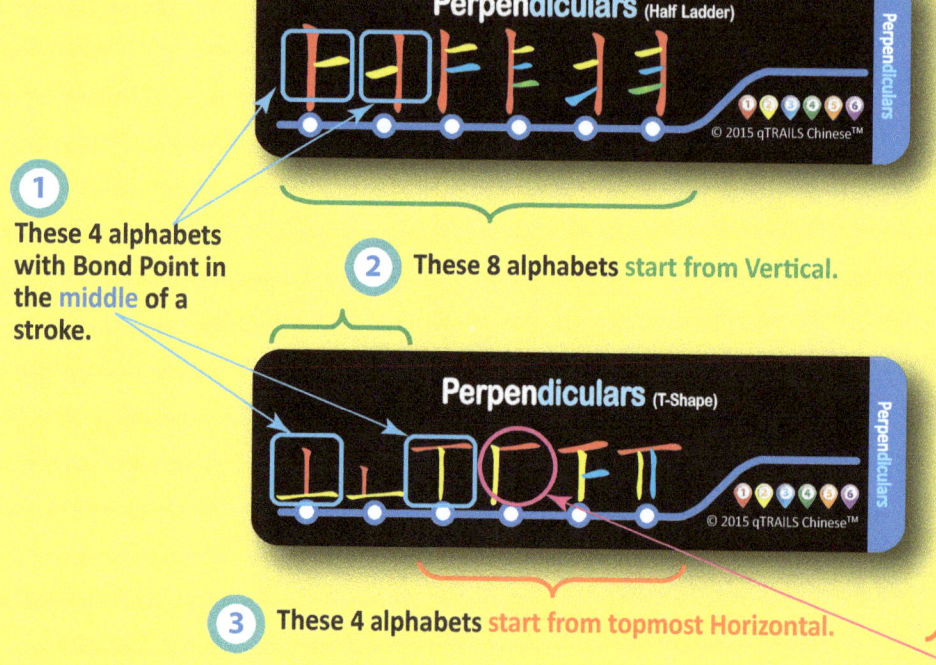

Perpendiculars (Half Ladder)

Perpendiculars (T-Shape)

© 2015 qTRAILS Chinese™

1 These 4 alphabets with Bond Point in the middle of a stroke.

2 These 8 alphabets start from Vertical.

3 These 4 alphabets start from topmost Horizontal.

4 All the alphabets have strokes that are bonded and perpendicular (90°) to one another (i.e. all AOJs are 90°.

5 The only alphabet with Head to Head (HH) bond.

Intersections

Intersections

① Intersections (Single Leg)

Stroke Order
① ② ③ ④ ⑤ ⑥

Anatomy of Chinese Alphabets
Applying Triple ABCs Concept

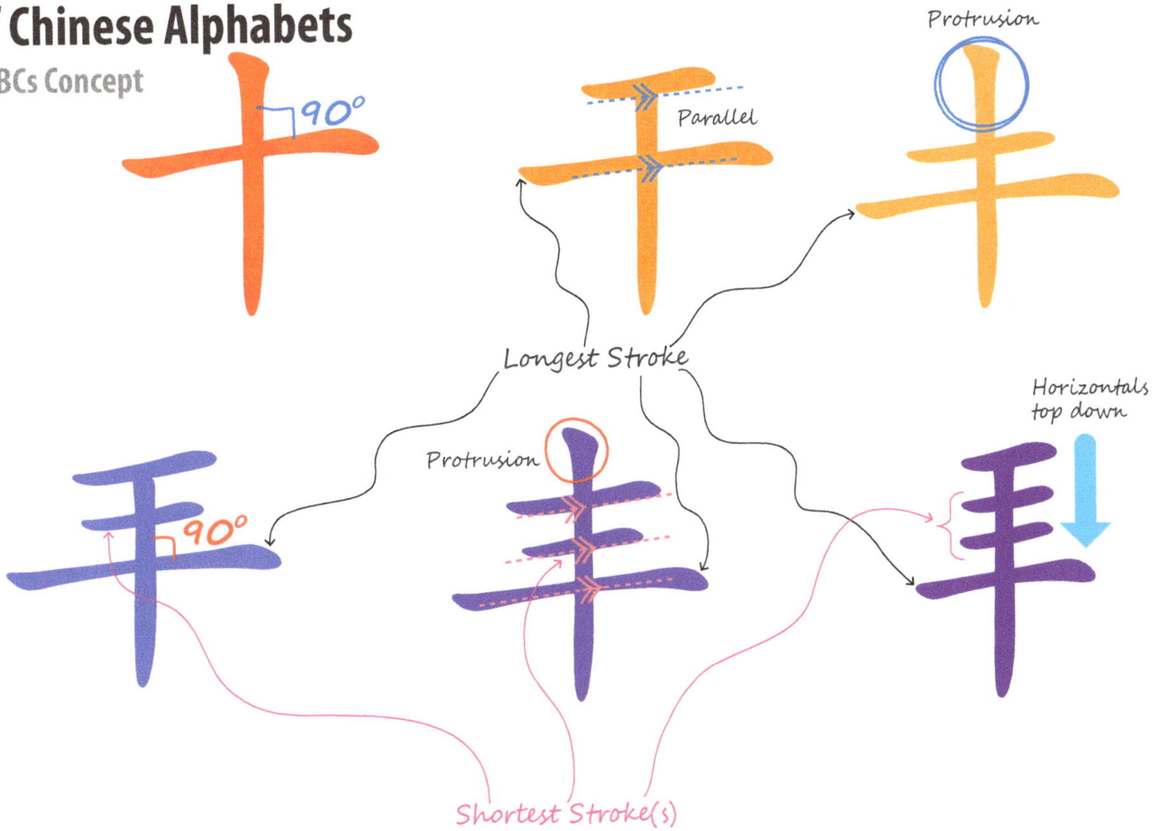

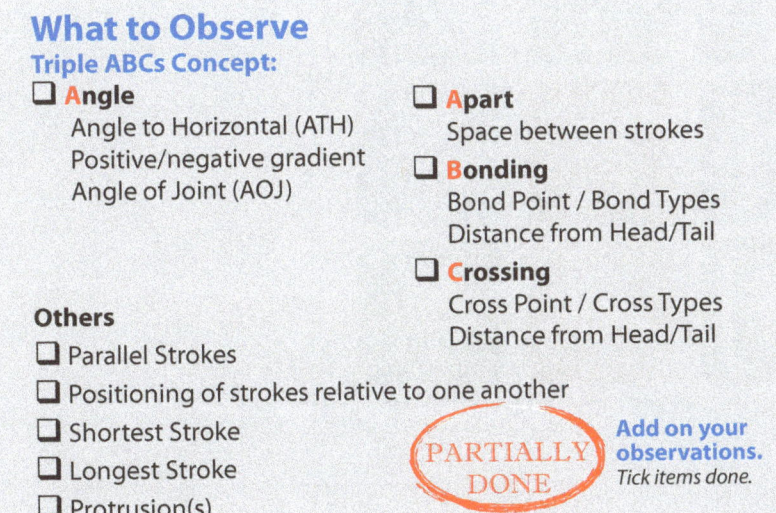

Protrusion

90°

Parallel

Longest Stroke

Protrusion

Horizontals top down

90°

Protrusion

Shortest Stroke(s)

Common Features: Horizontal(s) intersecting with a Vertical

What to Observe
Triple ABCs Concept:

☐ **A**ngle
  Angle to Horizontal (ATH)
  Positive/negative gradient
  Angle of Joint (AOJ)

☐ **A**part
  Space between strokes

☐ **B**onding
  Bond Point / Bond Types
  Distance from Head/Tail

☐ **C**rossing
  Cross Point / Cross Types
  Distance from Head/Tail

Others
☐ Parallel Strokes
☐ Positioning of strokes relative to one another
☐ Shortest Stroke
☐ Longest Stroke
☐ Protrusion(s)

PARTIALLY DONE

Add on your observations.
Tick items done.

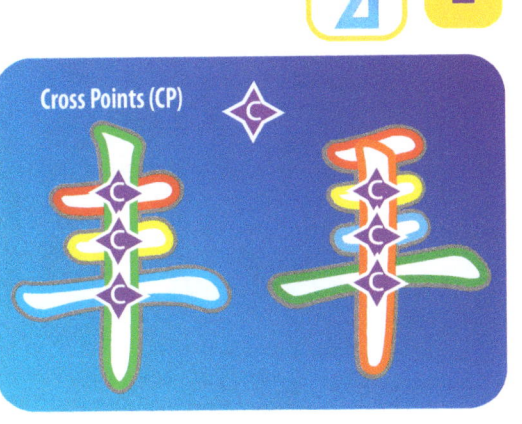

Cross Points (CP)

2

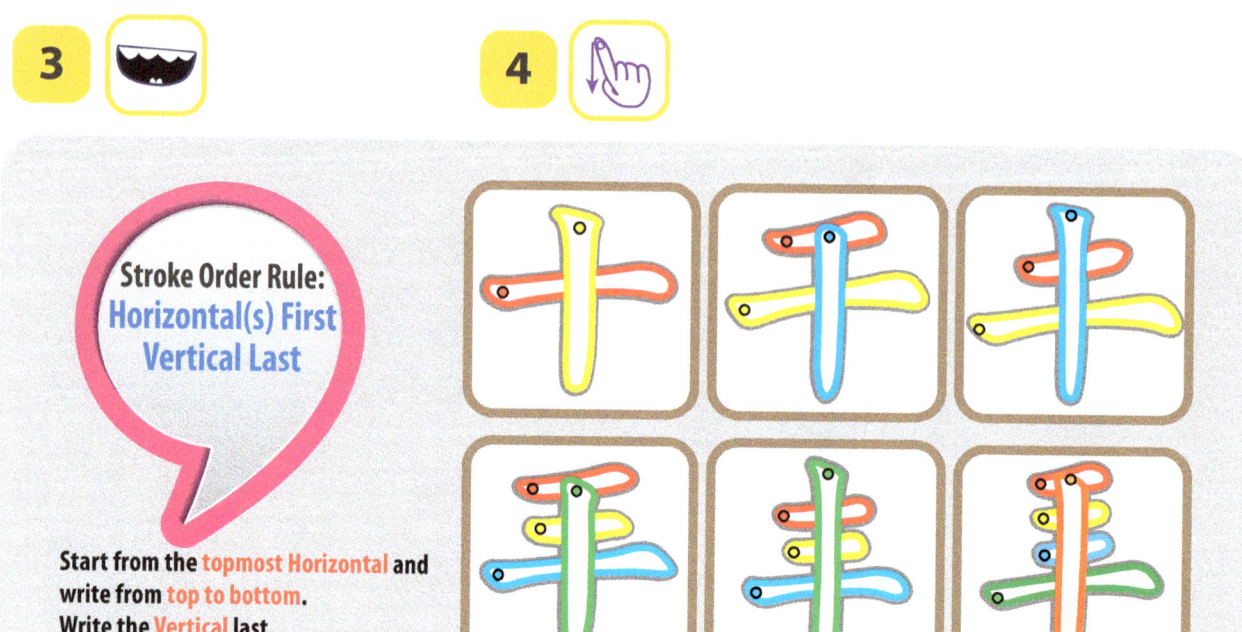

Stroke Order Rule:
Horizontal(s) First
Vertical Last

Start from the topmost Horizontal and write from top to bottom. Write the Vertical last.

5 车 午 斗 卖 岸 拜 害 牛 夆 用 举 羊

Activity 7

⑧ Inter**sections** (Multiple Legs)

Stroke Order
① ② ③ ④ ⑤ ⑥

Anatomy of Chinese Alphabets
Applying Triple ABCs Concept

Common Features:
Horizontals intersecting with 2 to 4 Verticals / RL-Slash

Protrusions

RL-Slash

2

What to Observe
Triple ABCs Concept:

Illustrate the features of these parts in the diagram above. Add on more features you observe.

- ☐ **A**ngle
  Angle to Horizontal (ATH)
  Positive/negative gradient
  Angle of Joint (AOJ)

- ☐ **A**part
  Space between strokes
- ☐ **B**onding
  Bond Point / Bond Types
  Distance from Head/Tail
- ☐ **C**rossing
  Cross Point / Cross Types
  Distance from Head/Tail

Others
- ☐ Parallel Strokes
- ☐ Positioning of strokes relative to one another
- ☐ Shortest Stroke
- ☐ Longest Stroke
- ☐ Protrusion(s)

Add on your observations
Tick items done

3

4

Stroke Order Rule:
Horizontal(s) First
Verticals Last

Start from **topmost Horizontal** and write from **top down**.
Start from **leftmost Vertical/RL-Slash** and write from **left to right**.

花　讲　贡
草　带　舞

5

并　进　刑

Activity 8

⑨ Inter**sections** (Split)

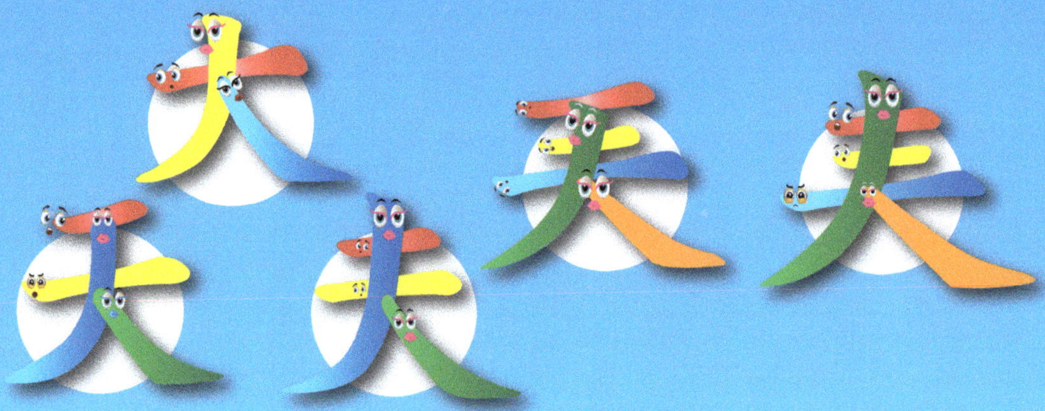

Stroke Order
① ② ③ ④ ⑤ ⑥

Anatomy of Chinese Alphabets
Applying Triple ABCs Concept

 2

What to Observe
Triple ABCs Concept:

Illustrate the features of these parts in the diagram above. Add on more features you observe.

☐ **A**ngle
  Angle to Horizontal (ATH)
  Positive/negative gradient
  Angle of Joint (AOJ)
☐ **C**urve
  Curvature

☐ **A**part
  Space between strokes
☐ **B**onding
  Bond Point / Bond Types
  Distance from Head/Tail
☐ **C**rossing
  Cross Point / Cross Types
  Distance from Head/Tail

Others
☐ Parallel Strokes
☐ Positioning of strokes relative to one another
☐ Shortest Stroke
☐ Longest Stroke
☐ Protrusion(s)

Do your own analysis
Tick items done

3

4

Stroke Order Rule:
Horizontal(s) First
Split Last

Start from topmost Horizontal and write top down.
Write Split (RL-Slash then LR-Slash) last.

5

Activity 9

10 Intersections (Tripod)

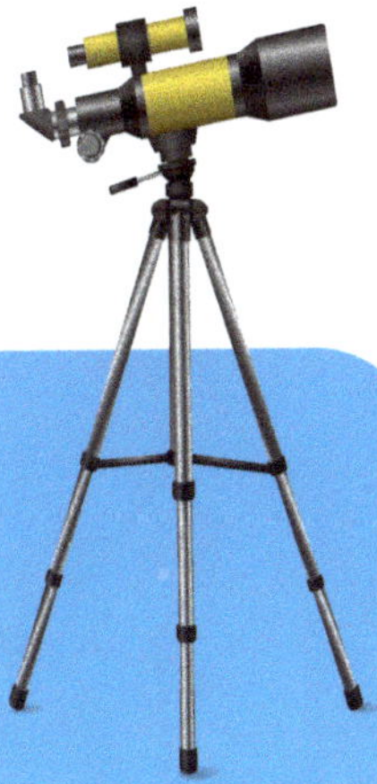

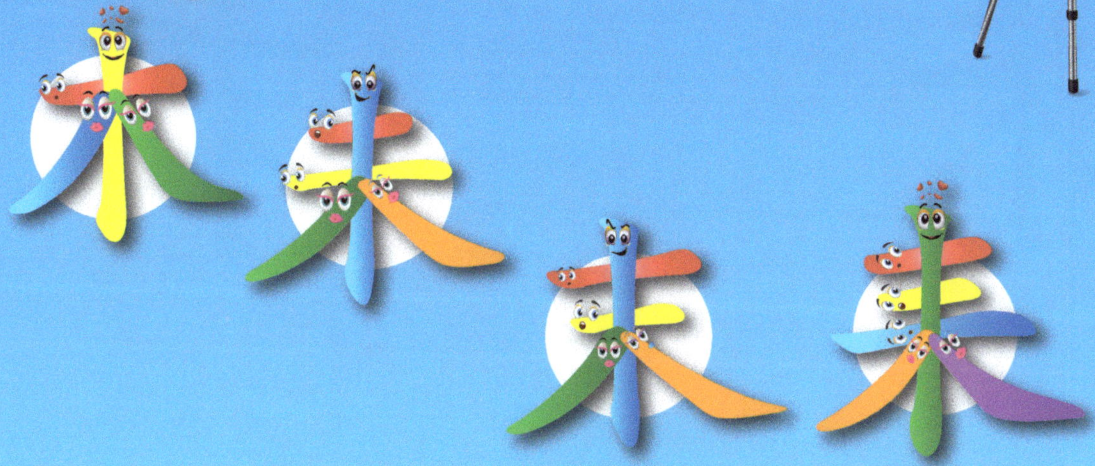

Stroke Order
1
2
3
4
5
6

1

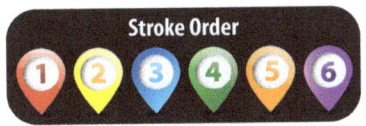

Anatomy of Chinese Alphabets
Applying Triple ABCs Concept

Common Features:
Horizontals intersecting with a tripod.

(A tripod is made by bonding a vertical, RL-Slash and LR-Slash to form a 'three-legged' stand)

 **2**

What to Observe
Triple ABCs Concept:

Illustrate the features of these parts in the diagram above. Add on more features you observe.

☐ **Angle**
Angle to Horizontal (ATH)
Positive/negative gradient
Angle of Joint (AOJ)

☐ **Curve**
Curvature

☐ **Apart**
Space between strokes

☐ **Bonding**
Bond Point / Bond Types
Distance from Head/Tail

☐ **Crossing**
Cross Point / Cross Types
Distance from Head/Tail

Others
☐ Parallel Strokes
☐ Positioning of strokes relative to one another
☐ Shortest Stroke
☐ Longest Stroke
☐ Protrusion(s)

Do your own analysis
Tick items done

3

Stroke Order Rule:
Horizontal(s) First
Tripod Last

Start from **topmost Horizontal** and write **top down**.
Write **Tripod** (Vertical, RL-Slash then LR-Slash).

4

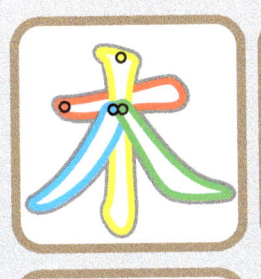 
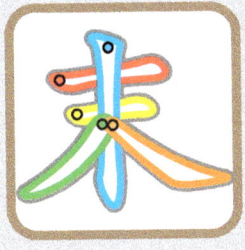 

5

Activity 10

⑪ Inter**sections** (Flat Bottom)

Stroke Order
1 2 3 4 5 6

1

Common Features: Horizontals intersecting with vertical(s) and all alphabets have flat base.

What to Observe
Triple ABCs Concept:

Colour the parts. Illustrate the features of these parts in the diagram above.
Add on more features you observe.

☐ **A**ngle
Positive/negative gradient
Angle of Joint (AOJ)

☐ **A**part
Space between strokes

☐ **B**onding
Bond Point / Bond Types
Distance from Head/Tail

☐ **C**rossing
Cross Point / Cross Types
Distance from Head/Tail

Others
☐ Parallel Strokes
☐ Positioning of strokes relative to one another
☐ Shortest Stroke
☐ Longest Stroke
☐ Protrusion(s)

Do your own analysis
Tick items done

Stroke Order Rule:
Horizontal(s) Top Down
Vertical(s) from Left to Right
Bottommost Horizontal Last

Start from Horizontal from top to bottom
Write Vertical(s) and write from left to right.
Write bottommost Horizontal last.

Activity 11

Comparison across qTRAILS 7 - 11

 1. Write all the horizontal lines first, starting from top down
2. All the parts have at least one Horizontal intersecting with Vertical(s) / Split / Tripod
3. All the alphabets 'stand on legs'.
4. All AOJs are 90°.

 **Maximum number of Horizontals**

 Intersects with

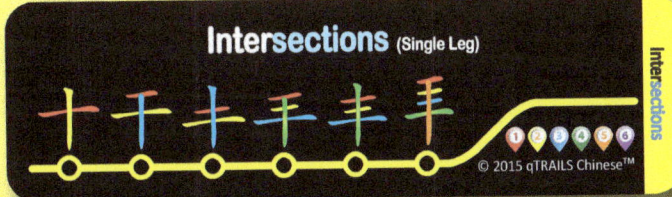

4 horizontals **1 vertical** (2 legs)

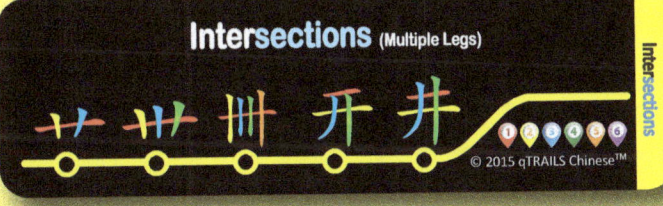

2 horizontals **2 to 4 verticals** (2 to 4 legs)

3 horizontals **'Split'** (2 legs) (RL Slash and LR-Slash)

3 horizontals **'Tripod'** (3 legs) (RL Slash, Vertical and LR-Slash)

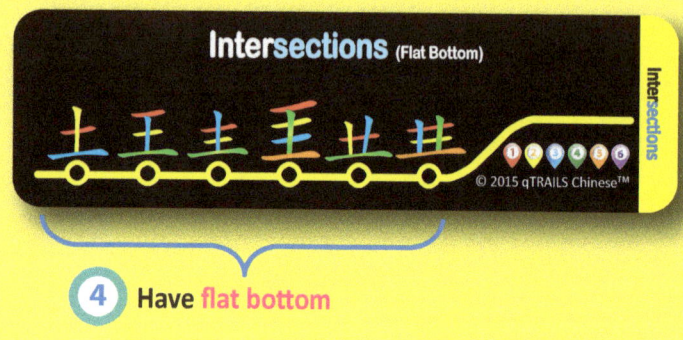

Intersections (Flat Bottom)

© 2015 qTRAILS Chinese™

4 Have flat bottom

Maximum number of Horizontals	Intersects with
4 horizontals	1-2 verticals

Activity 12

Alphabets from qTRAILS you have learnt so far are shown below without referring back to previous pages. Indicate the starting point of the first stroke with the symbol. See example.

Activity 13

Basic qTRAIL Alphabets from different qTRAILS are mixed up. Circle the qTRAIL Alphabets from the **same qTRAIL** using the given symbols. See examples.

Activity 14

Recall the basic qTRAILS Alphabets you have learnt so far. They are broken down into individual strokes in the order that they should be written. Write down the **basic qTRAIL Alphabets** that are written with the given strokes and in the same stroke order. See examples.

Example 1: ⼀ ⼀ ⼀ | 三 | Example 2: ⼀ ⼀ | | 干 午 |

1. ⼀ | List 3 qTRAILS Alphabets

2. | ⼀   List 2 qTRAILS Alphabets

3. ⼀ | | List 2 qTRAILS Alphabets

4. ⼀ | | | List 1 qTRAILS Alphabet

5. ⼀ | | ⼀   List 1 qTRAILS Alphabet

6. ⼀ | | | | List 1 qTRAILS Alphabet

7. ⼀ ⼀ | ⼀   List 2 qTRAILS Alphabets

8. ⼀ ⼀ | | ⼀   List 1 qTRAILS Alphabet

9.  List 2 qTRAILS Alphabets

10. List 2 qTRAILS Alphabets

11. List 1 qTRAILS Alphabets

12. List 1 qTRAILS Alphabet

13. List 3 qTRAILS Alphabet

14. List 2 qTRAILS Alphabet

15. List 2 qTRAILS Alphabets

16. List 1 qTRAILS Alphabet

Feel free to describe and illustrate in your own way in the next 2 pages.

qTRAILS 5 to 11

1. List the **qTRAILS Alphabets**

    a) standing on 1 leg (vertical)

    b) standing on 2 legs (include RL-Slash)

    c) standing on 3 legs (include RL-Slash and LR-Slash)

    d) standing on 4 legs

    e) with 1 horizontal

    f) with 2 horizontals

    g) with 3 horizontals

    h) with 4 horizontals

    i) with protrusions

2. List the **qTRAILS Alphabets** with the stroke order

    a) starting with horizontal

    b) ending with vertical and/or Slash(es)

    a) ending with horizontal

My Questions:
Write down your own questions.

My
Reflection

Match the Stroke Order Rules to the qTRAILS. Note you can match the rules more than once. See example.

Stroke Order Rules

qTRAILS

1. **Horizontal(s) First Vertical(s) Last**

2. **Dot Last**

3. **Horizontal(s) First Tripod Last**

4. **Top down or Left to right**

5. **Left to right**

6. **Horizontal(s) First Split Last**

7. **Vertical First Horizontal(s) Last**

8. **Top down**

9. **Top Horizontal(s) First Vertical(s) Bottommost Horizontal Last**

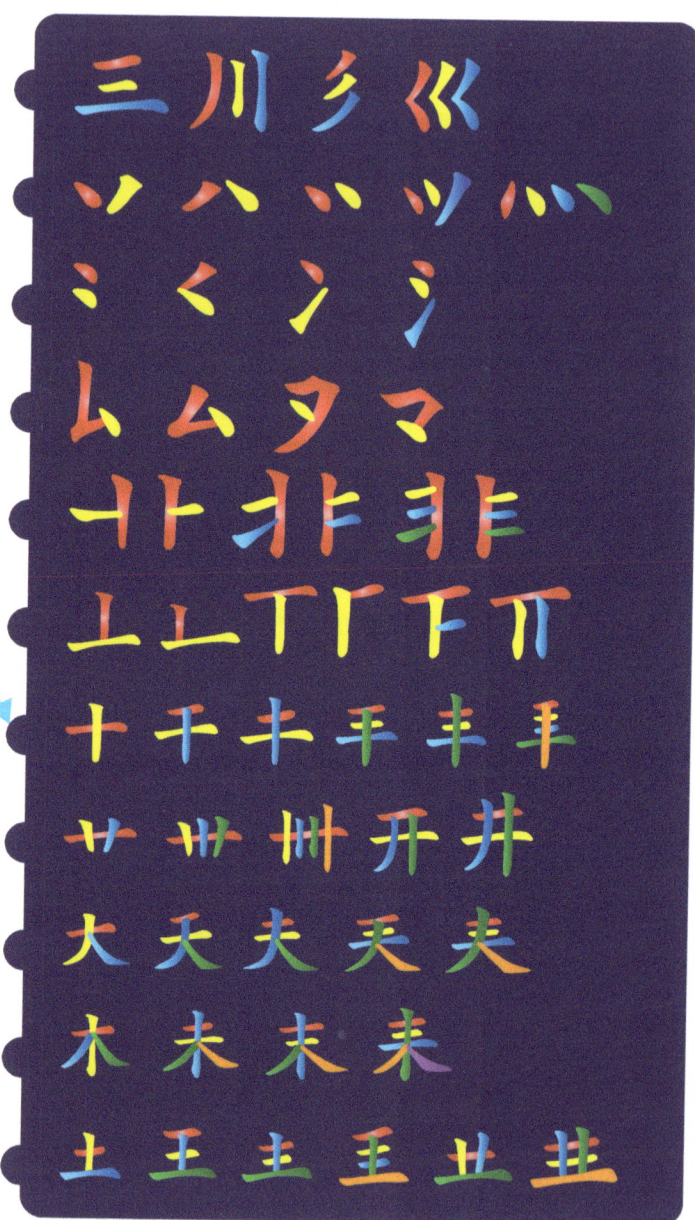

Sections
A5 & A6

Split & Cross

A5

Marching
&
Tick
A6

Flag, Frame
&
Skewer
A7

Enclosure

A8

Basic
qTRAILS

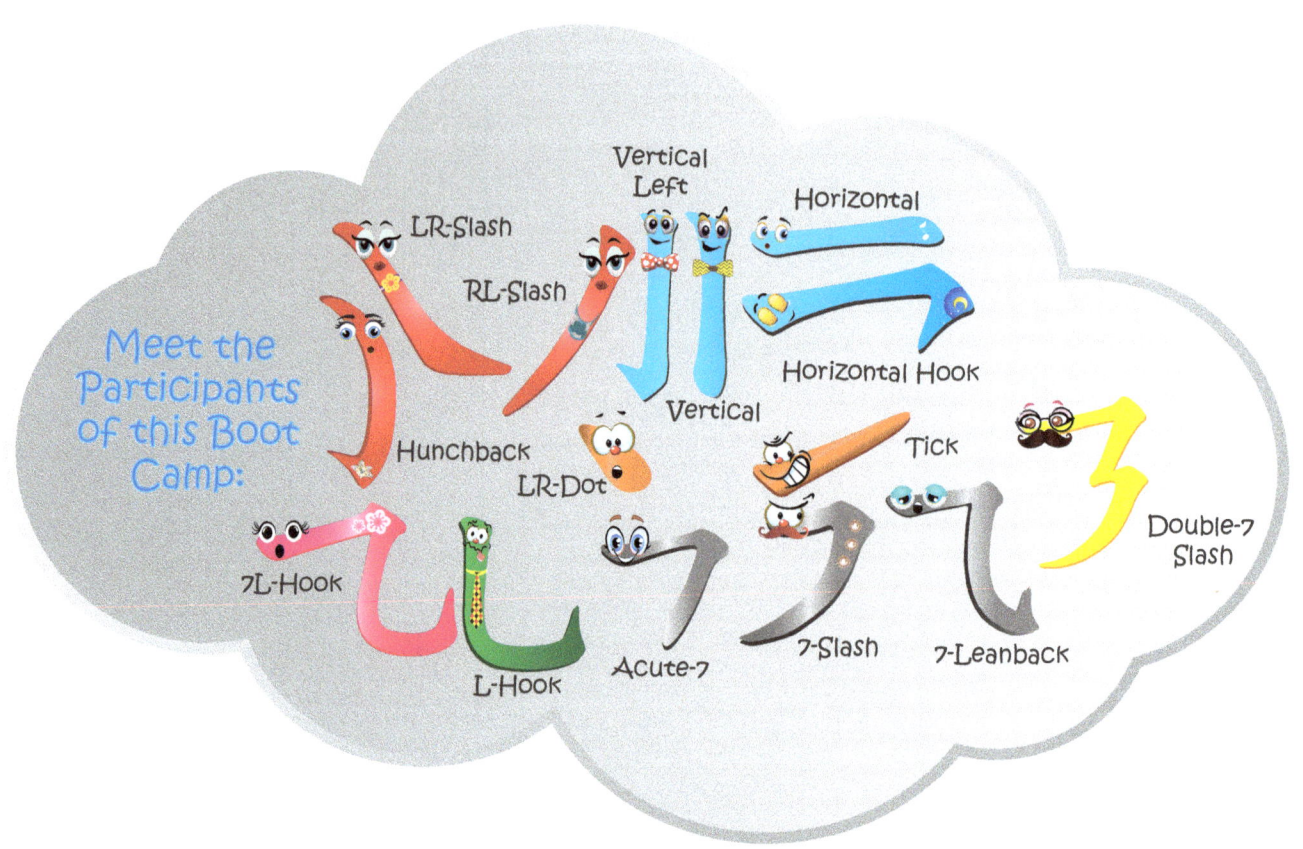

Meet the Participants of this Boot Camp:

LR-Slash
RL-Slash
Vertical Left
Horizontal
Horizontal Hook
Vertical
Hunchback
LR-Dot
Tick
Double-7 Slash
7L-Hook
L-Hook
Acute-7
7-Slash
7-Leanback

Boot Camp 3
Split & Cross
Marching & Tick
In Boot Camp 3, 15 performers are participating.

Split & Cross

Split

Cross

Split and Cross
(12) Split (Simple)
(13) Split (with Vertical or Horizontal)
(14) Slide
(15) Cross (Simple)
(16) Slide & Cross (7-Slash)
(17) Split & Cross (L-Hook and 7L-Hook)

12 Split (Simple)

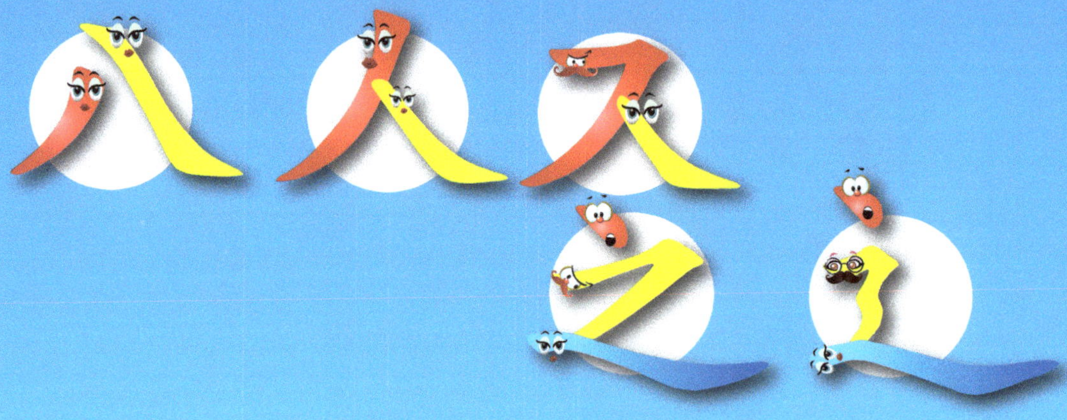

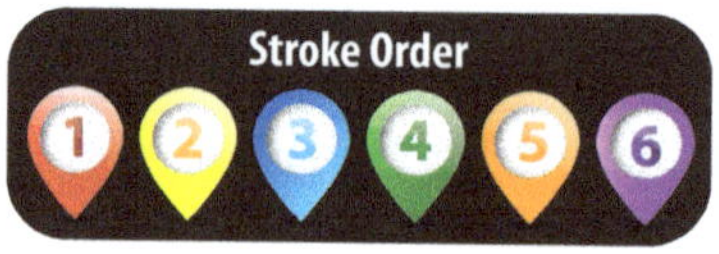
Stroke Order
1
2
3
4
5
6

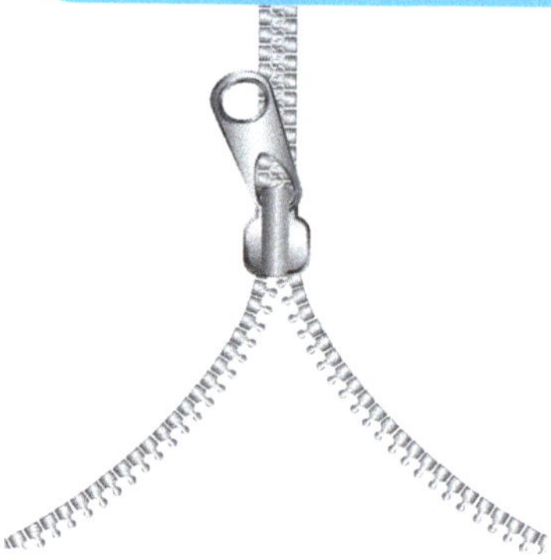

1

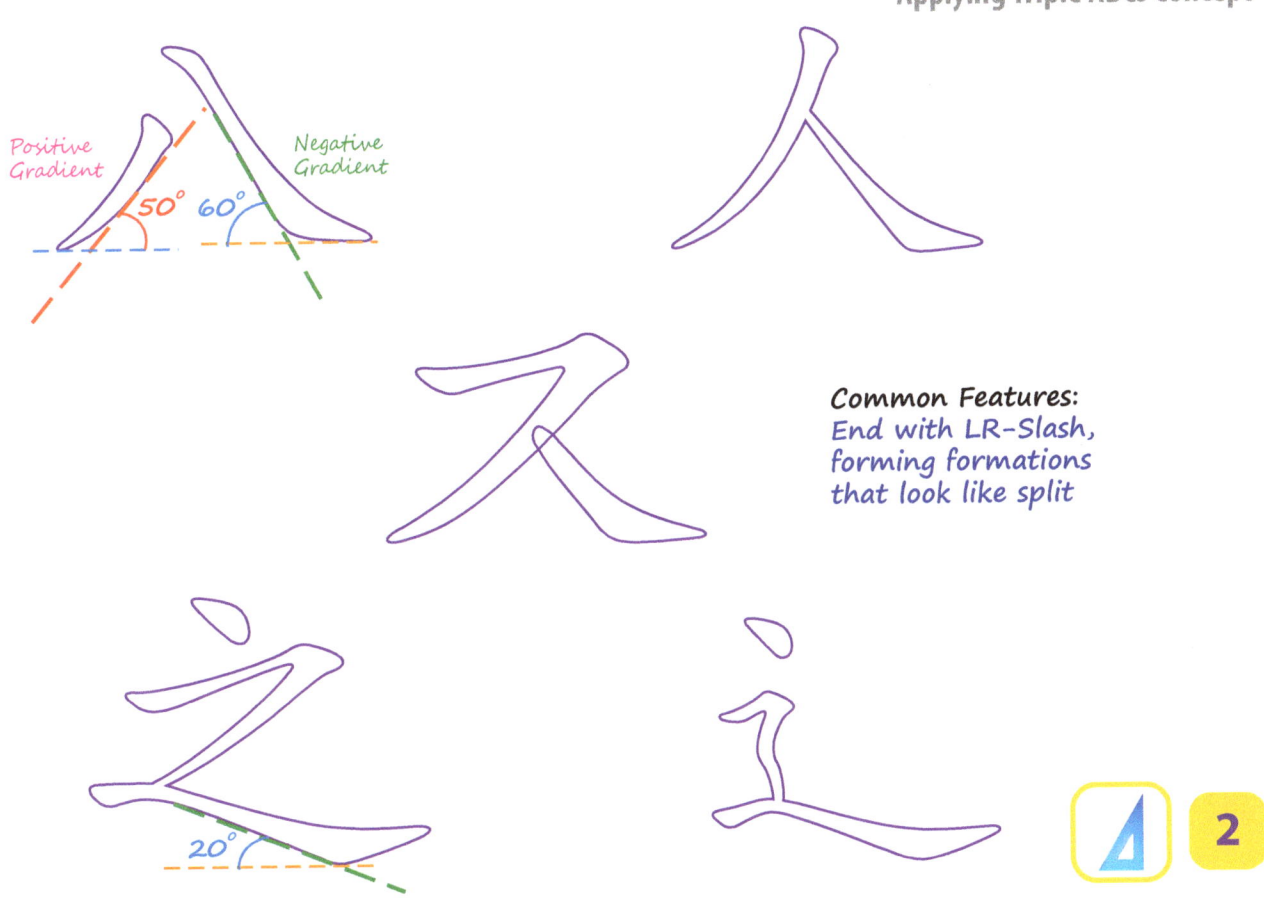

Positive Gradient

Negative Gradient

50° 60°

Common Features:
End with LR-Slash, forming formations that look like split

20°

2

What to Observe
Triple ABCs Concept:

Colour the parts. Illustrate the features of these parts in the diagram above.
Add on more features you observe.

❑ **A**ngle
Angle to Horizontal (ATH)
Positive/negative gradient
Angle of Joint (AOJ)

❑ **B**end
Angle of Bend (AOB)

❑ **C**urve
Curvature

❑ **A**part
Space between strokes

❑ **B**onding
Bond Point / Bond Types
Distance from Head/Tail

Others
❑ Positioning of strokes relative to one another

Do your own analysis
Tick items done

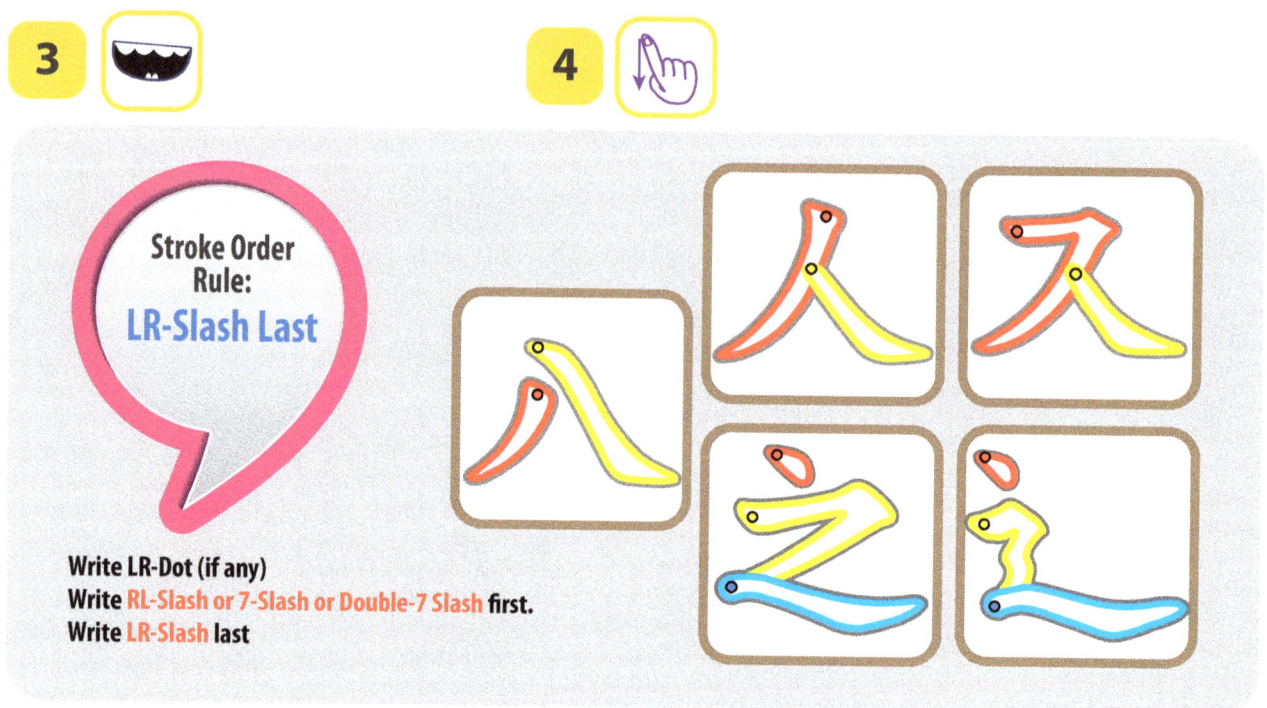

4

Stroke Order Rule:
LR-Slash Last

Write LR-Dot (if any)
Write RL-Slash or 7-Slash or Double-7 Slash first.
Write LR-Slash last

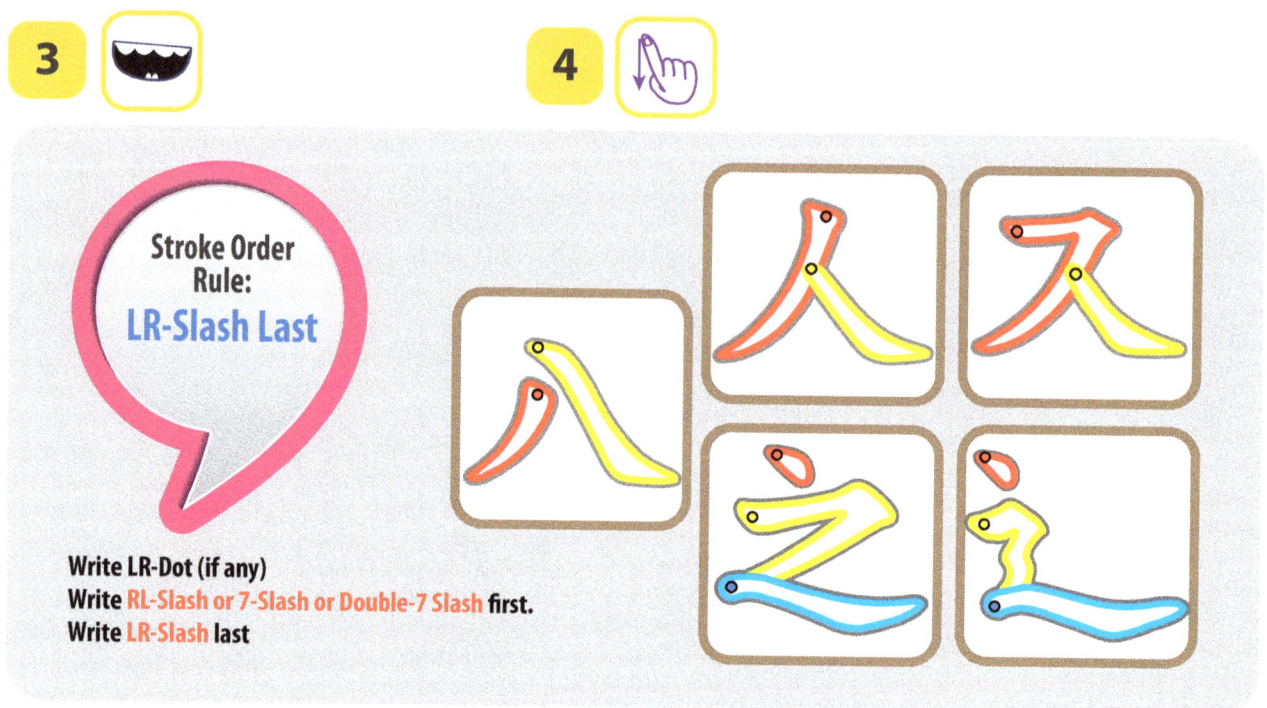

5

Activity 16

13 ## Split (with Vertical or Horizontal)

Stroke Order
①②③④⑤⑥

2

Common Features: Start with RL–Slash attached to a Vertical or Horizontal

What to Observe
Triple ABCs Concept:

Colour the parts. Illustrate the features of these parts in the diagram above.
Add on more features you observe.

☐ **A**ngle
  Angle to Horizontal (ATH)
  Positive/negative gradient
  Angle of Joint (AOJ)

☐ **C**urve
  Curvature

☐ **A**part
  Space between strokes

☐ **B**onding
  Bond Point / Bond Types
  Distance from Head/Tail

Others
☐ Parallel Strokes
☐ Positioning of strokes relative to one another

Do your
own analysis
Tick items done

3

4

Stroke Order Rule:
RL-Slash(es) First

Write RL-Slash(es) first.
Write Vertical or Horizontal attached to RL-Slash
Write LR-Dot (if any) last.

5

华 蓝 丘 行
作 吃 街 笑

Activity 17

⑭ Slide

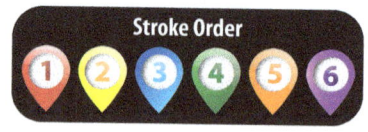

Stroke Order
1 2 3 4 5 6

 1

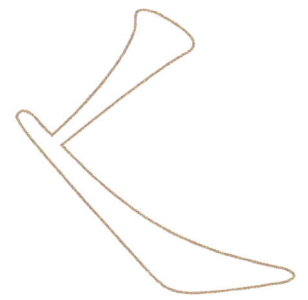

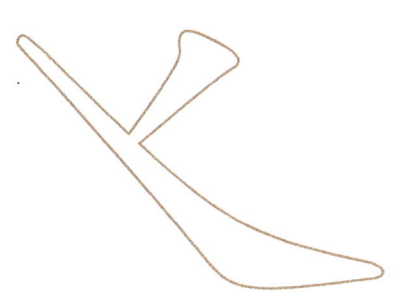

2

Common Features: RL-Slash(es) attached to LR-Slash and shaped like a slide

What to Observe
Triple ABCs Concept:

Colour the parts. Illustrate the features of these parts in the diagram above. Add on more features you observe.

☐ **A**ngle
Angle to Horizontal (ATH)
Positive/negative gradient
Angle of Joint (AOJ)

☐ **C**urve
Curvature

☐ **A**part
Space between strokes

☐ **B**onding
Bond Point / Bond Types
Distance from Head/Tail

Others
☐ Parallel Strokes
☐ Positioning of strokes relative to one another

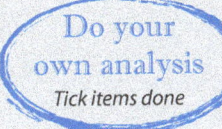

Do your own analysis
Tick items done

3

4

Stroke Order Rule:
RL-Slash(es) First
LR-Slash Last

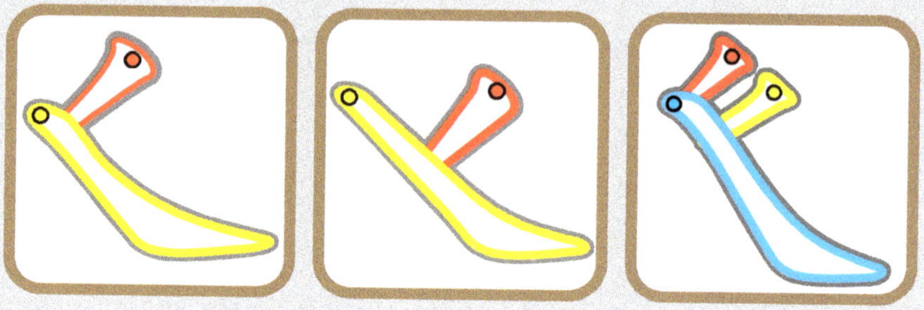

Write RL-Slash(es) first.
Write LR-Slash last and bonded to RL-Slash(es).

5 水 衣 家 橙

Activity 18

15 Cross (Simple)

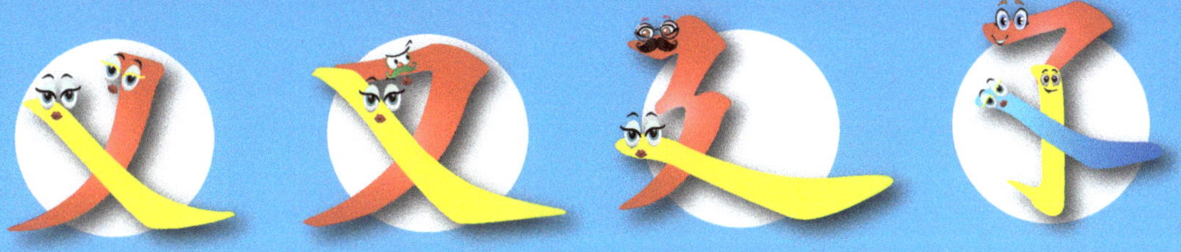

Stroke Order
1 2 3 4 5 6

1

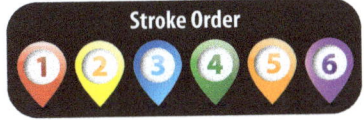

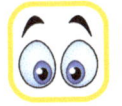

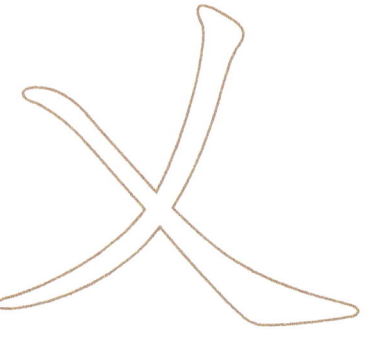

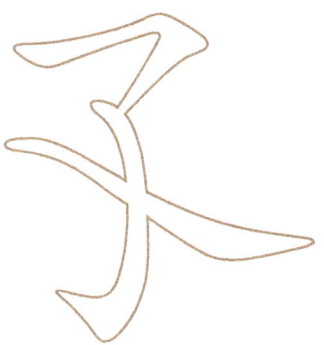

Common Features: End with LR–Slash intersecting another stroke

What to Observe
Triple ABCs Concept:

☐ **Angle**
Angle to Horizontal (ATH)
Positive/negative gradient
Angle of Joint (AOJ)

☐ **Bend**
Angle of Bend (AOB)

☐ **Curve**
Curvature

Colour the parts. Illustrate the features of these parts in the diagram above.
Add on more features you observe.

☐ **Bonding**
Bond Point / Bond Types
Distance from Head/Tail

☐ **Crossing**
Cross Point / Cross Types
Distance from Head/Tail

Others
☐ Positioning of strokes relative to one another

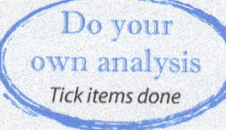

Do your own analysis
Tick items done

3

Stroke Order Rule:
LR-Slash Last

Start from **RL-Slash** or **7-Slash** or **Double-7 Slash** or **Acute-7**
Write the **LR-Slash** last **intersecting** the previous stroke

4

5

友 延 义
凶 廷 交

Activity 19

16 Slide & Cross (7-Slash)

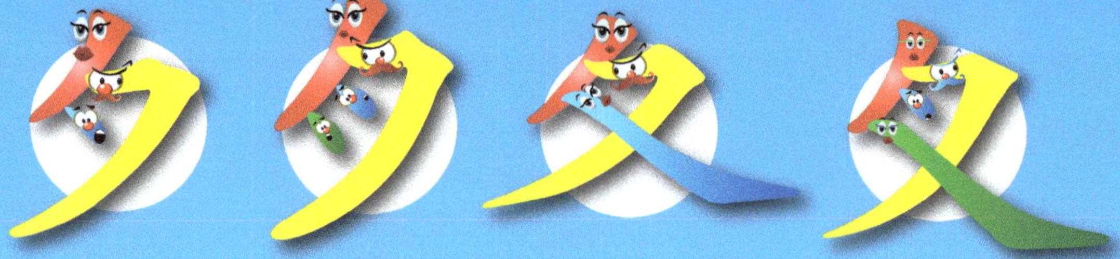

Stroke Order
1 2 3 4 5 6

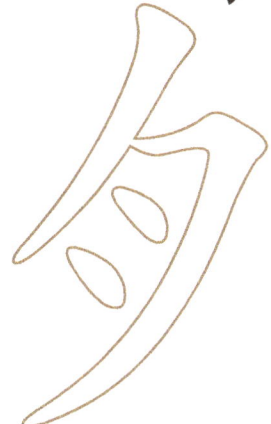

 **2**

Common Features: RL-Slash bonded to 7-Slash

What to Observe
Triple ABCs Concept:

Colour the parts. Illustrate the features of these parts in the diagram above.
Add on more features you observe.

☐ **A**ngle
  Angle to Horizontal (ATH)
  Positive/negative gradient
  Angle of Joint (AOJ)

☐ **B**end
  Angle of Bend (AOB)

☐ **C**urve
  Curvature

☐ **A**part
  Space between strokes

☐ **B**onding
  Bond Point / Bond Types
  Distance from Head/Tail

☐ **C**rossing
  Cross Point / Cross Types
  Distance from Head/Tail

Others

☐ Parallel Strokes

☐ Positioning of strokes relative to one another

Do your own analysis
Tick items done

3

4

Stroke Order Rule:

RL-Slash First

Start from RL-Slash then 7-Slash.
Then write LR-Dot(s) (if any).
Write LR-Slash (if any) intersecting with 7-Slash

Activity 20

5

⑰ Split & Cross (L-Hook / 7L-Hook)

Stroke Order
① ② ③ ④ ⑤ ⑥

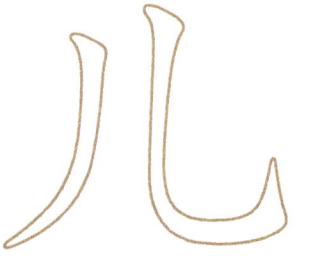
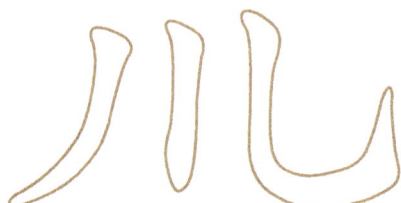
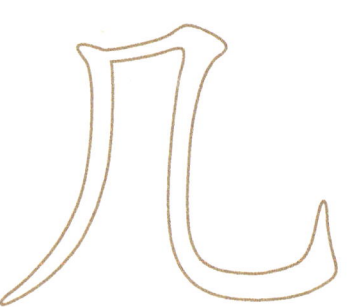

Common Features: RL-Slash and L-Hook/7L-Hook forming a Split/Cross

What to Observe
Triple ABCs Concept:

Colour the parts. Illustrate the features of these parts in the diagram above.
Add on more features you observe.

❏ **A**ngle
   Angle to Horizontal (ATH)
   Positive/negative gradient
   Angle of Joint (AOJ)
❏ **B**end
   Angle of Bend (AOB)
❏ **C**urve
   Curvature

❏ **A**part
   Space between strokes
❏ **B**onding
   Bond Point / Bond Types
   Distance from Head/Tail
❏ **C**rossing
   Cross Point / Cross Types
   Distance from Head/Tail

Others
❏ Parallel Strokes
❏ Positioning of strokes relative to one another
❏ Protrusion(s)

Do your own analysis
Tick items done

3

4

Start from **RL-Slash** first.
Then write **Vertical** (if any).
Write **L-Hook / 7L-Hook** last.

Stroke Order
Rule:
RL-Slash First

5

Activity 21

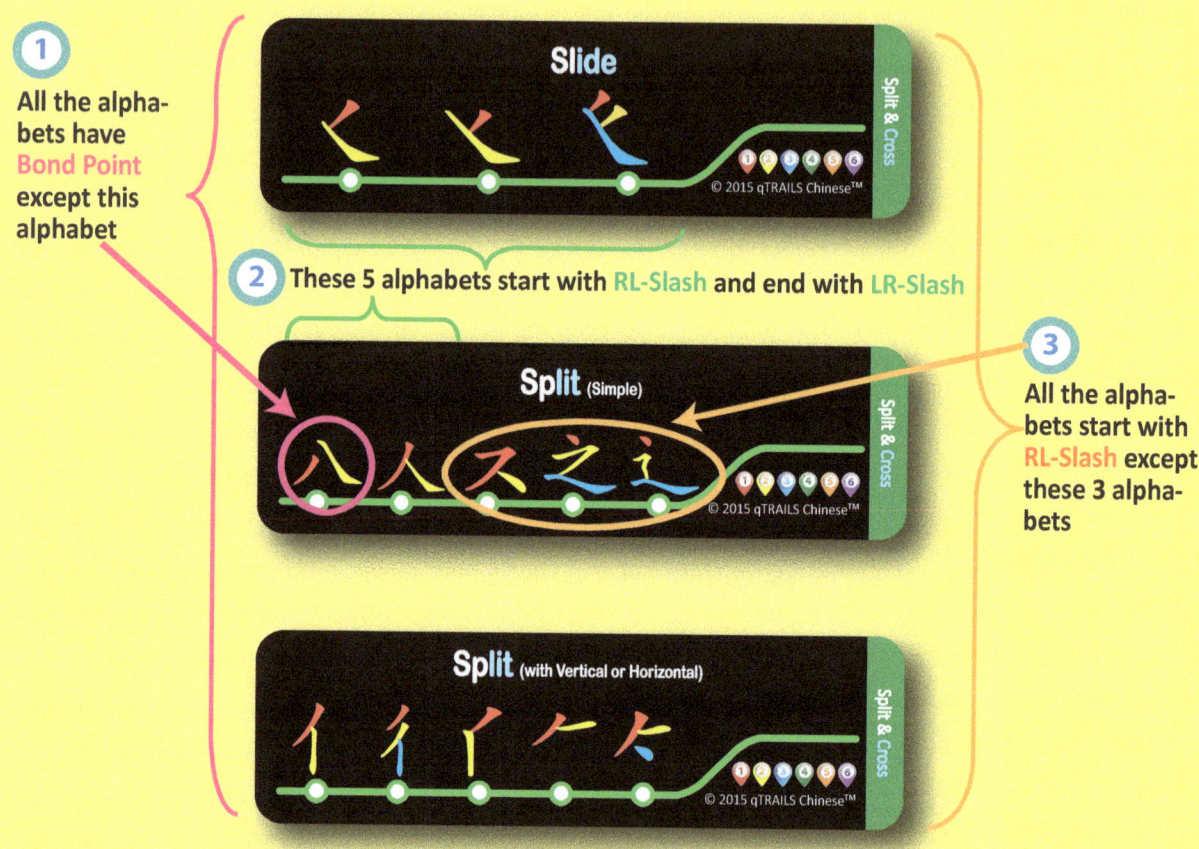

1 All the alphabets have **Bond Point** except this alphabet

2 These 5 alphabets start with **RL-Slash** and end with **LR-Slash**

3 All the alphabets start with **RL-Slash** except these 3 alphabets

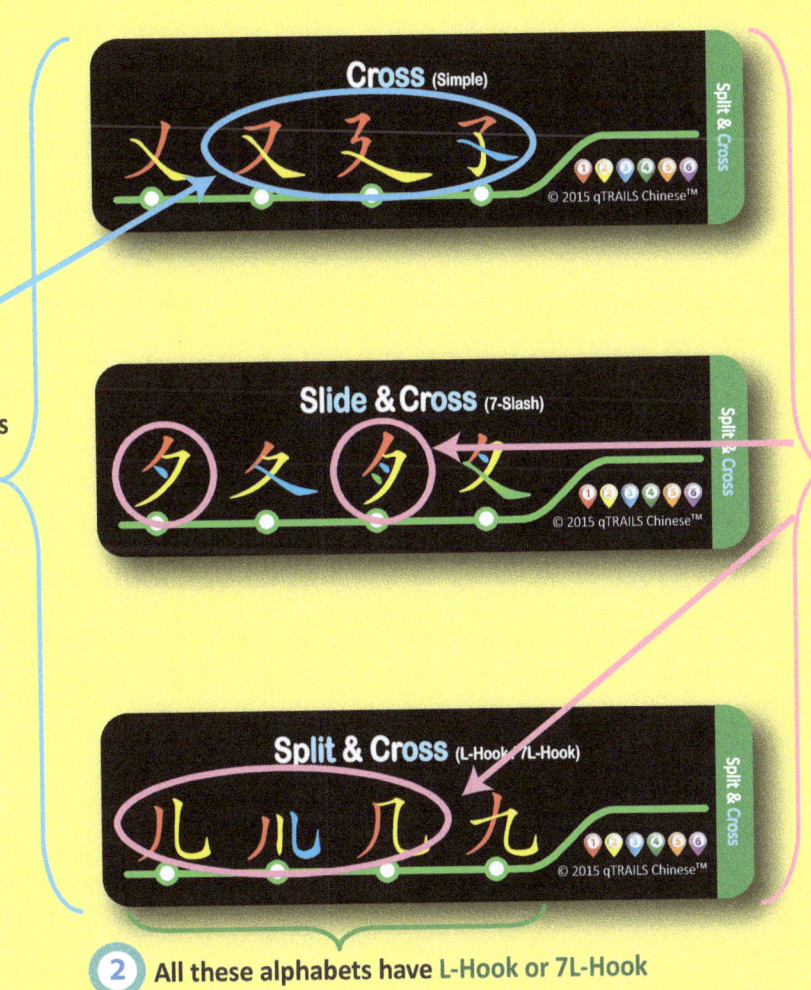

1 All the alphabets start with **RL-Slash** except these 3 alphabets

2 All these alphabets have **L-Hook** or **7L-Hook**

3 All the alphabets have **Cross Point** except these 5 alphabets

Cross (Simple)

Slide & Cross (7-Slash)

Split & Cross (L-Hook / 7L-Hook)

Split & Cross

© 2015 qTRAILS Chinese™

   Split & Cross

qTRAILS 12 to 17

1. List the **qTRAILS Alphabets**

    a) with Double-7 Slash

    b) with 7-Slash

    c) with LR-Dot(s)

    d) with Head-Head Bond point

    e) without Bond point and/or Cross point

2. List the **qTRAILS Alphabets** with the stroke order

    a) NOT starting with RL-Slash

    b) NOT ending with LR-Slash

My Questions:
Write down your own questions.

Create your own sketchbook! Add clippings. Doodle,
Make Notes, Summarise . . .

Activity 22

Basic qTRAIL Alphabets from different qTRAILS are mixed up. Circle the qTRAIL Alphabets from the **same qTRAIL** using the given symbols.

Activity 23

Recall the basic qTRAILS Alphabets you have learnt so far, which of them have these strokes within them, <u>not</u> considering the stroke order. See examples.

E.g. 丿乙 　丿乚 几九

List **8** basic qTRAILS Alphabets. One example is given.

夂

List **5** basic qTRAILS Alphabets. One example is given.

夂

List **2** basic qTRAILS Alphabets

List **2** basic qTRAILS Alphabets

ノ丨

List **11** basic qTRAILS Alphabets.

ノフ

List **4** basic qTRAILS Alphabets.

丶フ

List **4** basic qTRAILS Alphabets

ノ一

List **13** basic qTRAILS Alphabets

Marching & Tick

Marching

Tick

Marching and Tick
(18) Marching
(19) Tick

⑱ Marching

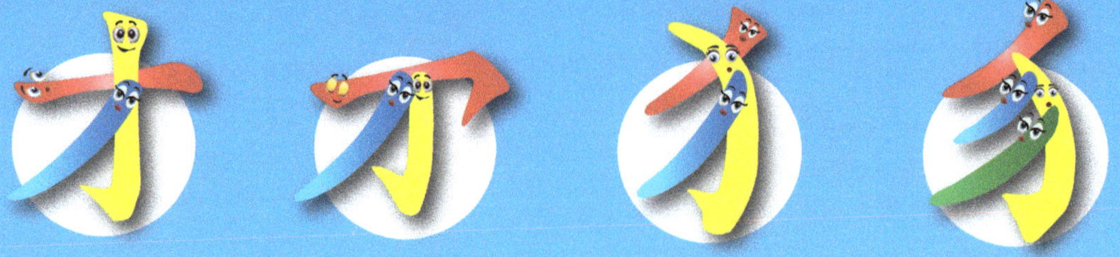

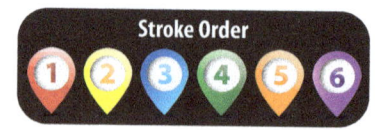

Stroke Order

① ② ③ ④ ⑤ ⑥

 1

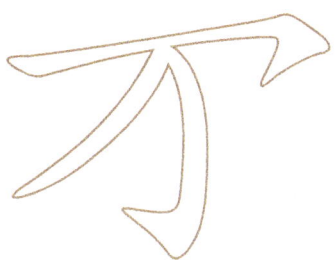

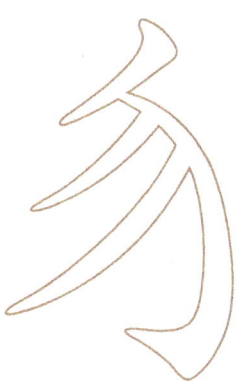

Common Features:
End with RL-Slash(es) attached to a Vertical Left / Hunchback, creating a formation like a soldier marching with one leg forward

 **2**

What to Observe
Triple ABCs Concept:

Colour the parts. Illustrate the features of these parts in the diagram above. Add on more features you observe.

☐ **Angle**
Angle to Horizontal (ATH)
Positive/negative gradient
Angle of Joint (AOJ)

☐ **Curve**
Curvature

☐ **Apart**
Space between strokes

☐ **Bonding**
Bond Point / Bond Types
Distance from Head/Tail

☐ **Crossing**
Cross Point / Cross Types
Distance from Head/Tail

Others
☐ Parallel Strokes
☐ Positioning of strokes relative to one another
☐ Protrusion(s)

Do your own analysis
Tick items done

Stroke Order Rule:
RL-Slash(es) Last

Start from Horizontal or Horizontal Hook or topmost RL-Slash first.
Then write Vertical Left or Hunchback.
Write RL-Slash(es) last.

5      Activity 24

Stroke Order
1 2 3 4 5 6

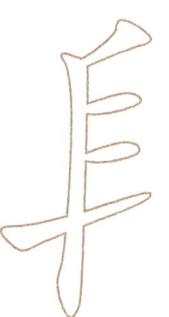

Common Features: A Tick intersecting with a Vertical or Vertical Left

What to Observe
Triple ABCs Concept:

Colour the parts. Illustrate the features of these parts in the diagram above.
Add on more features you observe.

☐ **A**ngle
Angle to Horizontal (ATH)
Positive/negative gradient
Angle of Joint (AOJ)

☐ **B**end
Angle of Bend (AOB)

☐ **A**part
Space between strokes

☐ **B**onding
Bond Point / Bond Types
Distance from Head/Tail

☐ **C**rossing
Cross Point / Cross Types
Distance from Head/Tail

Others
☐ Parallel Strokes
☐ Positioning of strokes relative to one another
☐ Shortest Stroke
☐ Longest Stroke
☐ Protrusion(s)

*Do your
own analysis*
Tick items done

Stroke Order Rule:

Tick Last

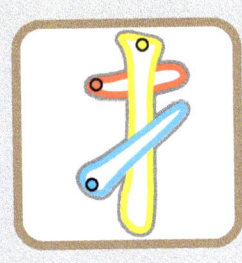 

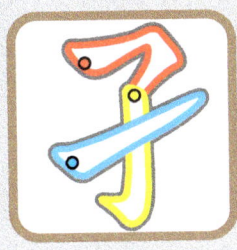 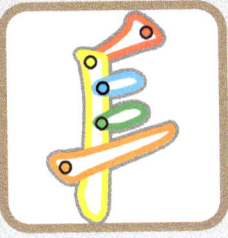

Start from Horizontal or Acute-7 or RL-Slash first
Then write Vertical or Vertical left.
Write Horizontals (if any).
Write Tick last.

  Activity 25

1 All the alphabets stand on Hunchback or Vertical Left or Vertical

2 These 2 alphabets stand on Hunchback

3 These 4 alphabets stand on Vertical Left.

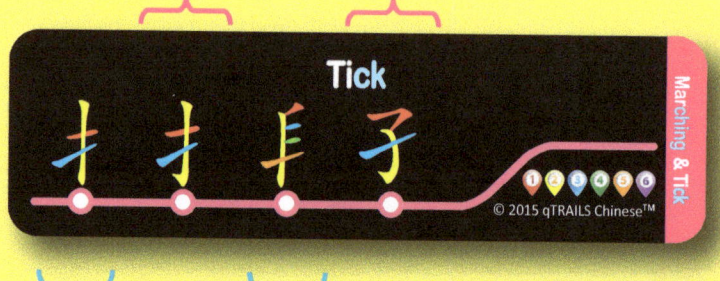

4 These 2 alphabets stand on Vertical.

Activity 26

Recall the basic qTRAILS Alphabets you have learnt so far, which of them have these strokes within them, <u>not</u> considering the stroke order. Write two basic qTRAIL alphabets for each question.

Activity 27

Alphabets from qTRAILS you have learnt so far are shown below. Indicate the starting point of the first stroke with the symbol. 1

Activity 28

Basic qTRAIL Alphabets from different qTRAILS are mixed up. Circle the qTRAIL Alphabets from the **same qTRAIL** using the given symbols. See examples.

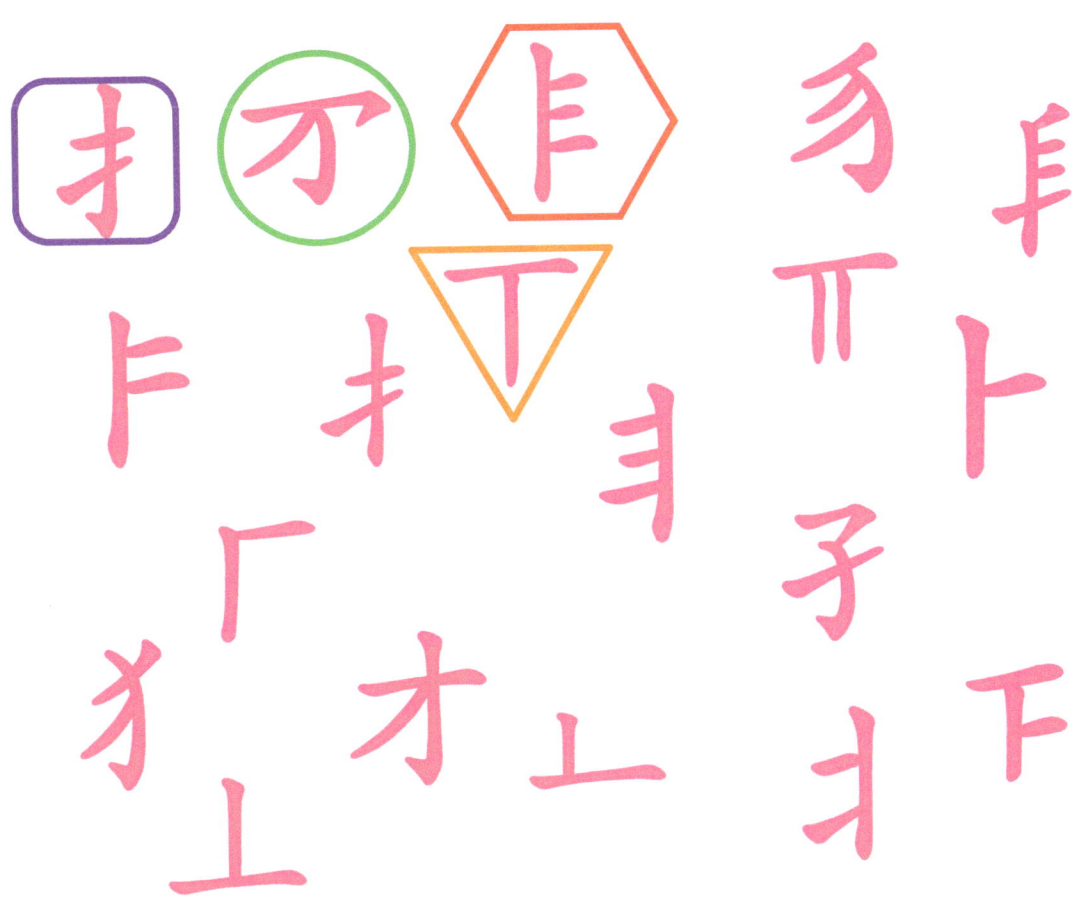

qTRAILS Stroke Order Rules (2)

Match the Stroke Order Rules to the qTRAILS.

Stroke Order Rules

1. **RL-Slash(es) First**
   LR-Slash Last •

2. **RL-Slash(es) First**
   Then vertical or horizontal
   Dot (if any) Last •

3. **RL-Slash or 7-Slash or 7-Hunchback**
   First
   LR-Slash Last •

4. **RL-Slash or 7-Slash or Double 7-Slash**
   or Acute-7 First
   LR-Slash Last •

5. **RL-Slash and 7-Slash First**
   Dot(s) (if any)
   LR-Slash (if any) Last •

6. **RL-Slash First**
   L-Hook or 7L-Hook Last •

7. **Horizontal or Acute-7 or RL-Slash First**
   Vertical or Vertical Left
   Horizontals (if any)
   Tick Last •

8. **Horizontal/Horizontal Hook or**
   topmost RL-Slash First
   Vertical left or Hunchback
   RL-Slash(es) Last •

qTRAILS

Create your own sketchbook! Add clippings. Doodle, Make Notes, Summarise . . . in the next 2 pages.

qTRAILS 18 to 19

1. List the **qTRAILS Alphabets**

    a) with hook

    b) with parallel strokes

    c) with Bond point and Cross point at the same point

    d) with Head-Head Bond point

2. List the **qTRAILS Alphabets** with the stroke order

    a) starting with RL-Slash

    b) starting with Horizontal or Horizontal Hook

My Questions:
Write down your own questions.

My Reflection

120

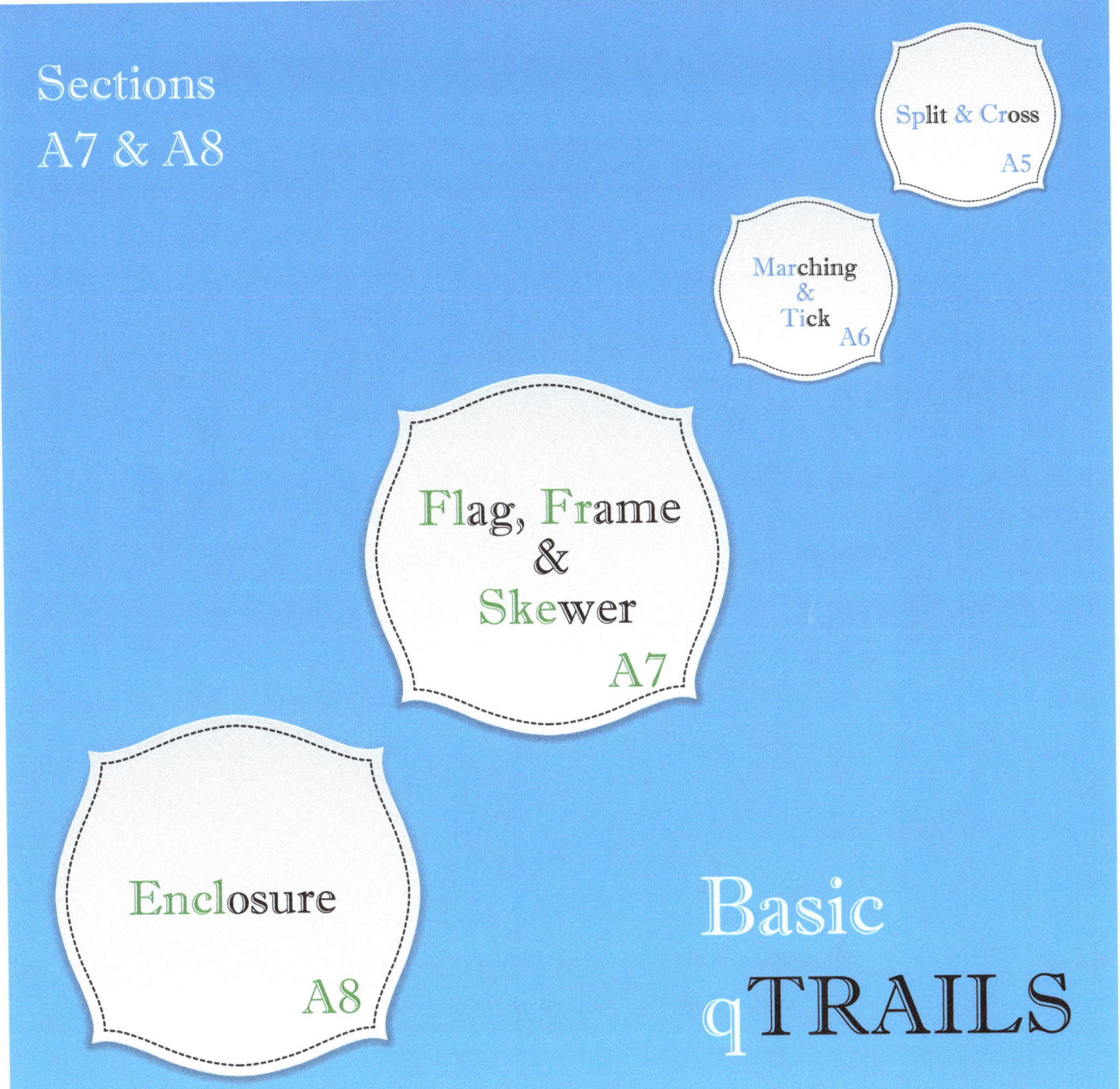

Sections
A7 & A8

Split & Cross
A5

Marching
&
Tick
A6

Flag, Frame
&
Skewer
A7

Enclosure
A8

Basic
qTRAILS

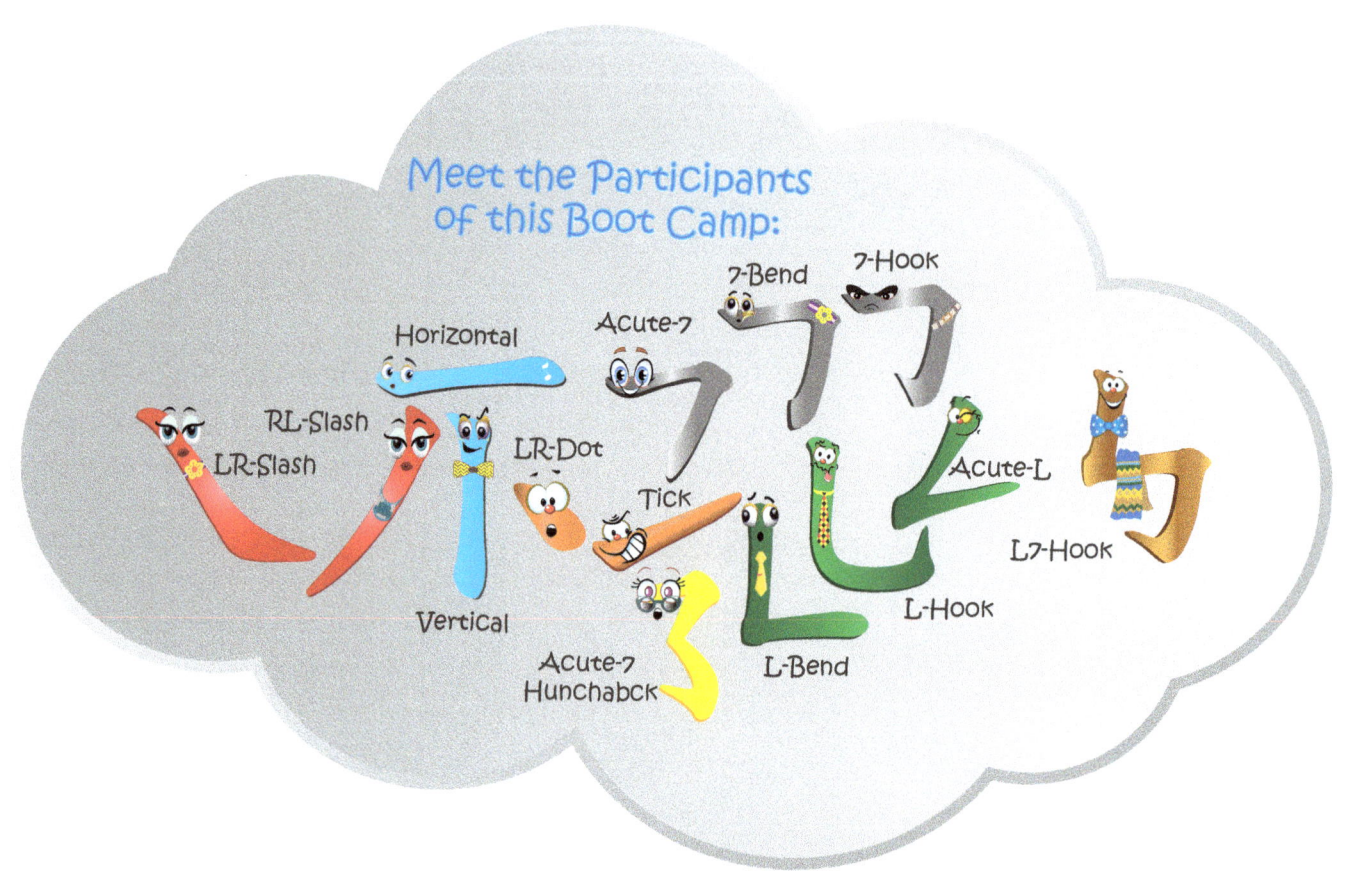

Meet the Participants of this Boot Camp:

LR-Slash · RL-Slash · Horizontal · LR-Dot · Vertical · Acute-7 · Tick · Acute-7 Hunchabck · 7-Bend · 7-Hook · L-Bend · L-Hook · Acute-L · L7-Hook

Boot Camp 4
Flag, Frame & Skewer Enclosure

In Boot Camp 4, 14 performers are participating.

Flag, Frame & Skewer

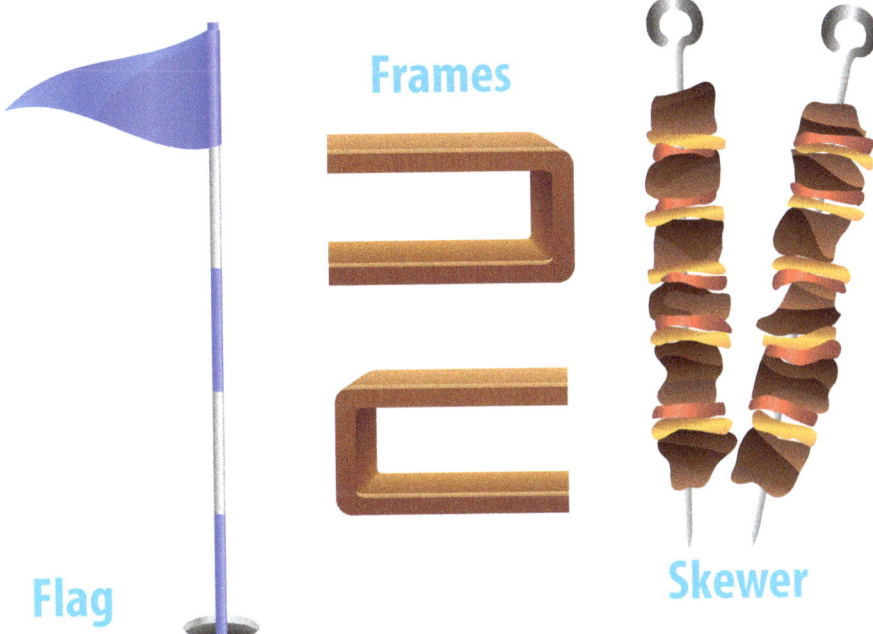

Frames

Flag

Skewer

Flag, Frame & Skewer
(20) Flag (7-Hook)
(21) Flag (L-Bend)
(22) L7-Hook
(23) 7-Hook Frame
(24) L-Frame and U-Frame
(25) C-Frame
(26) Flipped C-Frame
(27) h-Shape and n-Frame
(28) Skewer

20 Flag (7-Hook)

Stroke Order
1 2 3 4 5 6

 1

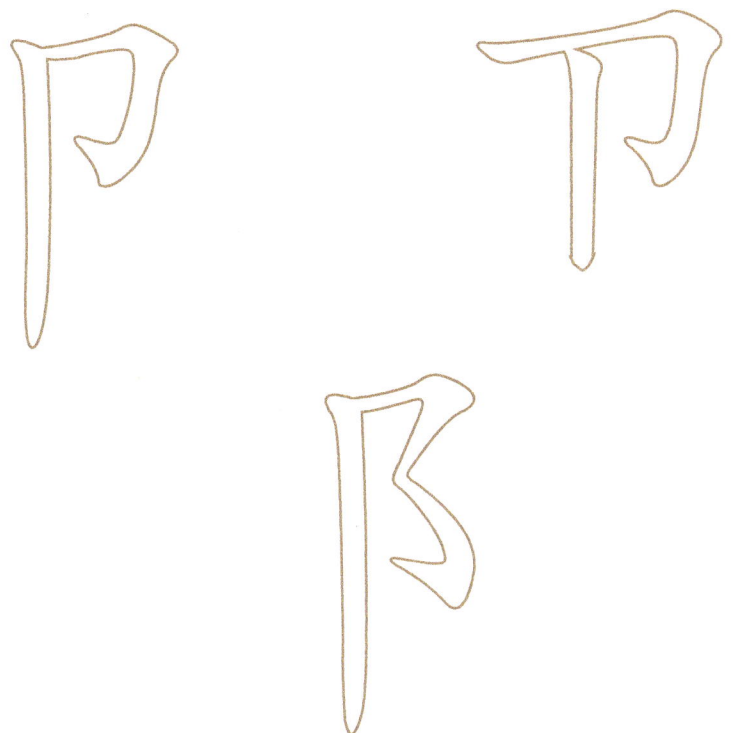

Common Features:
7-Hook or Acute-7 Hunchback bonded with a Vertical and shaped like a flag

What to Observe
Triple ABCs Concept:

Colour the parts. Illustrate the features of these parts in the diagram above.
Add on more features you observe.

Others

☐ **A**ngle
  Angle to Horizontal (ATH)
  Positive/negative gradient
  Angle of Joint (AOJ)

☐ **B**onding
  Bond Point / Bond Types
  Distance from Head/Tail

☐ **B**end
  Angle of Bend (AOB)

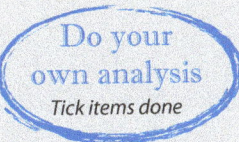

Do your own analysis
Tick items done

3

4

Stroke Order Rule:
7-Hook /
Acute-7 Hunchback First
Vertical Last

Write 7-Hook or Acute-7 Hunchback First.
Then write Vertical last

5

节 卯 郑
爷 帮 服

Activity 30

㉑ Flag (L-Bend)

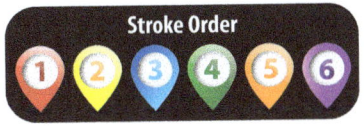

Stroke Order
1 2 3 4 5 6

 1

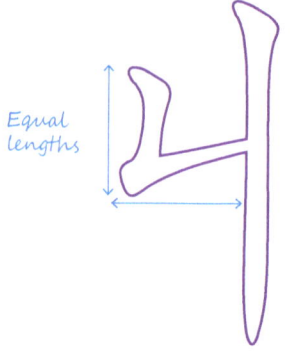

Equal lengths

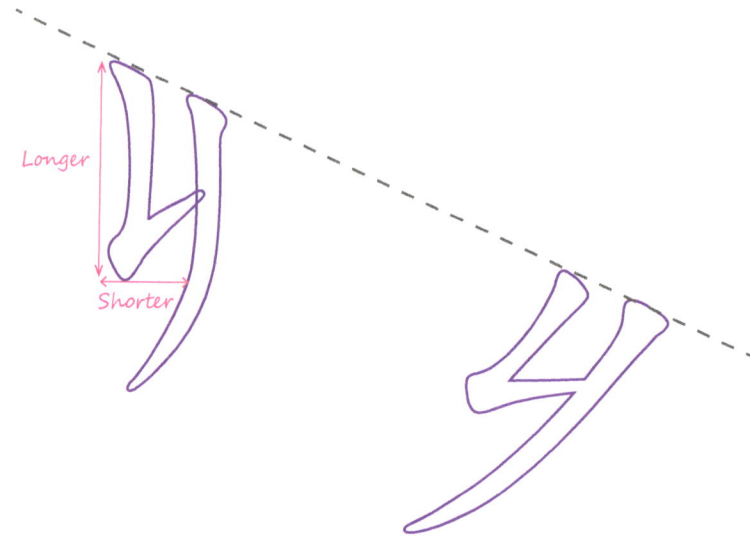

Longer

Shorter

Common Features:
L-Bend or Acute-L bonded with a RL-Slash or Vertical and shaped like a flag

 **2**

What to Observe
Triple ABCs Concept:

Colour the parts. Illustrate the features of these parts in the diagram above. Add on more features you observe.

☐ **A**ngle
Angle to Horizontal (ATH)
Positive/negative gradient
Angle of Joint (AOJ)

☐ **B**end
Angle of Bend (AOB)

☐ **C**urve
Curvature

☐ **B**onding
Bond Point / Bond Types
Distance from Head/Tail

Others
☐ Relative lengths of two stems in L-Bend and Acute-L

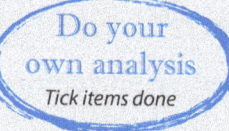

Do your own analysis
Tick items done

3    **4**

Stroke Order Rule:

L-Bend / Acute-L First
RL-Slash / Vertical Last

 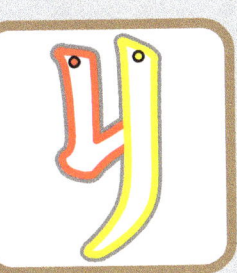 

Write L-Bend or Acute-L First.
Write RL-Slash and Vertical Last.

5         Activity 31

22 L7-Hook

ㄅ ㄅ ㄅ ㄣ 马 马

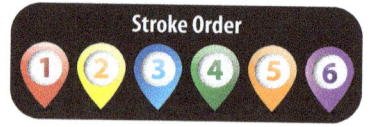

Stroke Order
1 2 3 4 5 6

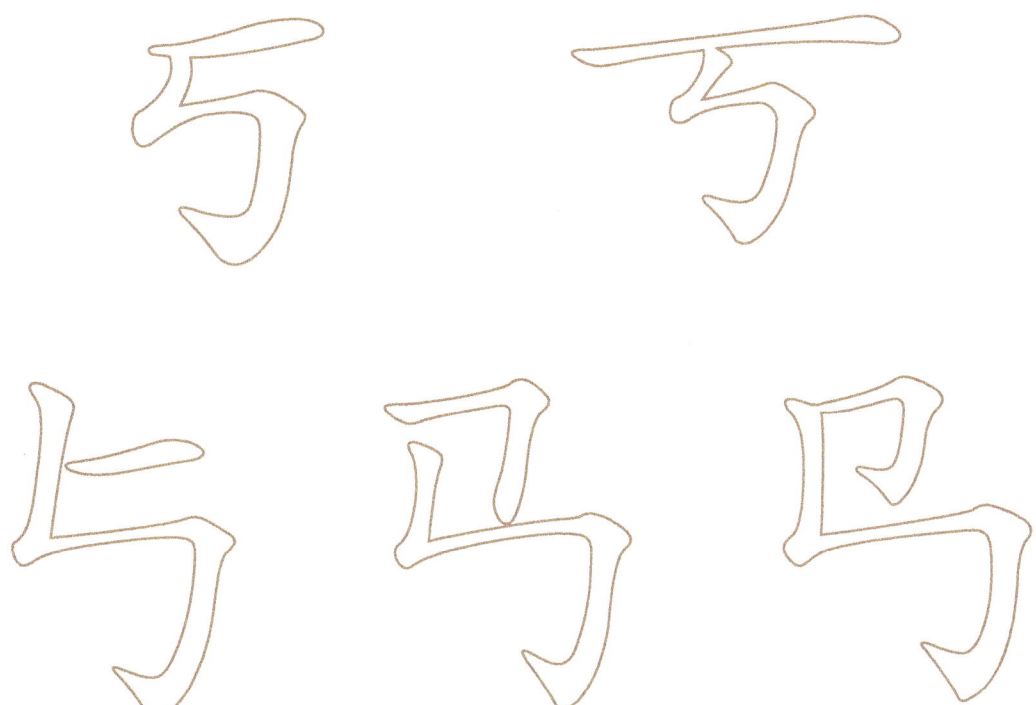

Common Features: *End with L7-Hook*

 **2**

What to Observe
Triple ABCs Concept:

Colour the parts. Illustrate the features of these parts in the diagram above. Add on more features you observe.

☐ **A**ngle
   Angle of Joint (AOJ)

☐ **B**end
   Angle of Bend (AOB)

☐ **A**part
   Space between strokes

☐ **B**onding
   Bond Point / Bond Types
   Distance from Head/Tail

Others

☐ Positioning of strokes relative to one another

☐ Relative lengths of the 3 stems of L7-Hook

Do your own analysis
Tick items done

Stroke Order Rule:

**Horizontal / 7-Bend /
7-Hook First
L7-Hook Last**

Write Horizontal or 7-Bend or7-Hook First.
Then write L7-Hook Last.

5

马　与　巧

考　号　鸟

Activity 32

23 7-Hook Frame

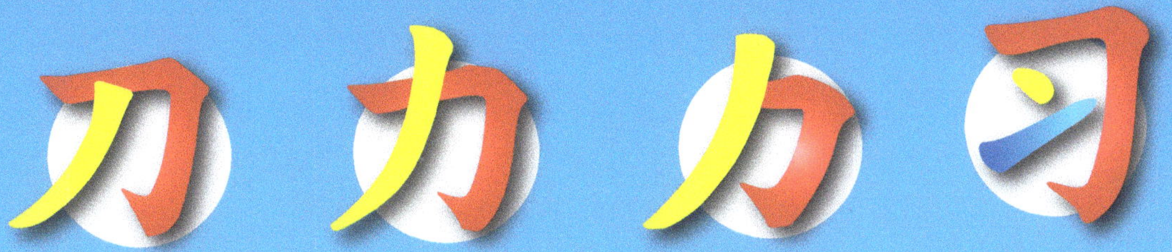

刀 力 力 习

Stroke Order

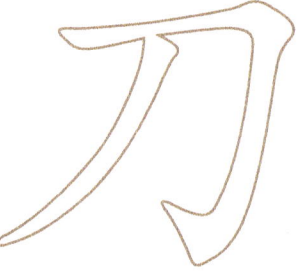

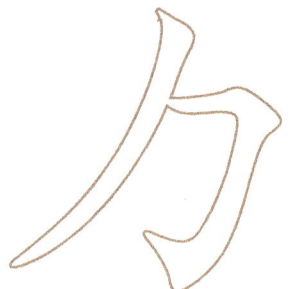

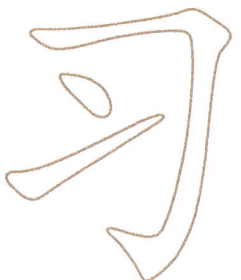

Common Features:
Start with a 7-Hook

 **2**

What to Observe
Triple ABCs Concept:

Colour the parts. Illustrate the features of these parts in the diagram above. Add on more features you observe.

☐ **A**ngle
   Angle to Horizontal (ATH)
   Positive/negative gradient
   Angle of Joint (AOJ)

☐ **B**end
   Angle of Bend (AOB)

☐ **C**urve
   Curvature

☐ **A**part
   Space between strokes

☐ **B**onding
   Bond Point / Bond Types
   Distance from Head/Tail

☐ **C**rossing
   Cross Point / Cross Types
   Distance from Head/Tail

Others
☐ Positioning of strokes relative to one another
☐ Protrusion(s)
☐ Relative lengths of the 2 stems of 7-Hook

Do your own analysis
Tick items done

3

Stroke Order Rule:

7-Hook First

Write **7-Hook** First.
Write the **inside or RL-Slash** last.

4

5

万 切 方 劳
别 历 扇 剪

Activity 33

Stroke Order

1 2 3 4 5 6

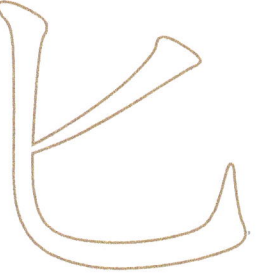
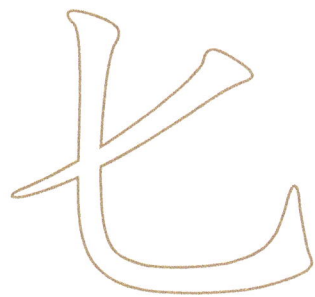

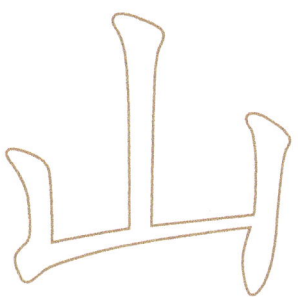

Common Features: End with L-Hook or U-Frame
(A U-Frame is created with L-Bend bonded to a Vertical)

 **2**

What to Observe
Triple ABCs Concept:

Colour the parts. Illustrate the features of these parts in the diagram above. Add on more features you observe.

Do your own analysis
Tick items done

☐ **A**ngle
   Angle of Joint (AOJ)

☐ **B**end
   Angle of Bend (AOB)

☐ **B**onding
   Bond Point / Bond Types
   Distance from Head/Tail

☐ **C**rossing
   Cross Point / Cross Types
   Distance from Head/Tail

Others

☐ Positioning of strokes relative to one another

☐ Protrusion(s)

☐ Relative lengths of the 2 stems of L-Bend

☐ Relative lengths of the 2 stems of Round-L

3

Stroke Order Rule:
Inside First
L-Hook / U-Frame
Last

Write Inside (if any) First.
Then L-Bend /L-Hook
Follwed by Vertical (if any)

4

它 岸 北 画
化 讪 出 龙

Activity 34

5

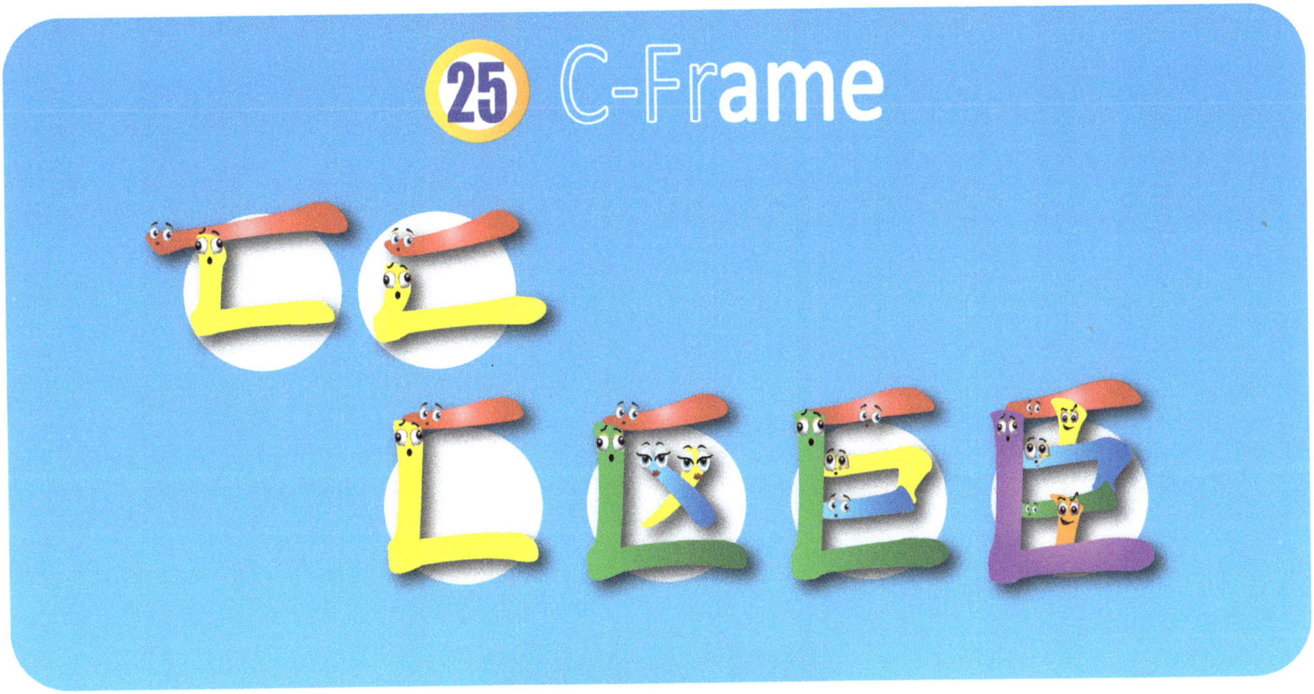
25 C-Frame

Stroke Order
1
2
3
4
5
6

1

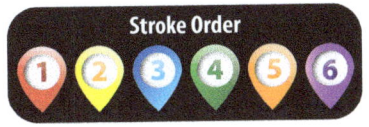

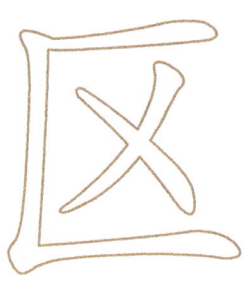

Common Features:
Horizontal and L-Bend
forming a C-Frame

 **2**

What to Observe
Triple ABCs Concept:

- ☐ **A**ngle
  Angle of Joint (AOJ)
- ☐ **B**end
  Angle of Bend (AOB)

Colour the parts. Illustrate the features of these parts in the diagram above.
Add on more features you observe.

- ☐ **A**part
  Space between strokes
- ☐ **B**onding
  Bond Point / Bond Types
  Distance from Head/Tail
- ☐ **C**rossing
  Cross Point / Cross Types
  Distance from Head/Tail

Others
- ☐ Parallel Strokes
- ☐ Positioning of strokes relative to one another
- ☐ Relative lengths of the 2 stems of L-Bend

Do your own analysis
Tick items done

3  **4**

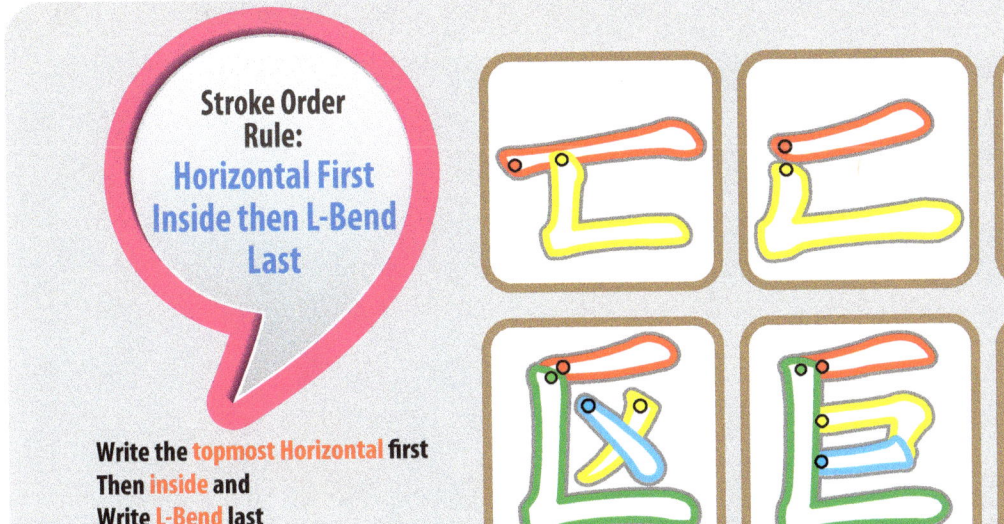

Stroke Order Rule:
Horizontal First
Inside then L-Bend
Last

Write the **topmost Horizontal** first
Then **inside** and
Write **L-Bend** last

5       Activity 35

26 Flipped C-Frame

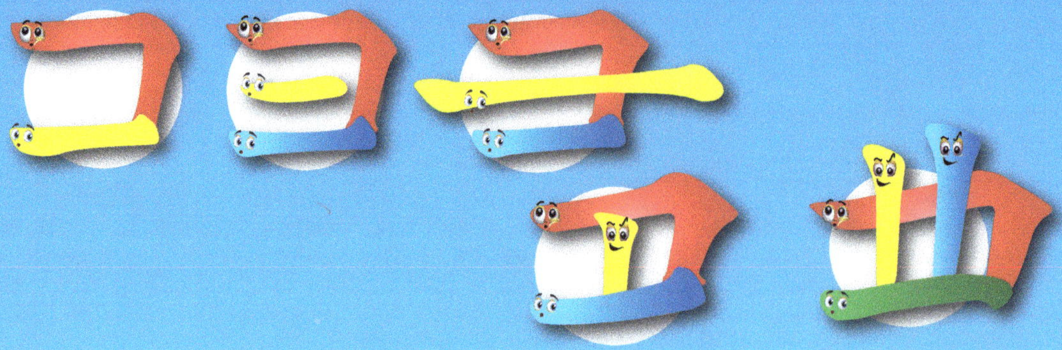

Stroke Order
1 2 3 4 5 6

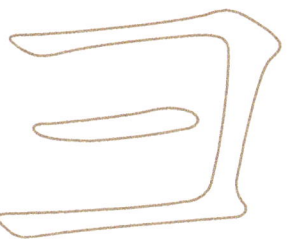

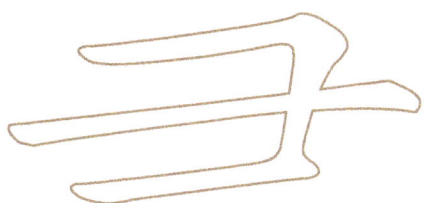

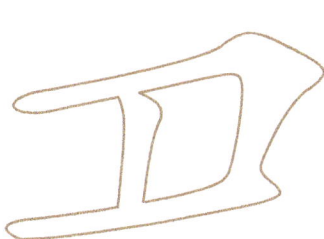

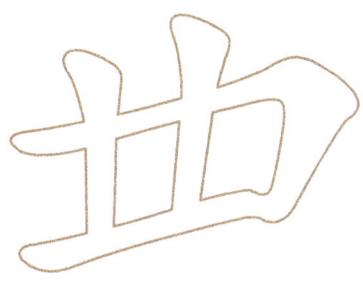

 2

Common Features: 7-Bend and Horizontal forming an inverted C-Frame

What to Observe
Triple ABCs Concept:

Colour the parts. Illustrate the features of these parts in the diagram above.
Add on more features you observe.

Do your own analysis
Tick items done

☐ **A**ngle
Angle of Joint (AOJ)

☐ **B**end
Angle of Bend (AOB)

☐ **A**part
Space between strokes

☐ **B**onding
Bond Point / Bond Types
Distance from Head/Tail

☐ **C**rossing
Cross Point / Cross Types
Distance from Head/Tail

Others
☐ Parallel Strokes
☐ Positioning of strokes relative to one another
☐ Protrusion(s)
☐ Relative lengths of the 2 stems of 7-Bend

Stroke Order Rule:
7-Bend First
Inside
Bottommost
Horizontal Last

Write **7-Bend** First.
Then write **Horizontal or Vertical(s)** inside.
Write **bottommost Horizontal** last.

5

事 扫 弓 声
弟 鹿 争 很

Activity 36

27 h-Shape & n-Frame

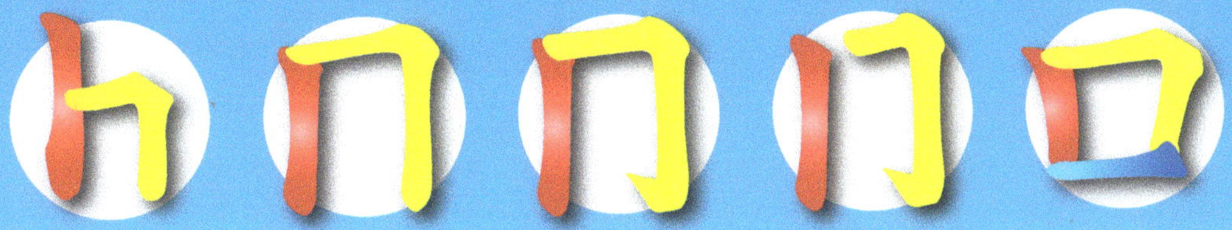

Stroke Order

1 2 3 4 5 6

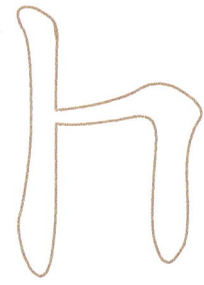
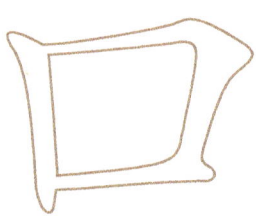

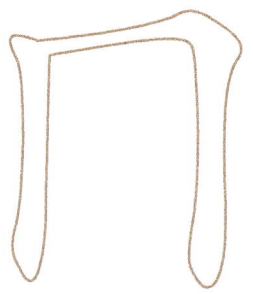
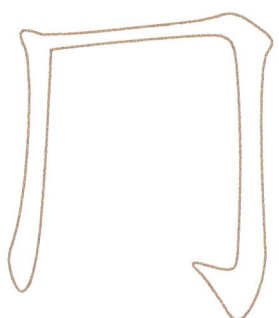
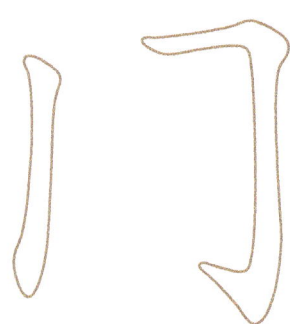

Common Features:
A Vertical bonded with a 7-Bend / 7-Hook to form a h-Shape or n-Frame

 2

What to Observe
Triple ABCs Concept:

Colour the parts. Illustrate the features of these parts in the diagram above. Add on more features you observe.

Do your own analysis
Tick items done

☐ **A**ngle
  Angle of Joint (AOJ)
☐ **B**end
  Angle of Bend (AOB)

☐ **A**part
  Space between strokes
☐ **B**onding
  Bond Point / Bond Types
  Distance from Head/Tail

Others
☐ Positioning of strokes relative to one another
☐ Relative lengths of the 2 stems of 7-Bend
☐ Relative lengths of the 2 stems of 7-Hook

3

4

Stroke Order Rule:
Vertical First
7-Bend / 7-Hook Next
Horizontal (if any) Last

Write Vertical first.
Then 7-Bend or 7-Hook
Close the frame with Horizontal (if any)

门　贝　只　同　内

5　问　园　丽　启　鼎　Activity 37

28 Skewer

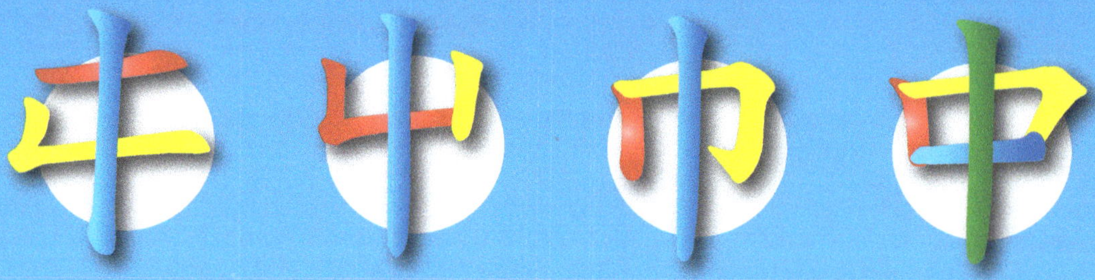

Stroke Order
1 2 3 4 5 6

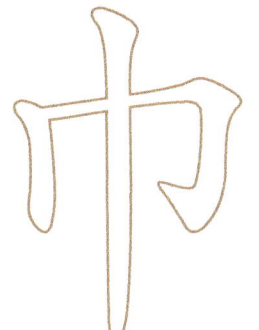

Common Features:
A Vertical intersecting a C-Frame, U-Frame or n-Frame in the middle.

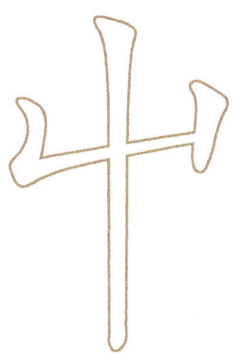
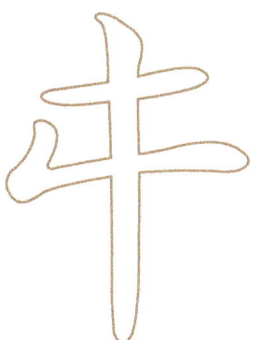

 2

What to Observe
Triple ABCs Concept:

☐ **A**ngle
Angle of Joint (AOJ)

☐ **B**end
Angle of Bend (AOB)

Do your own analysis
Tick items done

Colour the parts. Illustrate the features of these parts in the diagram above. Add on more features you observe.

☐ **B**onding
Bond Point / Bond Types
Distance from Head/Tail

☐ **C**rossing
Cross Point / Cross Types
Distance from Head/Tail

Others
☐ Parallel Strokes
☐ Positioning of strokes relative to one another
☐ Shortest Stroke
☐ Longest Stroke
☐ Protrusion(s)
☐ Relative lengths of the 2 stems of L-Bend
☐ Relative lengths of the 2 stems of 7-Bend
☐ Relative lengths of the 2 stems of 7-Hook

3

Stroke Order
Rule:

Frame/Enclosure First
Vertical Last

4

Write the C-Frame, U-Frame, n-Frame or Enclosure first.
Write Middle Vertical last to intersect the Frame/Enclosure

出 串 布

5 朿 舞 束

Activity 38

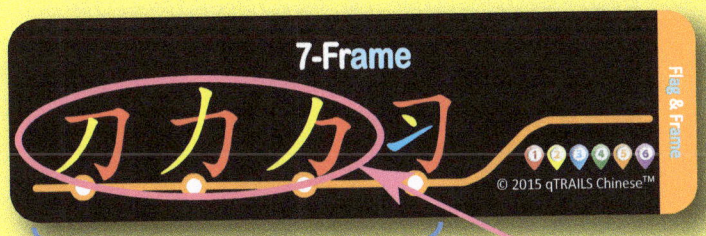

1 These 6 alphabets start with 7-Hook

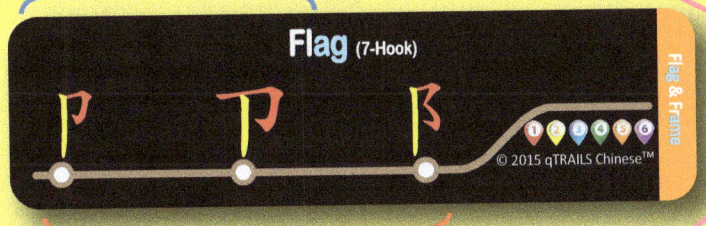

4 These 6 alphabets end with RL-Slash

2 These 4 alphabets end with Vertical

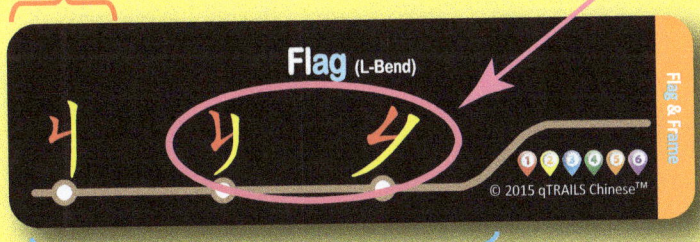

3 These 3 alphabets start with L-Bend / Acute-L

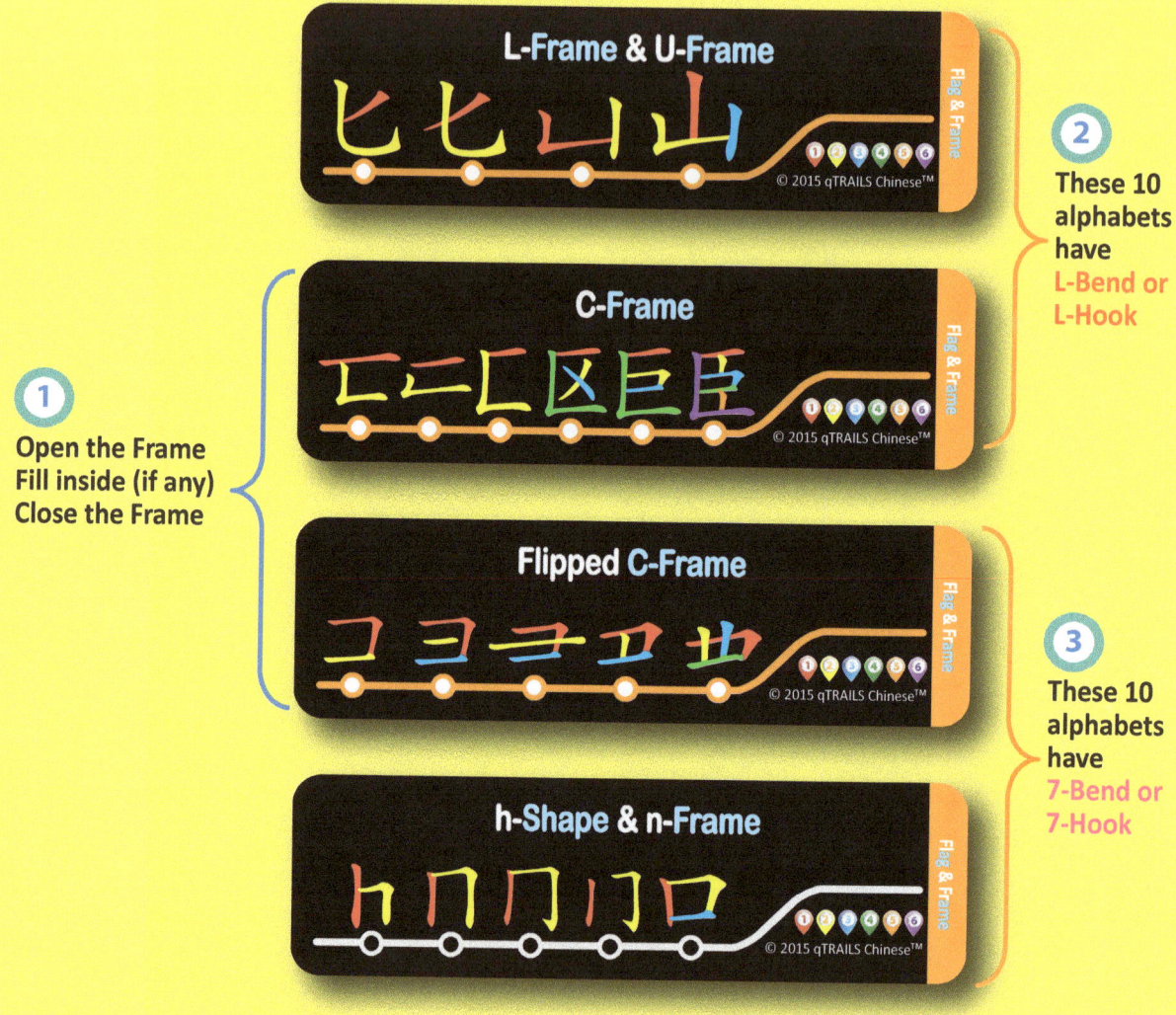

1

Open the Frame
Fill inside (if any)
Close the Frame

2

These 10
alphabets
have
L-Bend or
L-Hook

3

These 10
alphabets
have
7-Bend or
7-Hook

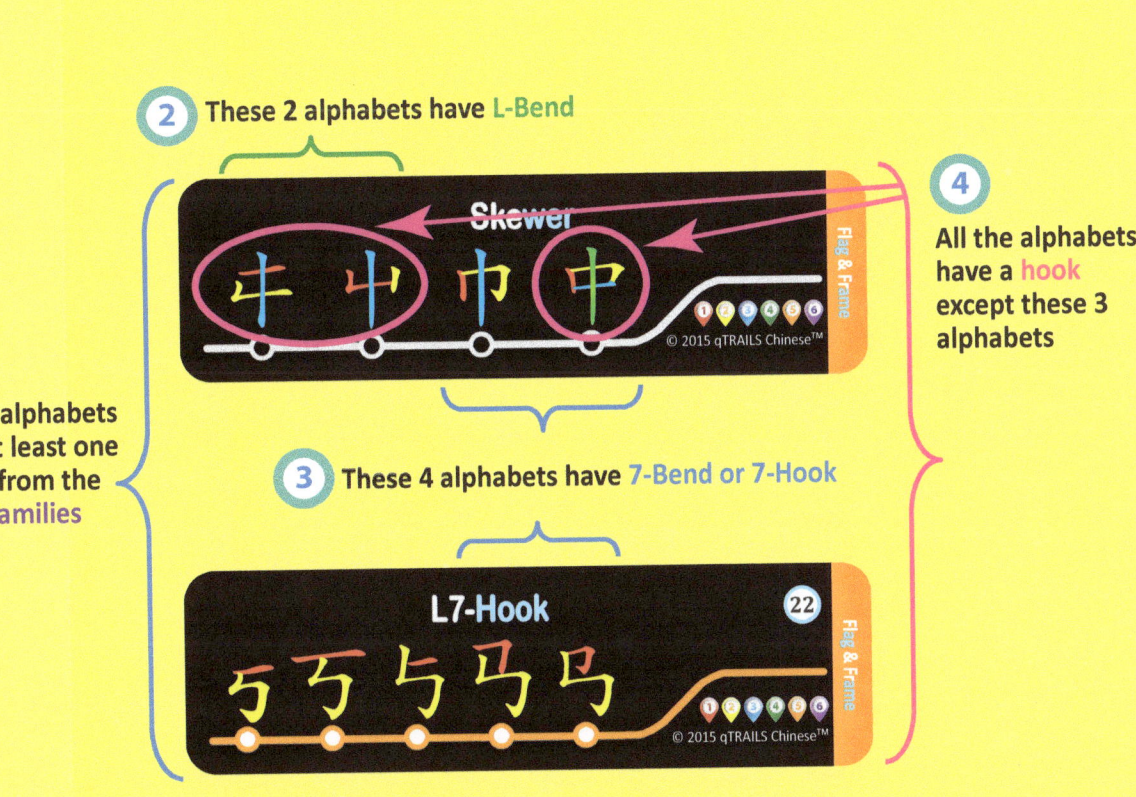

2 These 2 alphabets have L-Bend

1 All the alphabets have at least one stroke from the Bend Families

4 All the alphabets have a hook except these 3 alphabets

3 These 4 alphabets have 7-Bend or 7-Hook

Skewer

牛 屮 巾 中

© 2015 qTRAILS Chinese™

Flag & Frame

L7-Hook

22

ㄅ ㄆ ㄅ ㄢ ㄢ

© 2015 qTRAILS Chinese™

Flag & Frame

Activity 39

Recall the basic qTRAILS Alphabets you have learnt so far, which of them have these strokes within them, <u>not</u> considering the stroke order. See examples.

ノ コ

List **4** basic qTRAILS Alphabets.

丨 コ

List **4** basic qTRAILS Alphabets.

丨 コ

List **4** basic qTRAILS Alphabets

一 コ

List **4** basic qTRAILS Alphabets

ノ レ

List **6** basic qTRAILS Alphabets

丨 レ

List **7** basic qTRAILS Alphabets

154   **FLAG, FRAME & SKEWER**

Activity 40

Alphabets from qTRAILS you have learnt so far are shown below. Indicate the starting point of the first stroke with the symbol. 📍

Activity 41

Basic qTRAIL Alphabets from different qTRAILS are mixed up. Circle the qTRAIL Alphabets from the **same qTRAIL** using the given symbols. See examples.

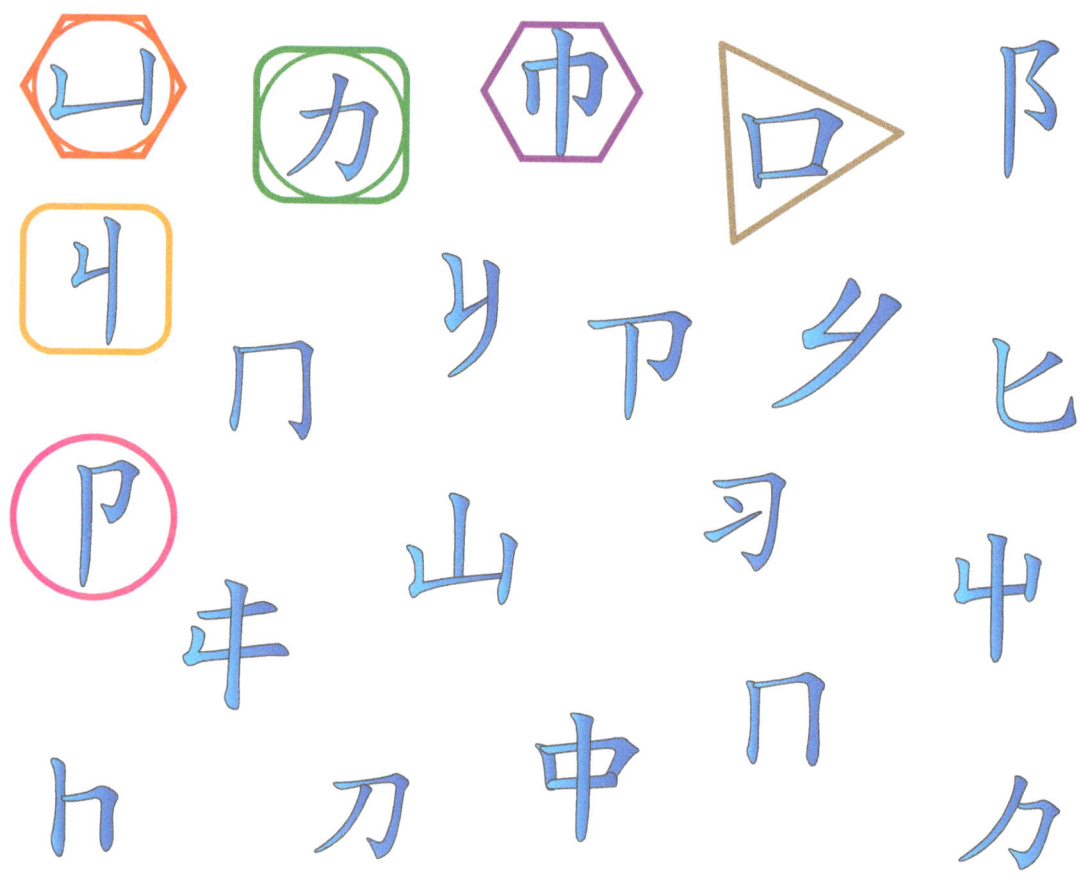

qTRAILS 20 to 28

1. List the **qTRAILS Alphabets**

    a) with 7-Hook

    b) with 7-Bend

    c) with L-Bend

    d) with a Cross Point

2. List the **qTRAILS Alphabets** with the stroke order

    a) starting with Horizontal

    b) starting with Vertical

    c) ending with Horizontal

    d) ending with Vertical

My Questions:
Write down your own questions.

My
Reflection

Create your own sketchbook! Add clippings. Doodle,
Make Notes, Summarise . . .

Flag, Frame & Skewer

Enclosure

Enclosure

29 Enclosure (Horizontals)

月 月 目 且 且

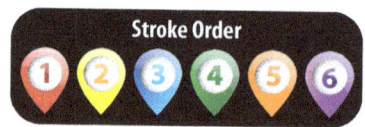

Stroke Order
1 2 3 4 5 6

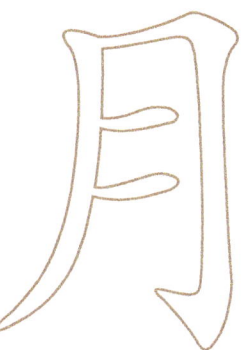

Common Features:
n-Frame with
Horizontal(s)
enclosed within

2

What to Observe
Triple ABCs Concept:

☐ **A**ngle
Angle of Joint (AOJ)

☐ **B**end
Angle of Bend (AOB)

Colour the parts. Illustrate the features of these parts in the diagram above.
Add on more features you observe.

☐ **A**part
Space between strokes

☐ **B**onding
Bond Point / Bond Types
Distance from Head/Tail

Others

☐ Parallel Strokes

☐ Positioning of strokes relative to one another

☐ Relative lengths of the 2 stems of 7-Bend

☐ Relative lengths of the 2 stems of 7-Hook

Do your own analysis
Tick items done

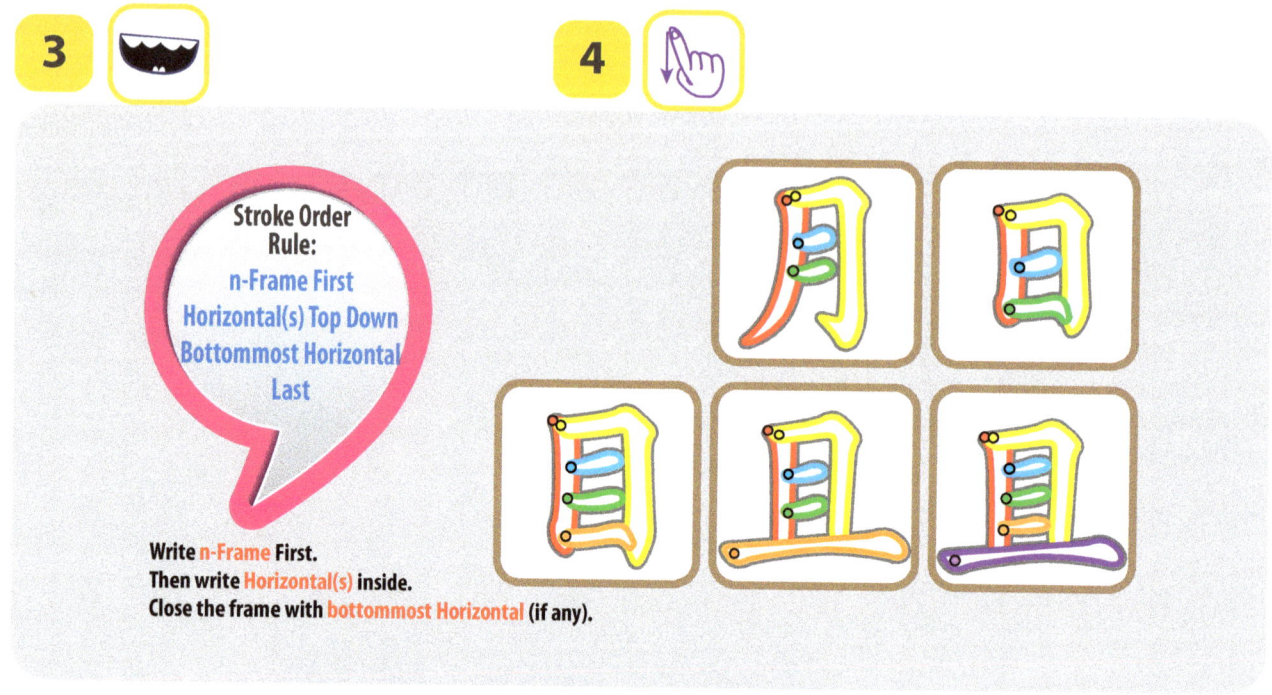
4

Stroke Order Rule:
n-Frame First
Horizontal(s) Top Down
Bottommost Horizontal Last

Write **n-Frame** First.
Then write **Horizontal(s)** inside.
Close the frame with **bottommost Horizontal** (if any).

月 日
目 且 亘

自 旧 睛
5
者 看 具

Activity 42

30 Enclosure (Verticals)

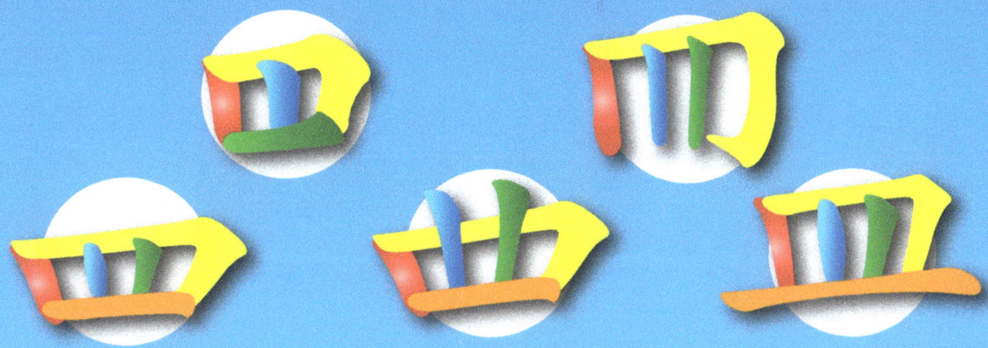

Stroke Order

1 2 3 4 5 6

Anatomy of Chinese Alphabets
Applying Triple ABCs Concept

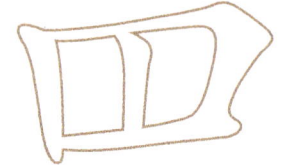

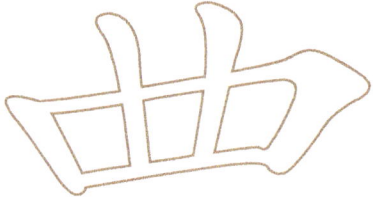

Common Features:
n–Frame with
Vertical(s) enclosed
within

What to Observe
Triple ABCs Concept:

☐ **A**ngle
Angle of Joint (AOJ)

☐ **B**end
Angle of Bend (AOB)

Colour the parts. Illustrate the features of these parts in the diagram above.
Add on more features you observe.

☐ **A**part
Space between strokes

☐ **B**onding
Bond Point / Bond Types
Distance from Head/Tail

☐ **C**rossing
Cross Point / Cross Types
Distance from Head/Tail

Others
☐ Parallel Strokes
☐ Positioning of strokes relative to one another
☐ Protrusion(s)
☐ Relative lengths of the 2 stems of 7-Bend
☐ Relative lengths of the 2 stems of 7-Hook

Do your own analysis
Tick items done

---

166   **ENCLOSURE**

3 **4**

Stroke Order Rule:
n-Frame
Vertical(s) inside
Horizontal Last

Write **n-Frame** First.
Write **Vertical(s) inside** from left to right.
Close the Enclosure by writing the **bottommost Horizontal** (if any).

而 罪 血 要
盒 临 栗 耍

5

Activity 43

㉛ Enclosure (Intersections)

Stroke Order
1 2 3 4 5 6

 1

Common Features:
n-Frame with
intersecting strokes
enclosed within

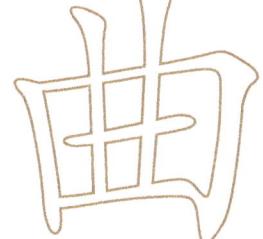

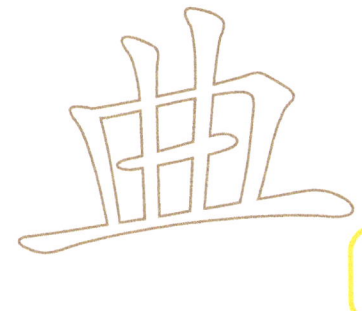

What to Observe
Triple ABCs Concept:

Colour the parts. Illustrate the features of these parts in the diagram above.
Add on more features you observe.

Do your own analysis
Tick items done

- ☐ **A**ngle
  Angle of Joint (AOJ)
- ☐ **B**end
  Angle of Bend (AOB)

- ☐ **A**part
  Space between strokes
- ☐ **B**onding
  Bond Point / Bond Types
  Distance from Head/Tail
- ☐ **C**rossing
  Cross Point / Cross Types
  Distance from Head/Tail

Others
- ☐ Parallel Strokes
- ☐ Positioning of strokes relative to one another
- ☐ Protrusion(s)
- ☐ Relative lengths of the 2 stems of 7-Bend
- ☐ Relative lengths of the 2 stems of 7-Hook

3

4

Stroke Order Rule:

n-Frame First

Intersection(s) Inside

Horizontal Last

Write **n-Frame** First.
Write **Intersections inside**.
Close the Enclosure by writing the
bottommost Horizontal (if any).

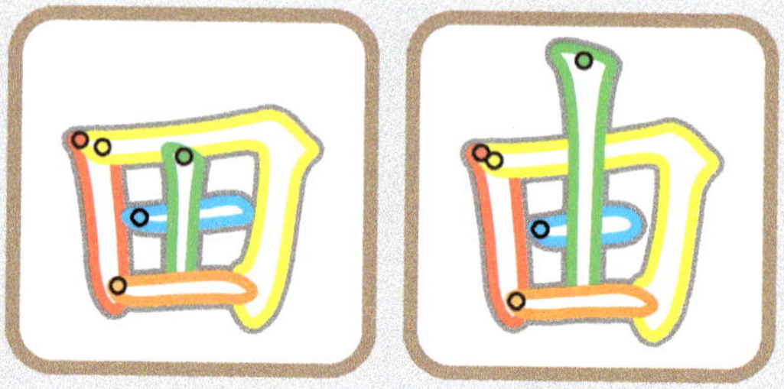

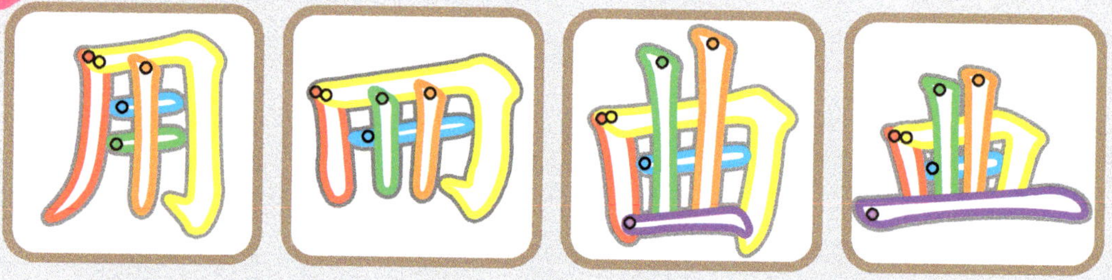

回 由

用 冊 曲 血

5

油 拥 蚰 庙

扁 奋 角 典

Activity 44

口 ㄅ 口 ㄅ

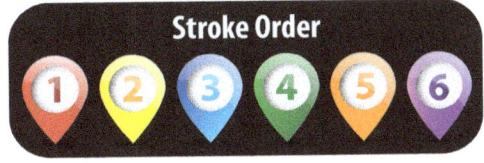

Stroke Order

① ② ③ ④ ⑤ ⑥

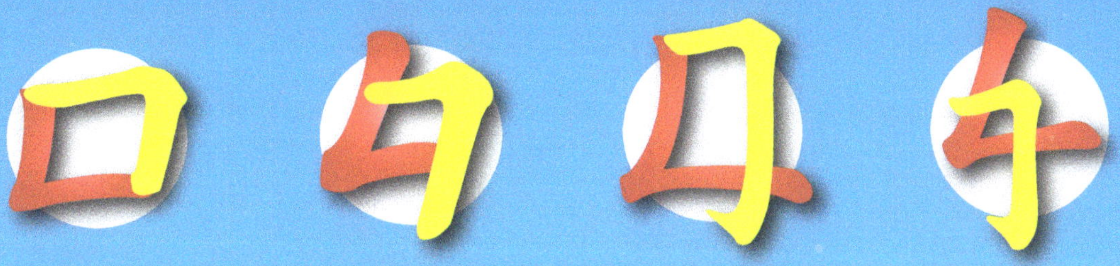

1

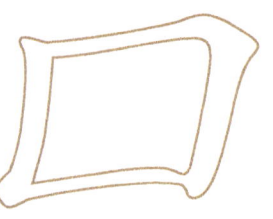

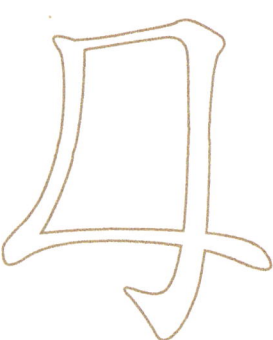

Common Features:

L–Bend or Acute–L bonded or intersected with 7–Bend or 7–Hook or Acute–7

What to Observe
Triple ABCs Concept:

Colour the parts. Illustrate the features of these parts in the diagram above. Add on more features you observe.

☐ **Angle**
  Angle of Joint (AOJ)

☐ **Bend**
  Angle of Bend (AOB)

Do your own analysis
Tick items done

☐ **Bonding**
  Bond Point / Bond Types
  Distance from Head/Tail

☐ **Crossing**
  Cross Point / Cross Types
  Distance from Head/Tail

Others

☐ Positioning of strokes relative to one another
☐ Protrusion(s)
☐ Relative lengths of the 2 stems of 7-Bend
☐ Relative lengths of the 2 stems of 7-Hook
☐ Relative lengths of the 2 stems of L-Bend
☐ Relative lengths of the 2 stems of Acute-L

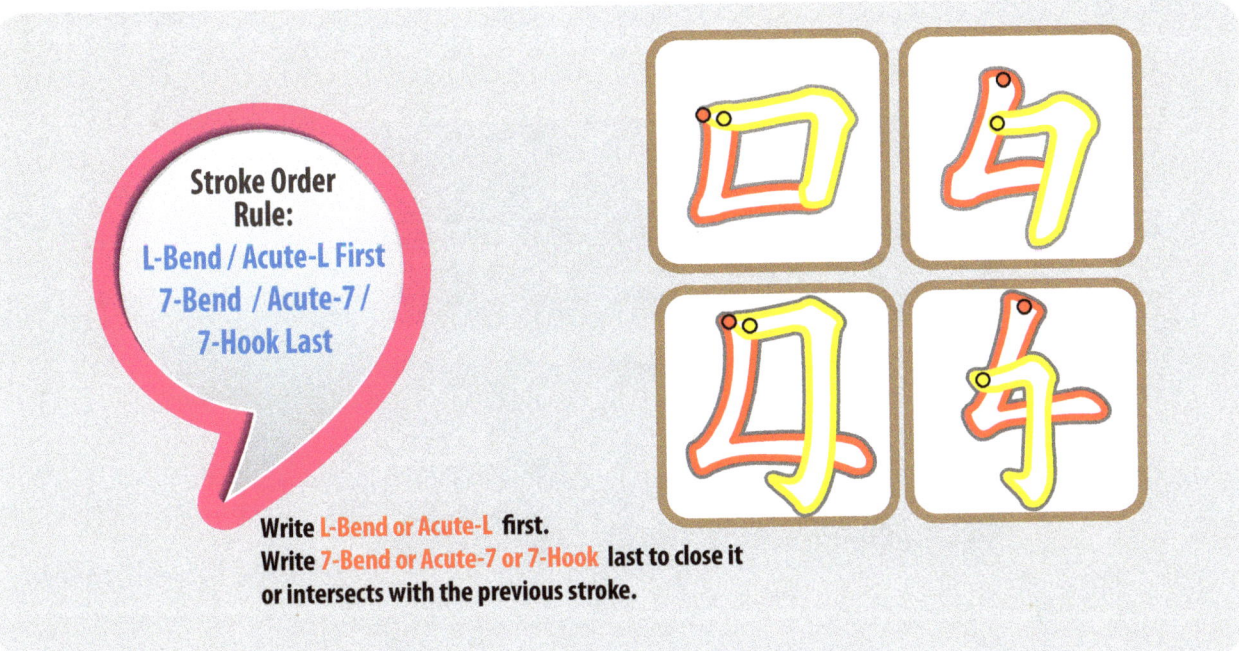

Stroke Order Rule:
L-Bend / Acute-L First
7-Bend / Acute-7 /
7-Hook Last

Write L-Bend or Acute-L first.
Write 7-Bend or Acute-7 or 7-Hook last to close it
or intersects with the previous stroke.

5

练 每 互

缘 贯 毒　　**Activity 45**

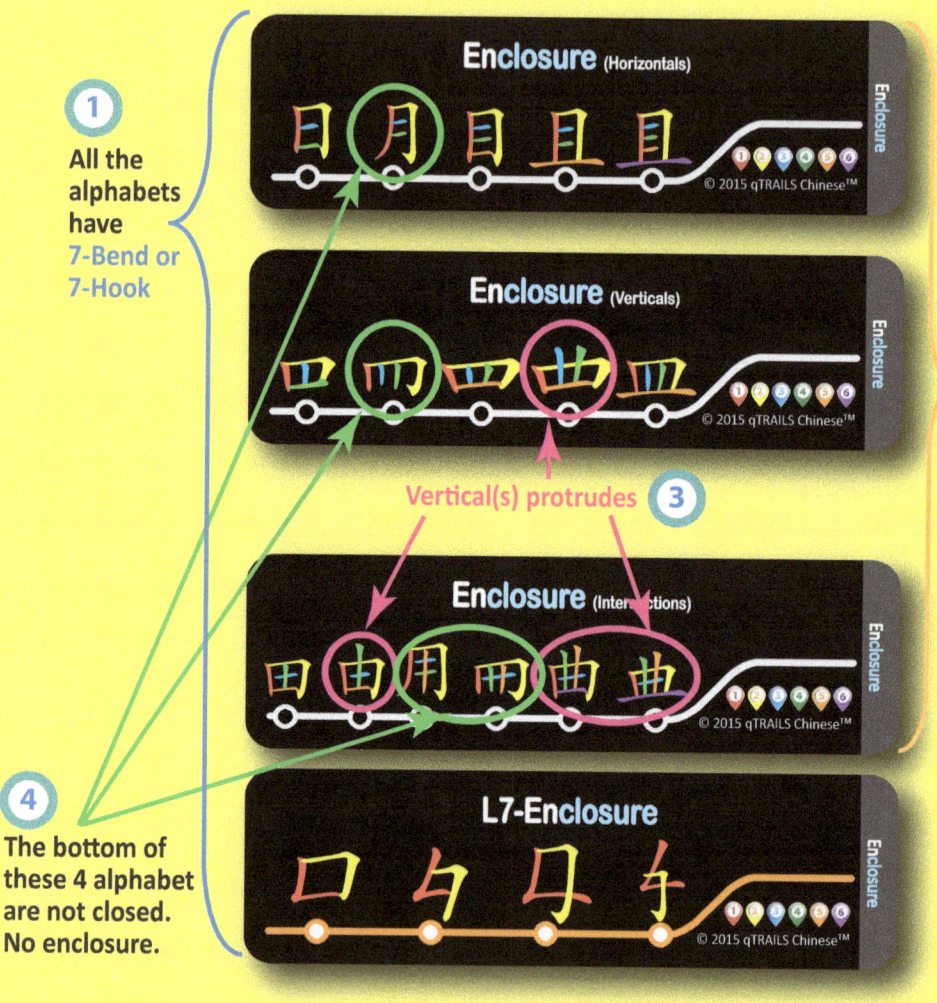

1 All the alphabets have **7-Bend or 7-Hook**

2 Open with **n-Frame** Fill inside Close frame (if required)

3 Vertical(s) protrudes

4 The bottom of these 4 alphabet are not closed. No enclosure.

Where do they belong? 5

Basic qTRAIL Alphabets from different qTRAILS are mixed up. Round up the qTRAIL Alphabets from the **same qTRAIL using the given symbols.**

qTRAILS Stroke Order Rules (3)

Match the Stroke Order Rules to the qTRAILS.

Stroke Order Rules

1. L-Bend or Acute-L First
   RL-Slash or Vertical Last •

2. L-Bend or Acute-L First
   7-Bend or Acute-7 or 7-Hook Last •

3. Horizontal First
   Inside
   L-Bend Last •

4. Horizontal or 7-Bend or 7-Hook First
   L7-Bends Last •

5. 7-Hook First •

6. 7-Hook or 7-Hunchback First
   Vertical Last •

7. 7-Bend First
   Horizontal or Vertical(s)
   Bottommost Horizontal Last •

8. Vertical First
   7-Bend or 7-Hook
   Horizontal (if any) •

9. n-Frame First
   Horizontal(s) inside
   Bottommost horizontal Last •

10. Inside First
    L-Frame or U-Frame Last •

11. n-Frame First
    Intersections inside
    Horizontal Last •

12. n-Frame First
    Vertical(s) inside
    Horizontal Last •

13. C-Frame, U-Frame, n-Frame or Enclosure First •
    Vertical Last

qTRAILS

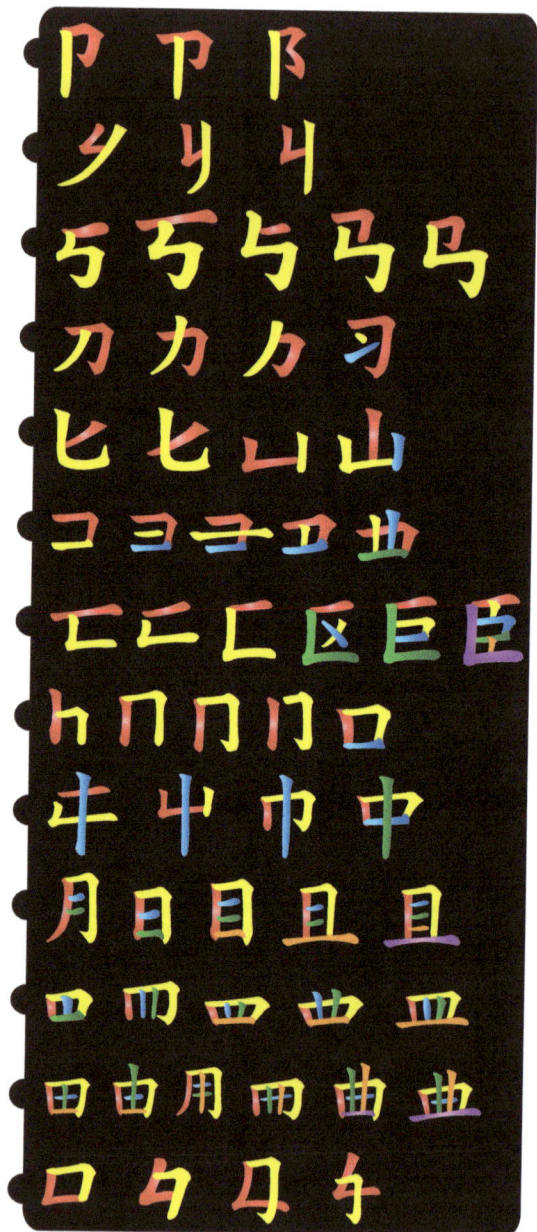

Recall the basic qTRAILS Alphabets you have learnt so far, which of them have these strokes within them, <u>not</u> considering the stroke order. Write two basic qTRAIL alphabets for each question.

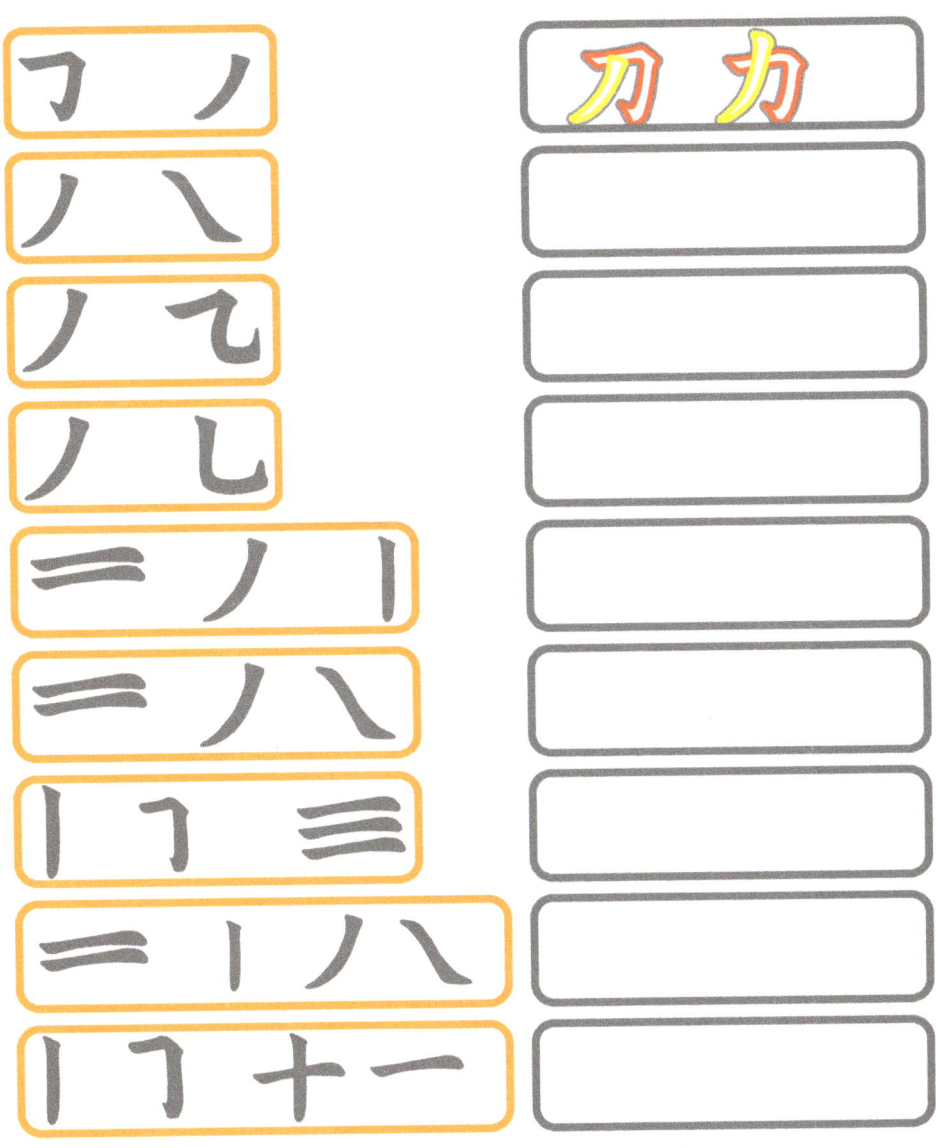

qTRAILS 29 to 32

1. List the **qTRAILS Alphabets**

    a) with 7-Hook

    b) with stroke from the L-Bend Family

    c) with Cross Point(s)

2. List the **qTRAILS Alphabets** with the stroke order

    a) starting with RL-Slash

    b) ending with 7-Hook

    c) ending with 7-Bend or Acute-7

Create your own sketchbook! Add clippings. Doodle,
Make Notes, Summarise . . .

Enclosure

My Questions:
Write down your own questions.

Basic qTRAILS Revision

Activity 49

Find the qTRAIL alphabet that does not fit into the qTRAIL. Write the number in the bracket.

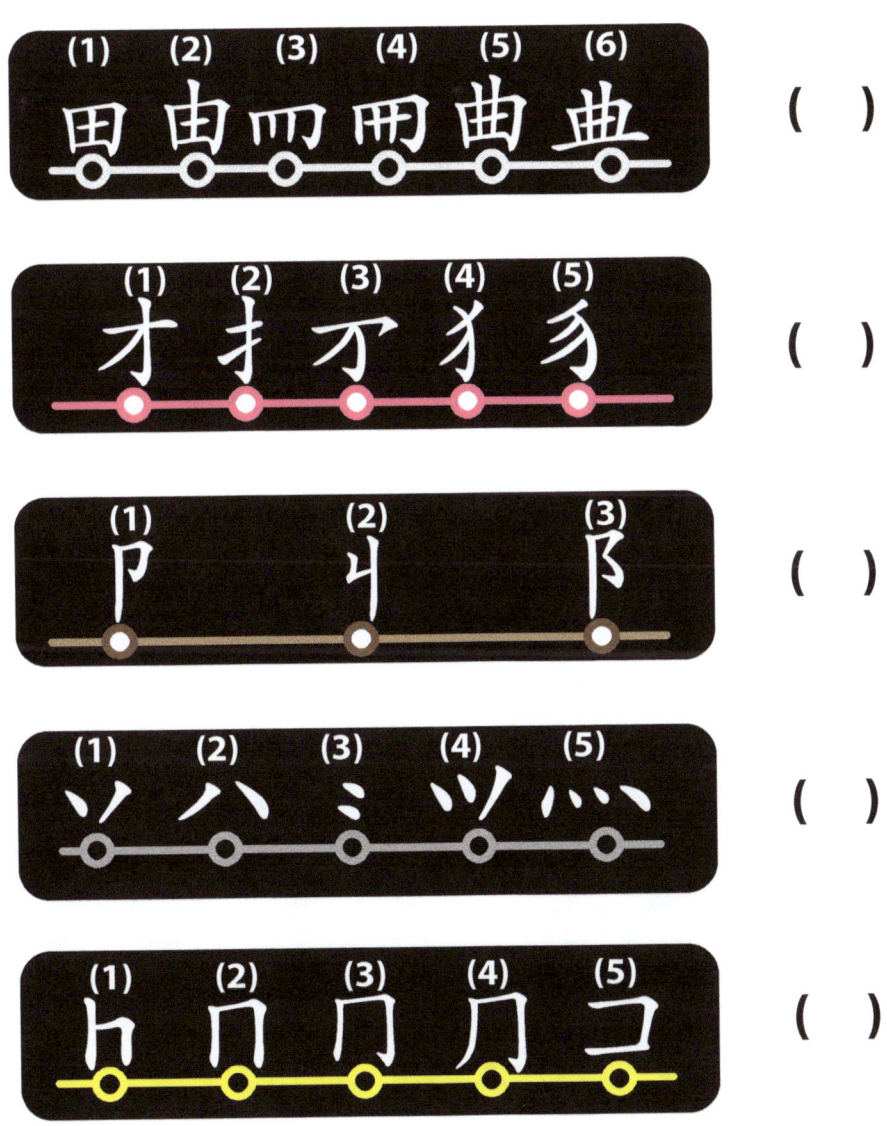

(1) (2) (3) (4) (5) (6)
田 由 皿 罒 曲 典   ( )

(1) (2) (3) (4) (5)
才 扌 才 犭 豸   ( )

(1) (2) (3)
卩 丩 阝   ( )

(1) (2) (3) (4) (5)
丷 八 氵 ⺍ 灬   ( )

(1) (2) (3) (4) (5)
𠃌 刀 刀 刀 コ   ( )

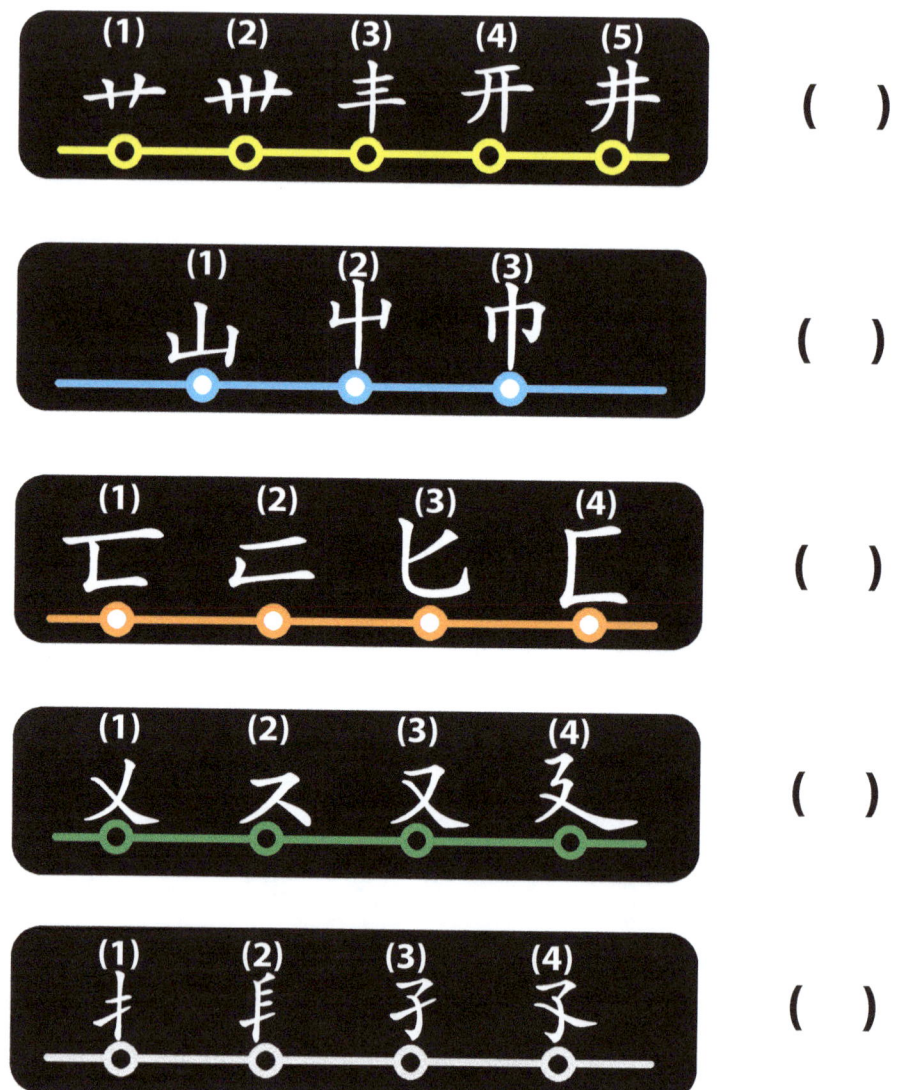

Recall all the **Basic Alphabets** with **6 strokes**. Fill them into the space given below according to their 'Shapes'. See example.

Recall all the **Basic Alphabets** with **5 strokes**. Fill them into the space given below according to their 'Shapes'. See examples.

These are basic qTRAILS Alphabets with 4 strokes.

开 井 八 八 卜 彑 彐 月 夕 夂

Recall the remaining **Basic Alphabets** with **4 strokes**. (i.e. those that do not appear above). Fill them into the space given below according to their 'Shapes'. See examples.

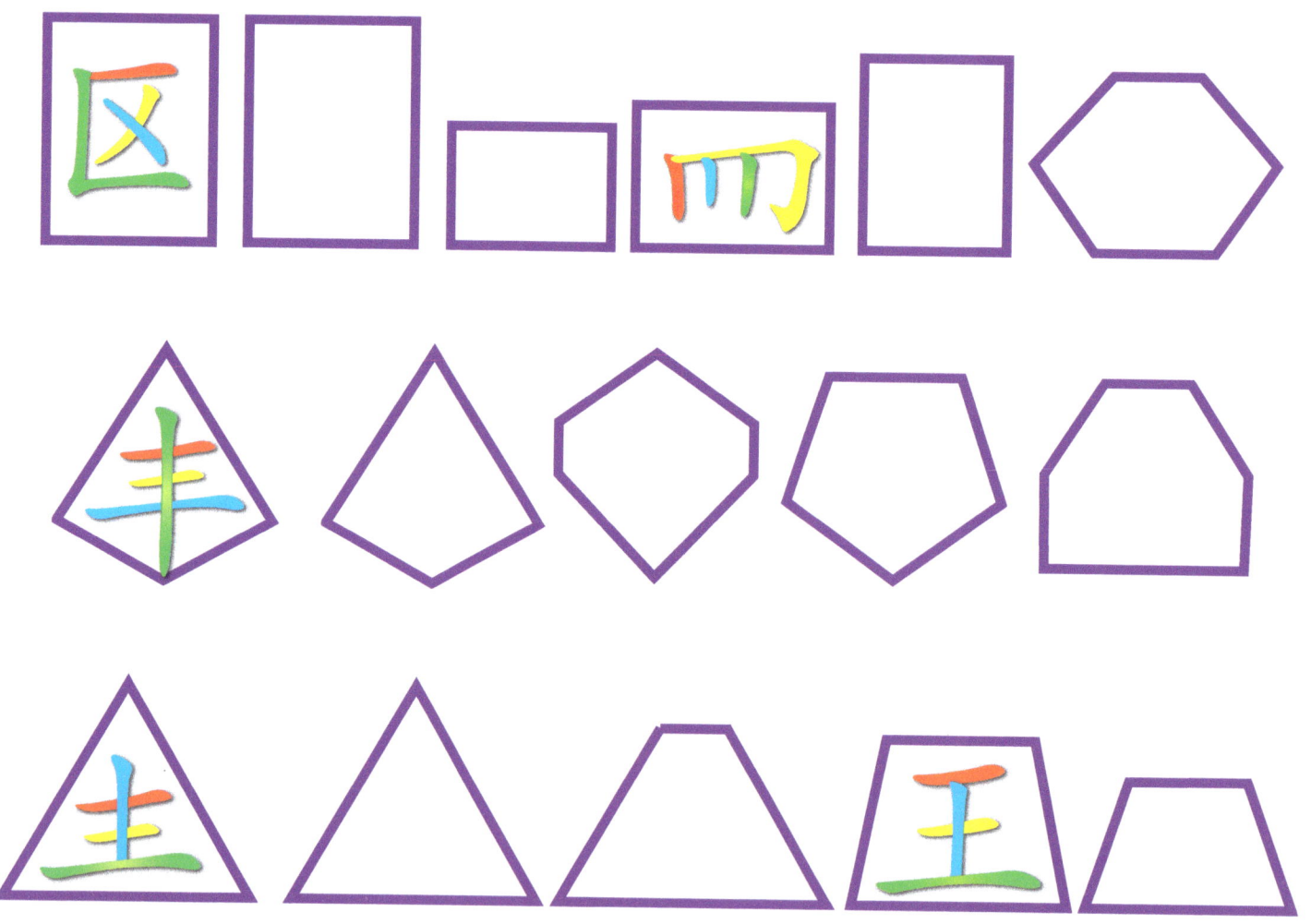

Section B

Variations

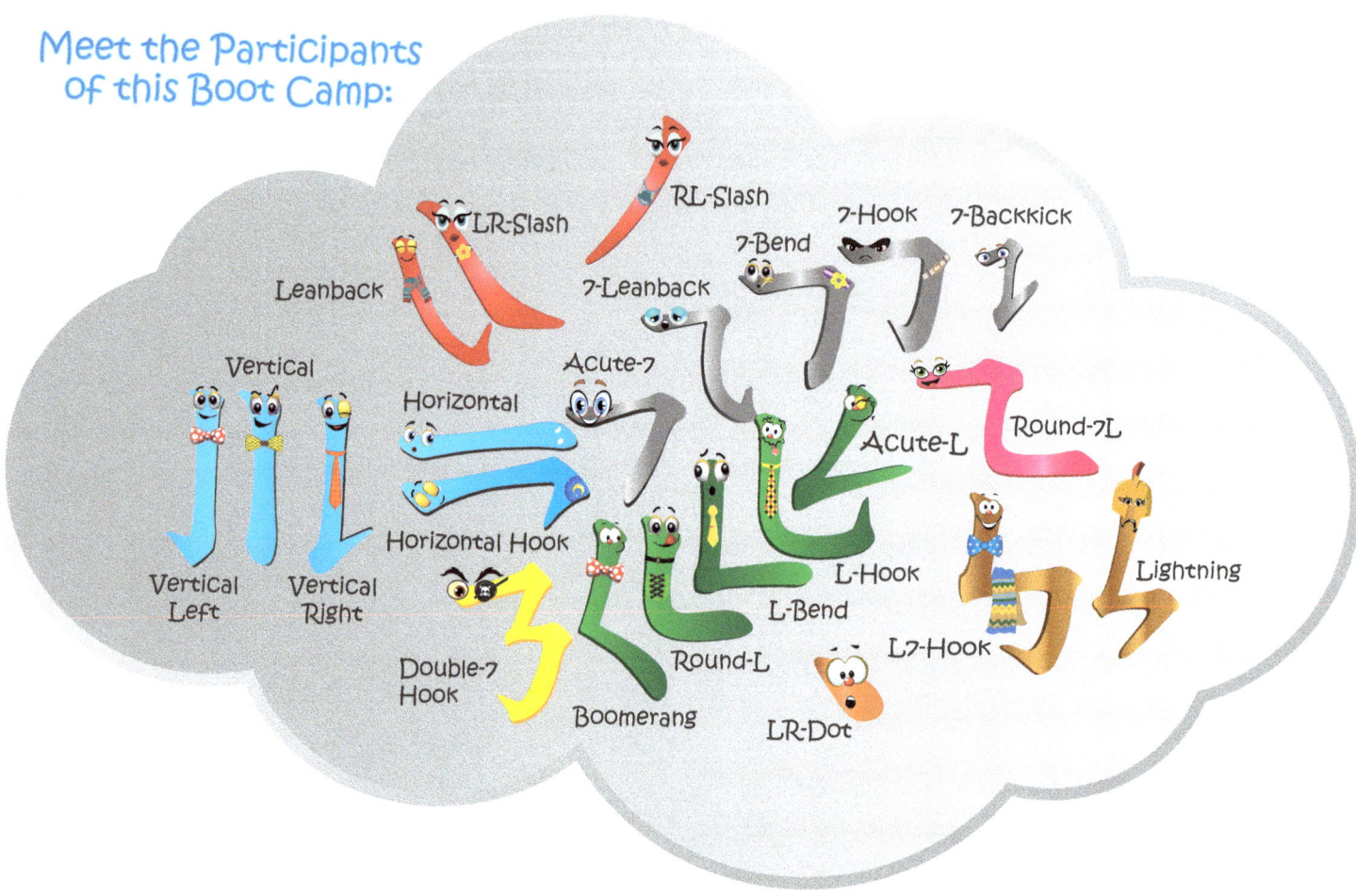

Meet the Participants of this Boot Camp:

RL-Slash
LR-Slash
7-Hook
7-Backkick
Leanback
7-Bend
7-Leanback
Vertical
Acute-7
Horizontal
Round-7L
Acute-L
Horizontal Hook
Vertical Left
Vertical Right
L-Hook
L-Bend
Lightning
Double-7 Hook
Round-L
L7-Hook
Boomerang
LR-Dot

Boot Camp 5
Variations and Exceptions
Boot Camp 5 has 23 performers, the biggest group.

Parallels

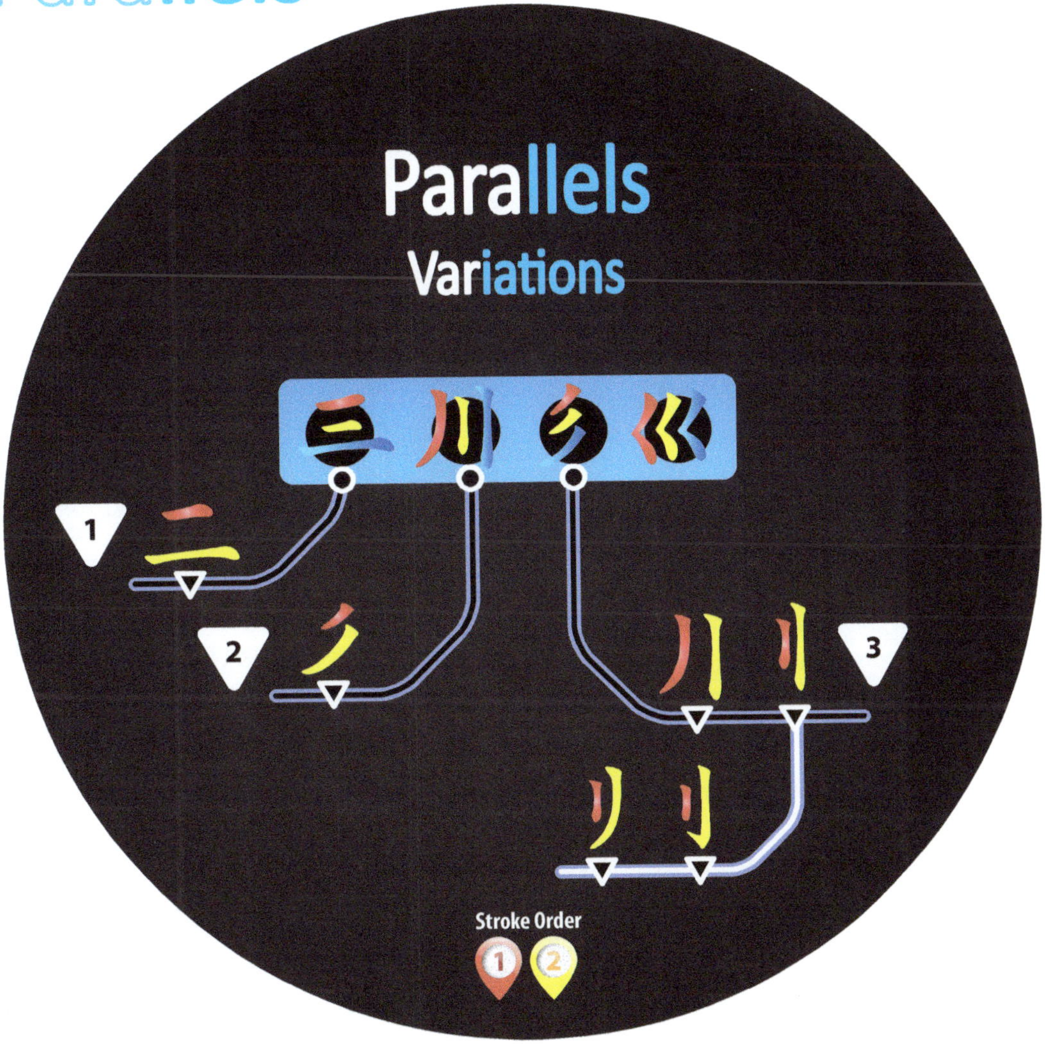

Parallels
Variations

(1) Close your eyes and visualise each variation in your mind.

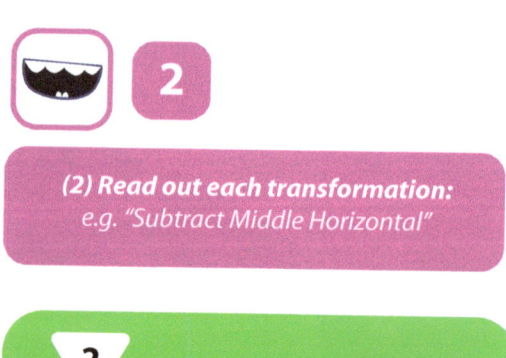

(2) Read out each transformation:
e.g. "Subtract Middle Horizontal"

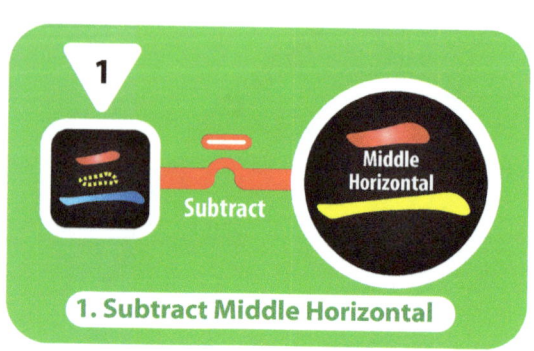

1. Subtract Middle Horizontal

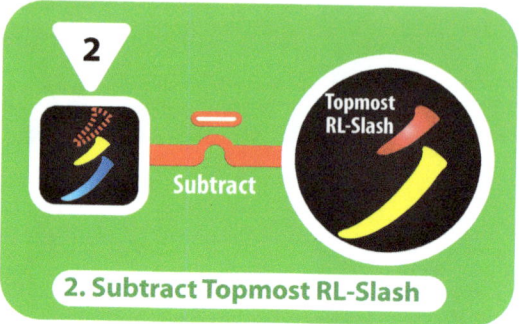

2. Subtract Topmost RL-Slash

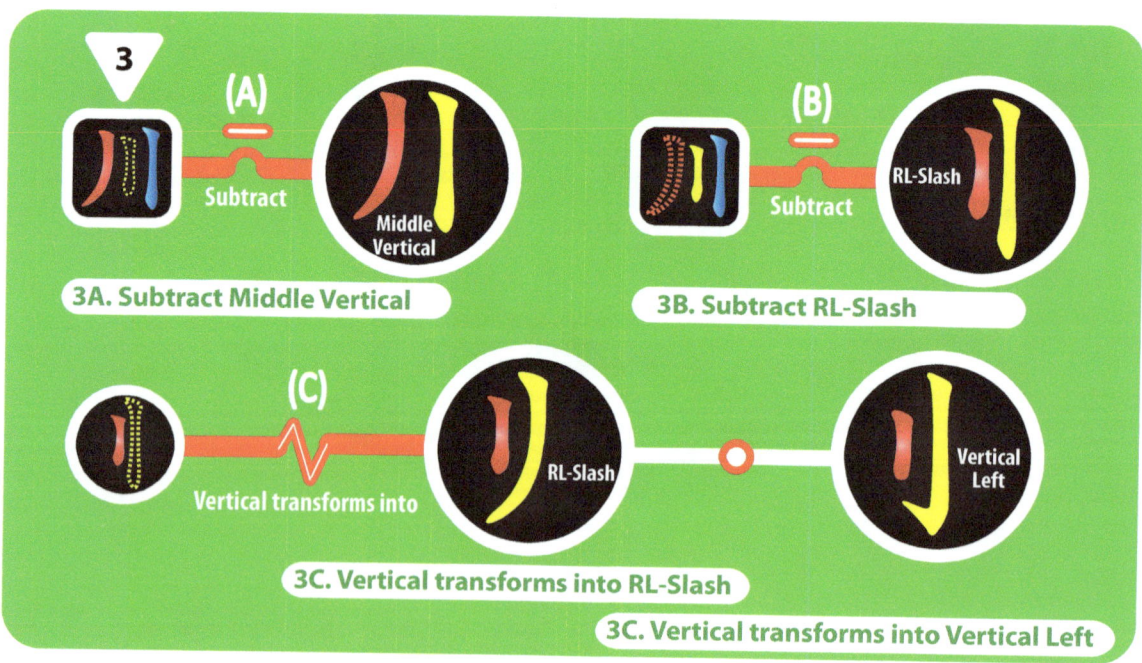

3A. Subtract Middle Vertical

3B. Subtract RL-Slash

3C. Vertical transforms into RL-Slash

3C. Vertical transforms into Vertical Left

3 (3) Trace the strokes with your finger or colour them according to the given stroke order.

Stroke Order 1 2

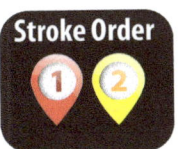

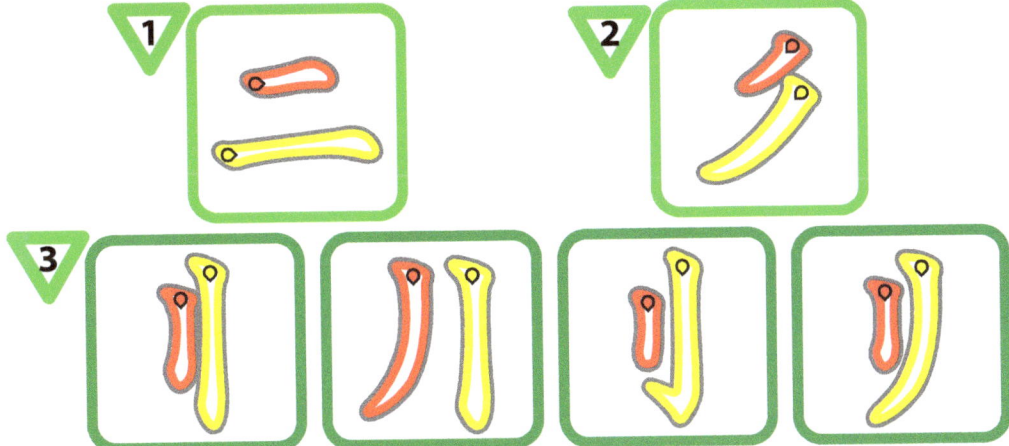

The Chinese alphabets you have just learnt appear in these characters.

4

(4) Colour the alphabets in the characters.

前	仁 Example:	聚	刊
介	师	齐	临
些	归	坚	监

Activity 51A

(6) Write the transformation in words. See examples.

Activity 51B

_____

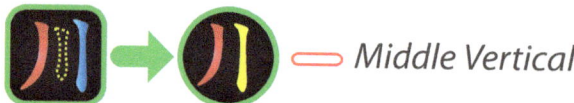 Middle Vertical

 Vertical Vertical Left

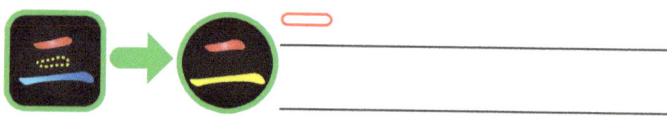

_____

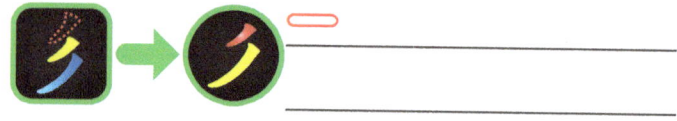

_____

 Vertical _____

_____

Final Dot

Variations

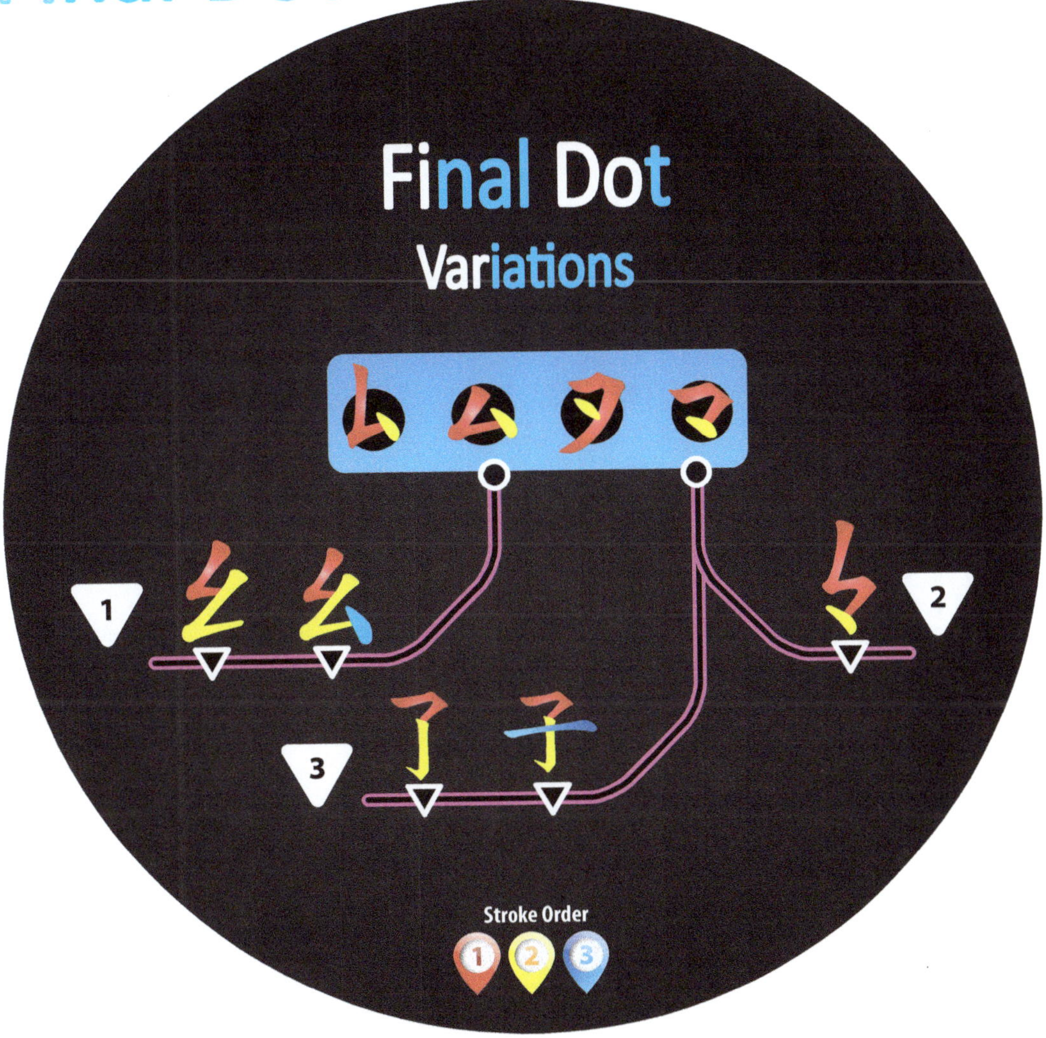

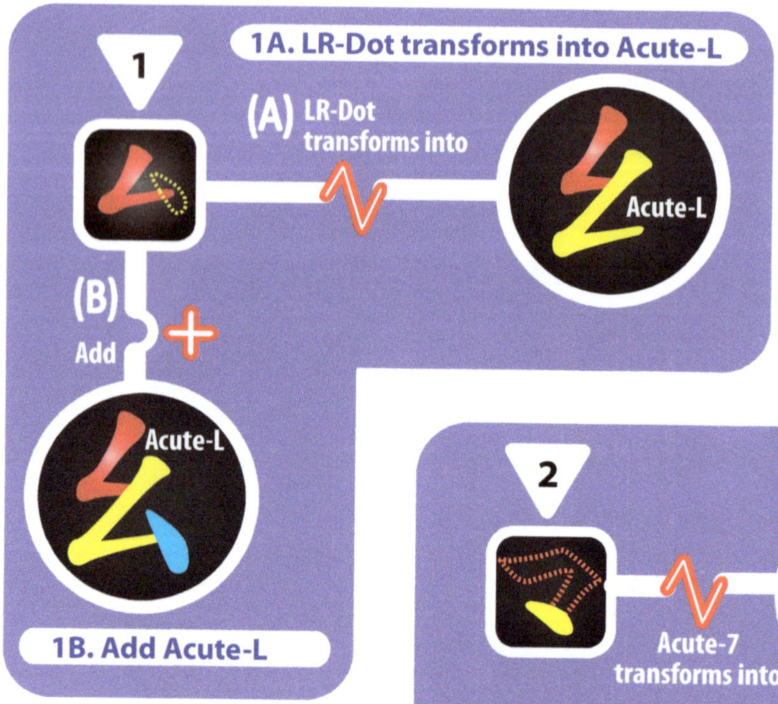

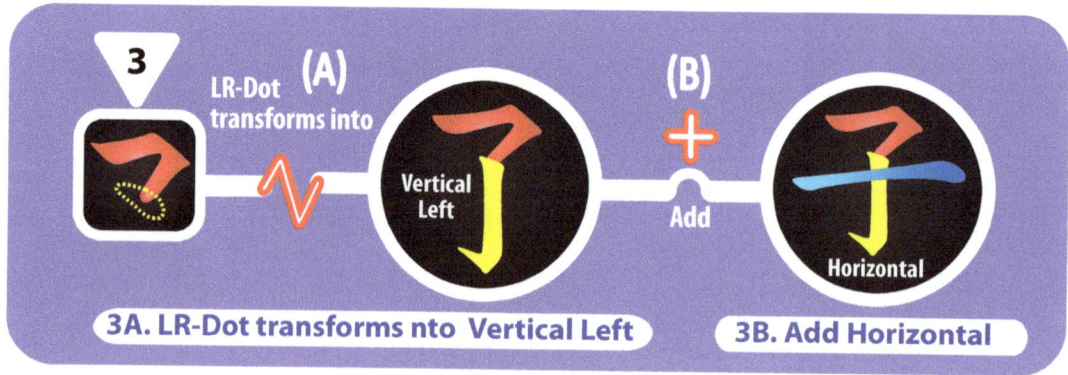

1A. LR-Dot transforms into Acute-L

1 (A) LR-Dot transforms into → Acute-L

(B) Add ➕

Acute-L

1B. Add Acute-L

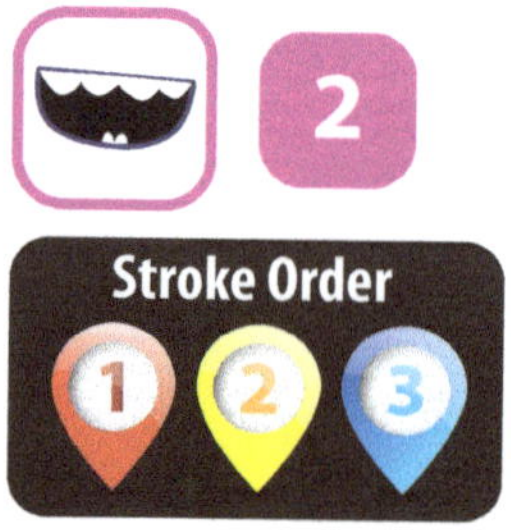

2. Acute-7 transforms into Lightning

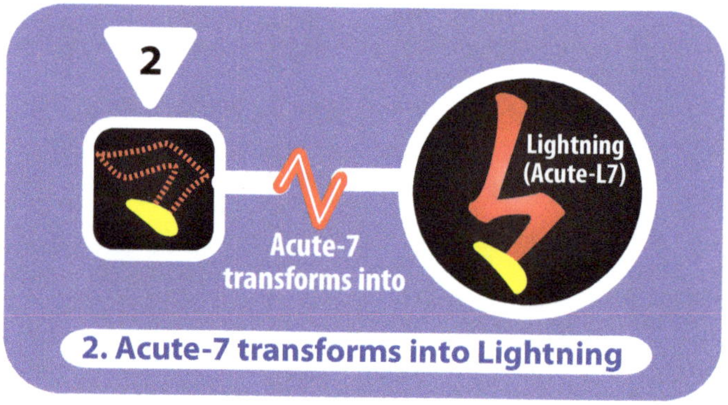

2 Acute-7 transforms into → Lightning (Acute-L7)

Stroke Order
1 2 3

3A. LR-Dot transforms into Vertical Left

3 (A) LR-Dot transforms into → Vertical Left ➕ Add → Horizontal (B)

3B. Add Horizontal

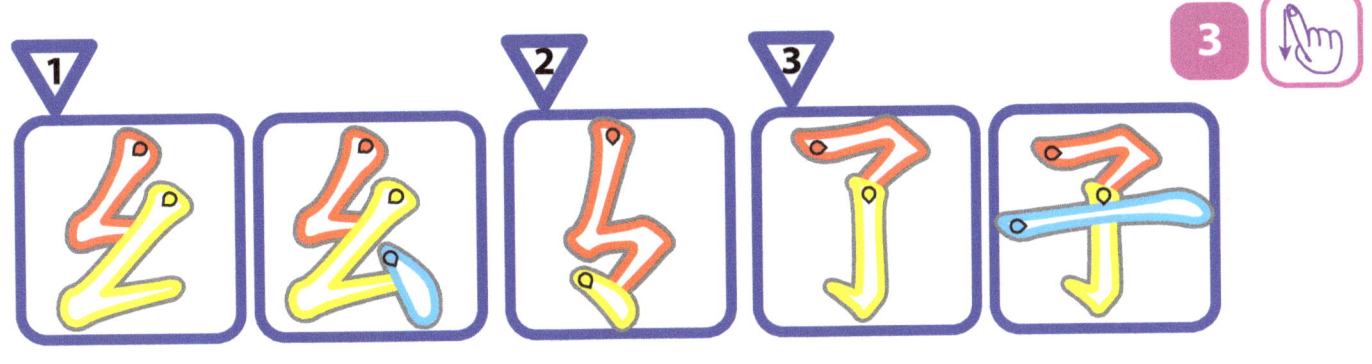

3

4

Activity 52A

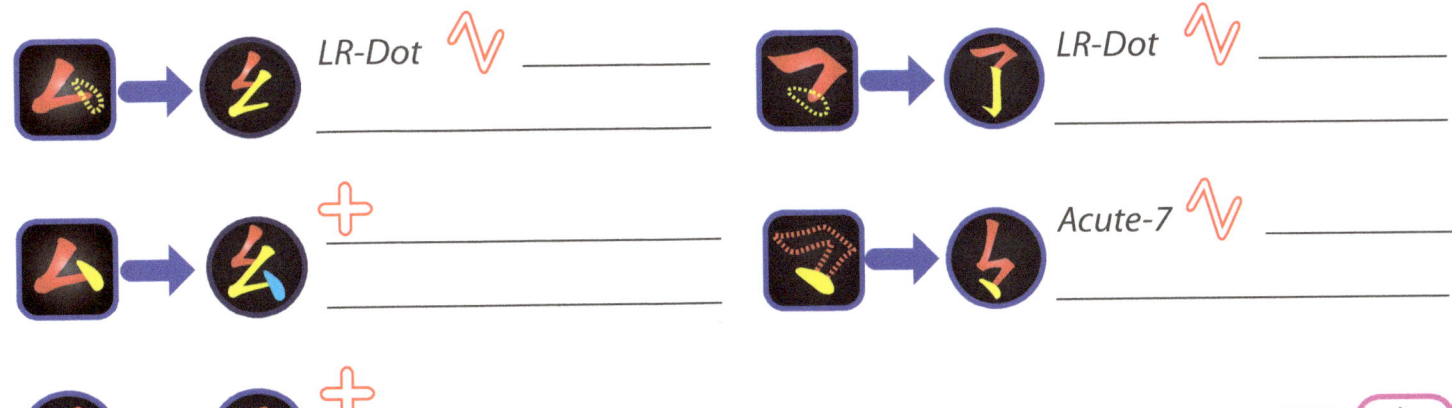

LR-Dot ⋀ _____

_____

LR-Dot ⋀ _____

_____

+ _____

_____

Acute-7 ⋀ _____

_____

+ _____

_____

Activity 52B **5**

③ Perpendiculars (Half Ladder)

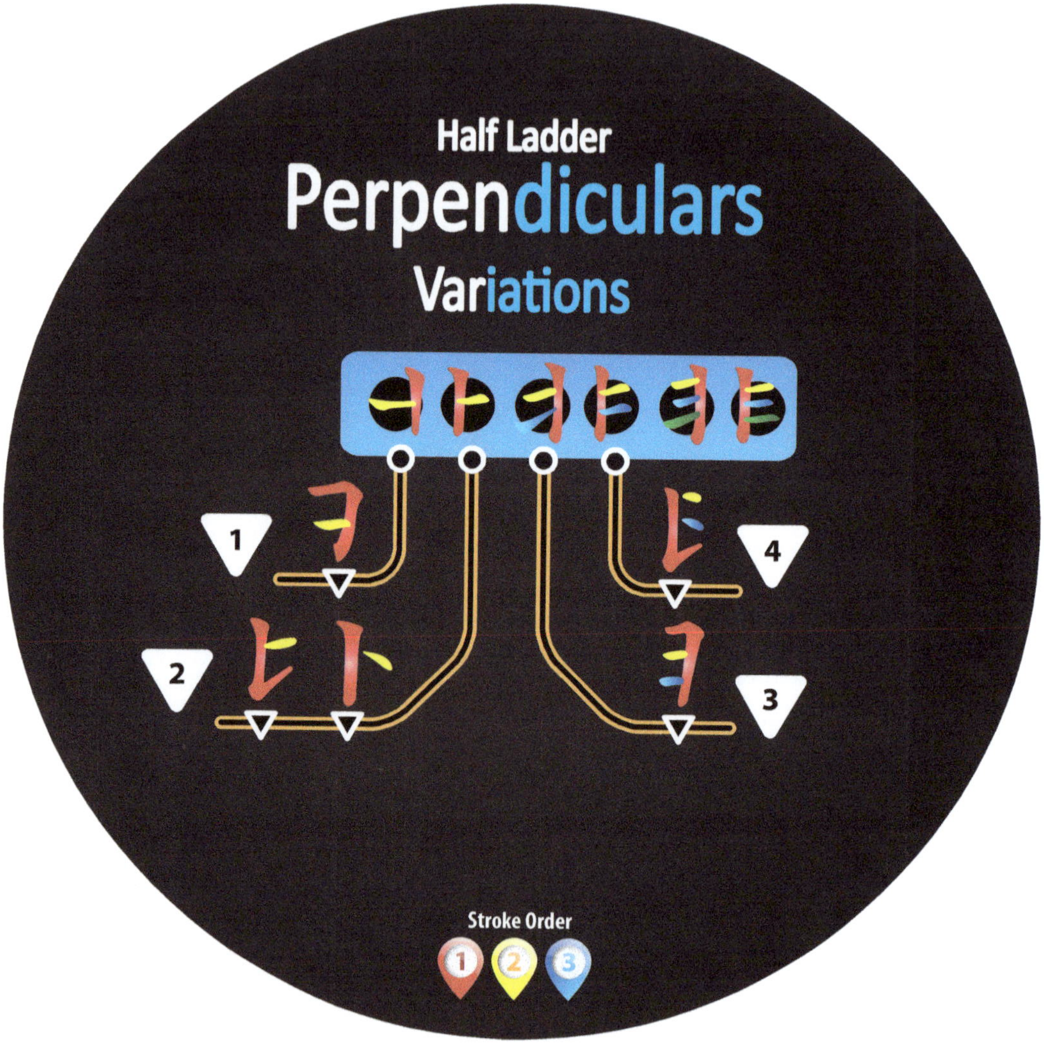

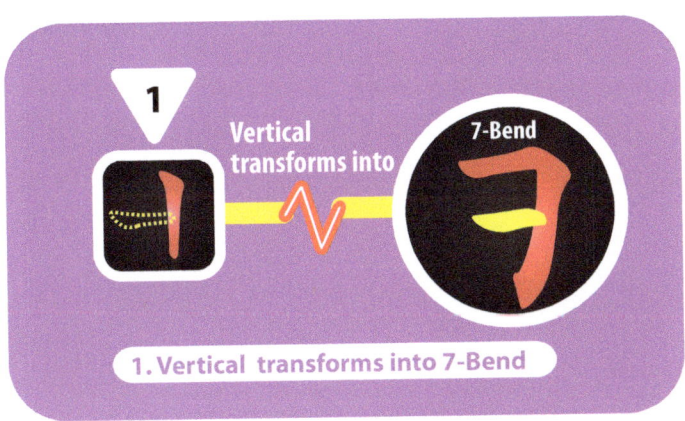

1. Vertical transforms into 7-Bend

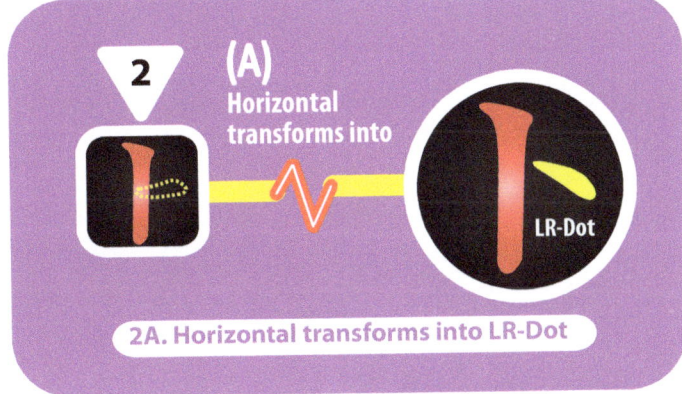

2A. Horizontal transforms into LR-Dot

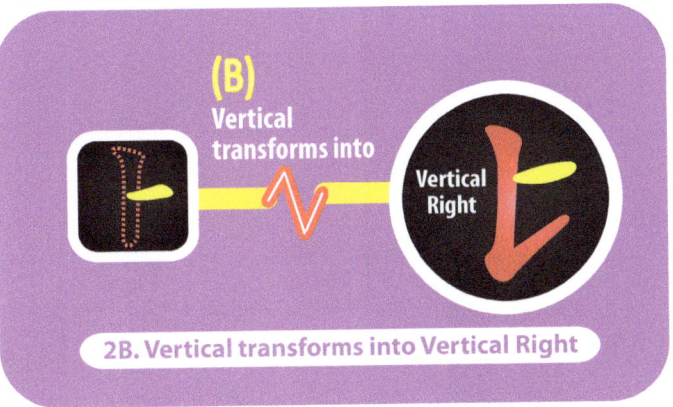

2B. Vertical transforms into Vertical Right

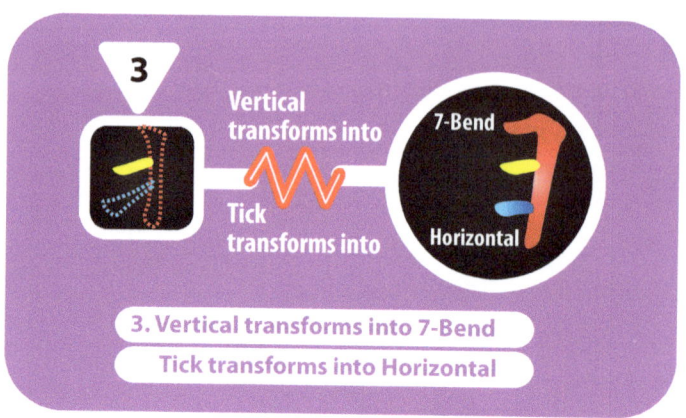

3

Vertical transforms into

Tick transforms into

7-Bend

Horizontal

3. Vertical transforms into 7-Bend

Tick transforms into Horizontal

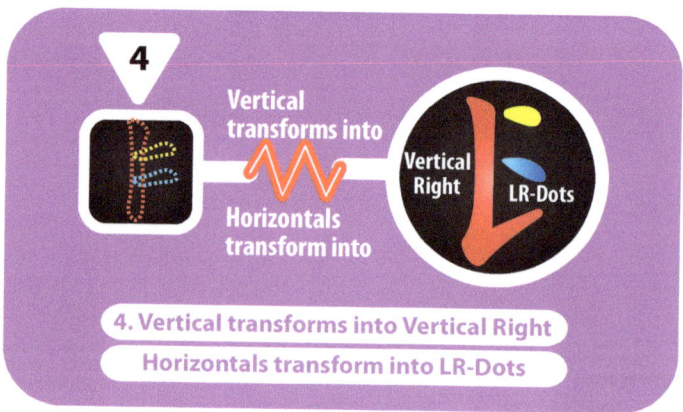

4

Vertical transforms into

Horizontals transform into

Vertical Right

LR-Dots

4. Vertical transforms into Vertical Right

Horizontals transform into LR-Dots

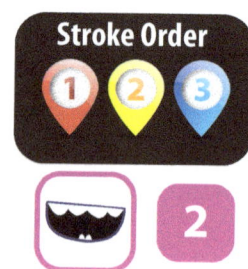

Stroke Order

1 2 3

2

3 🖐️

▽ 1

▽ 2

▽ 3

▽ 4

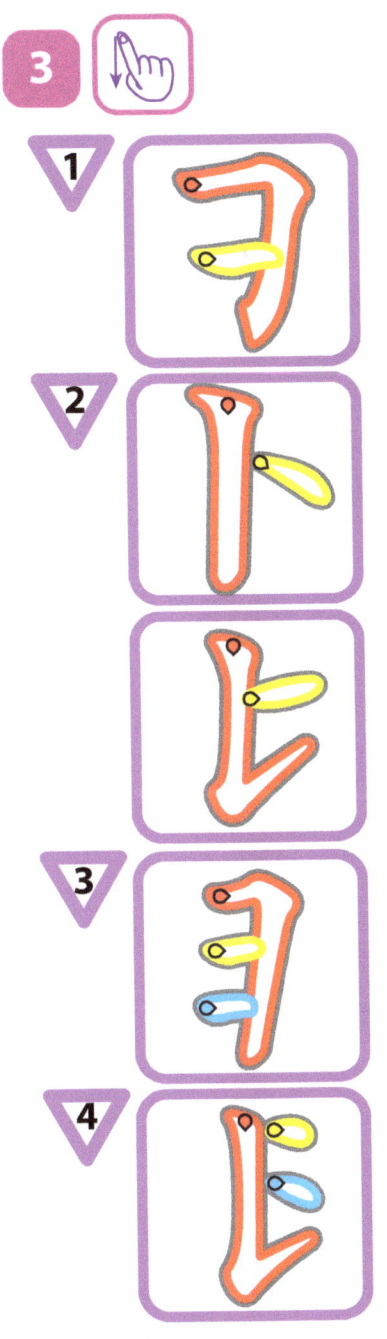

Activity 53A

4 🖍️

下　比　卡
白　　　毕
鼠　插　舆

5 ✏️

Activity 53B

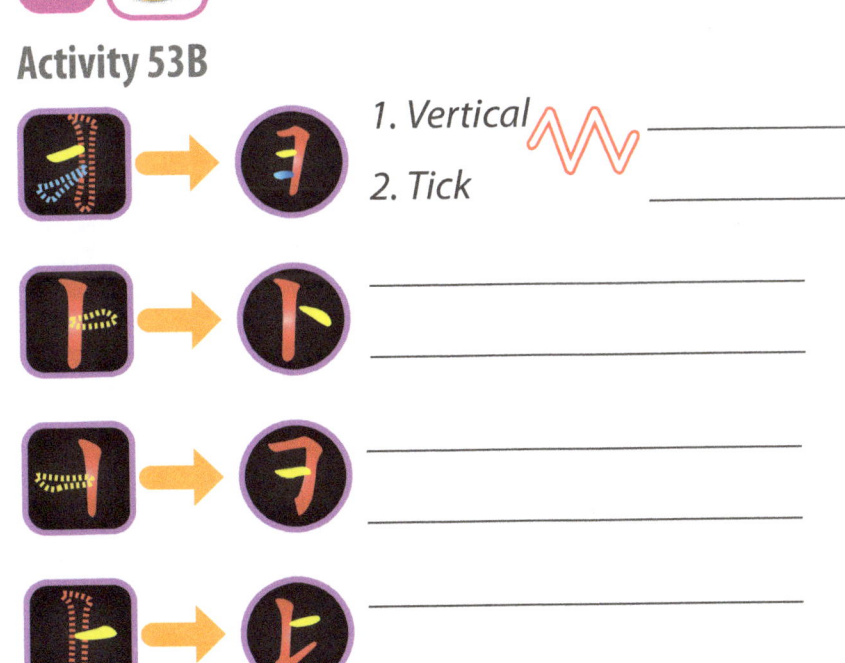

1. Vertical 〰️ _____
2. Tick _____

_____
_____

_____
_____

_____

1. Vertical 〰️ _____
2. Horizontals _____

④ Perpendiculars (T-Shape)

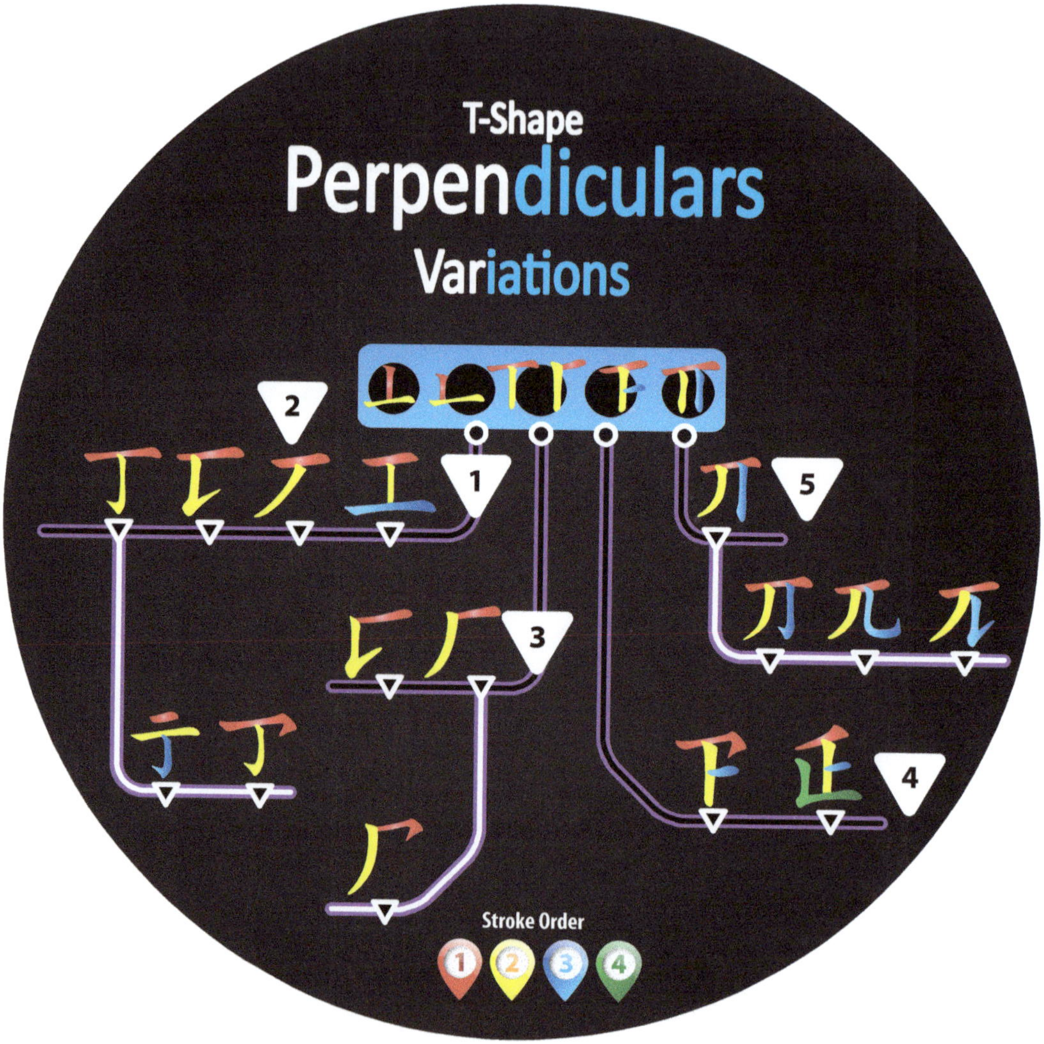

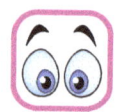

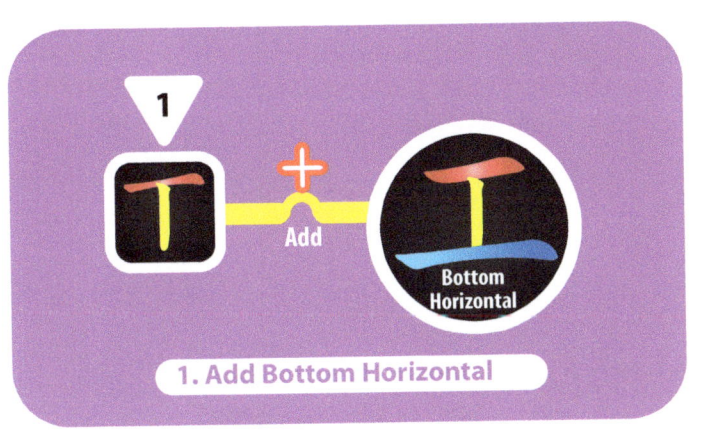

1. Add Bottom Horizontal

Stroke Order
1　2　3

2A. Vertical transforms into RL-Slash

2A. Vertical transforms into Vertical Right

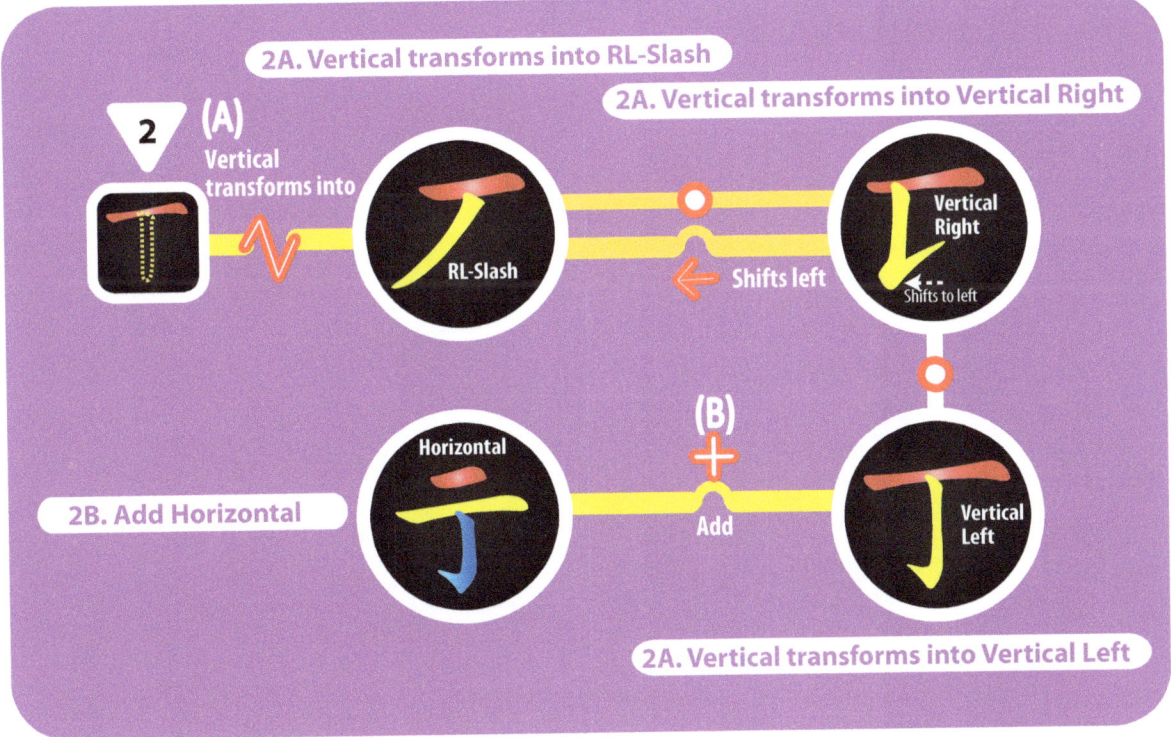

(A)
Vertical transforms into

RL-Slash

Shifts left

Vertical Right
Shifts to left

Horizontal

2B. Add Horizontal

(B)
Add

Vertical Left

2A. Vertical transforms into Vertical Left

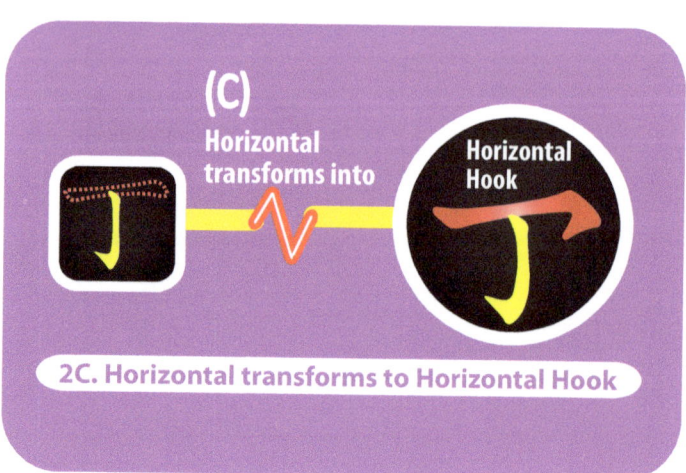

(C)

Horizontal transforms into → **Horizontal Hook**

2C. Horizontal transforms to Horizontal Hook

Activity 54A 4 🖍️

空 订 贡
瓦 行 辰
予 竹 石

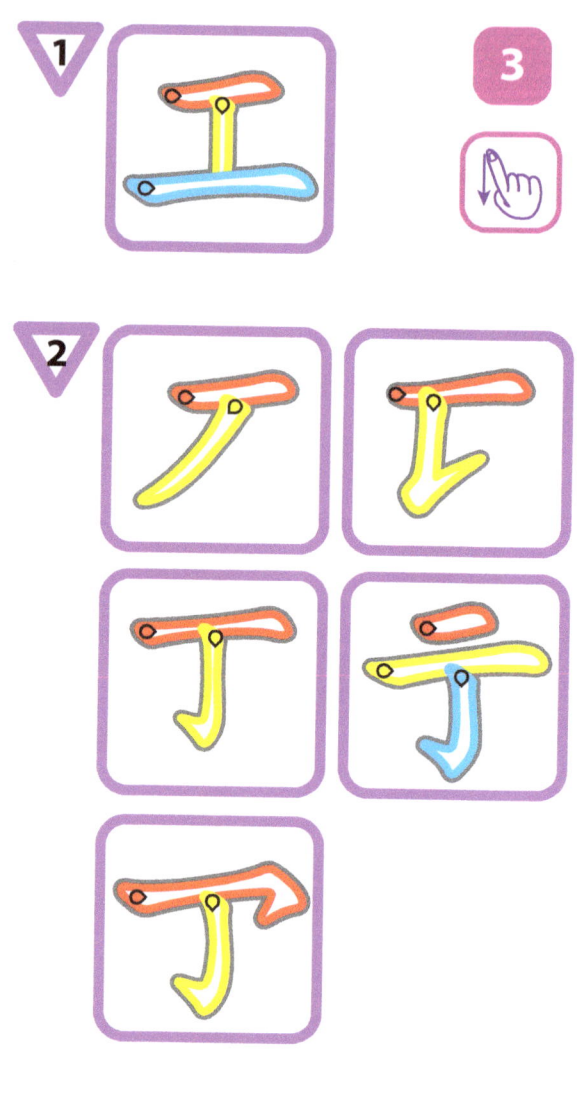

1

2

3 👆

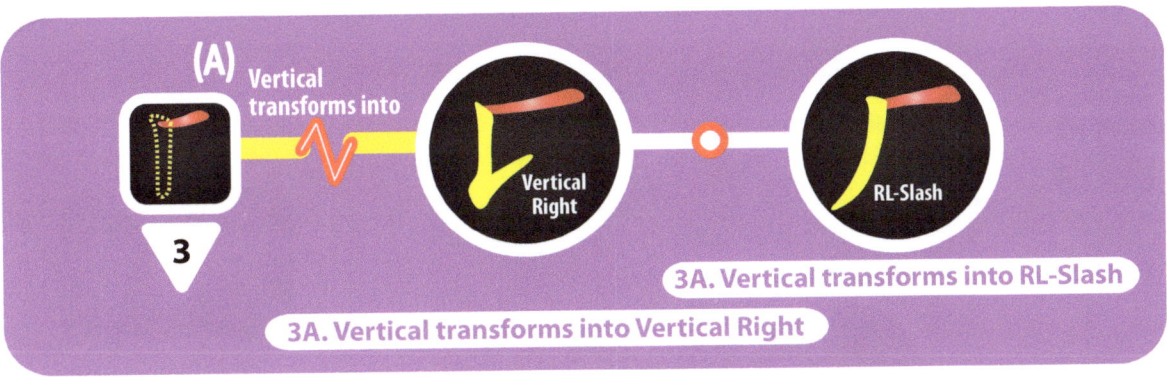

(A) Vertical transforms into

Vertical Right

RL-Slash

3A. Vertical transforms into RL-Slash

3A. Vertical transforms into Vertical Right

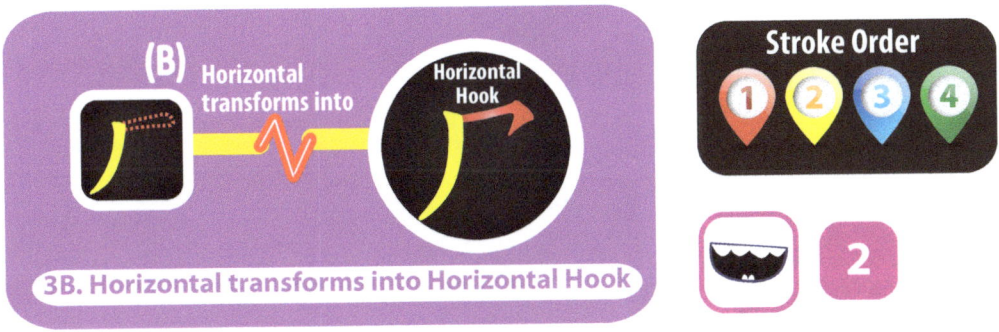

(B) Horizontal transforms into

Horizontal Hook

3B. Horizontal transforms into Horizontal Hook

Stroke Order

1 2 3 4

2

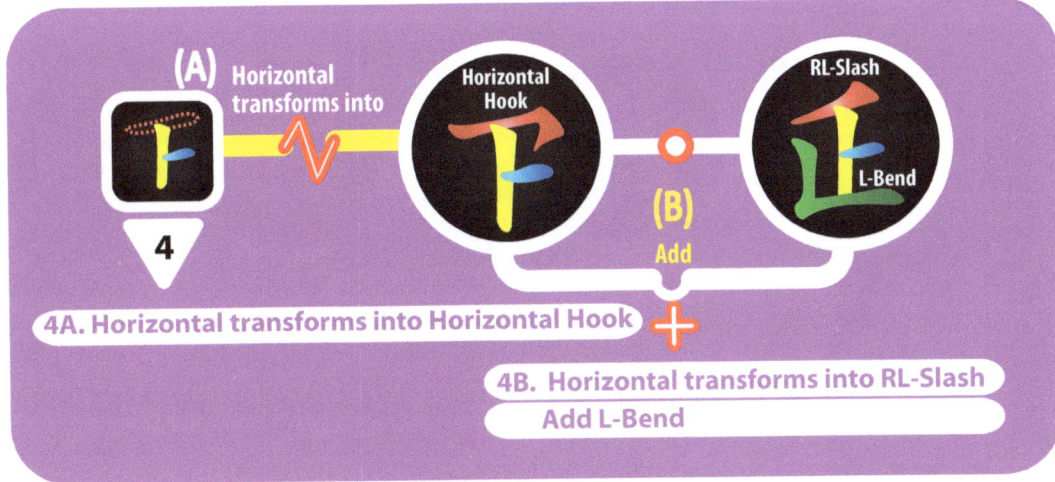

(A) Horizontal transforms into

Horizontal Hook

RL-Slash

L-Bend

(B)
Add

4A. Horizontal transforms into Horizontal Hook

+

4B. Horizontal transforms into RL-Slash

Add L-Bend

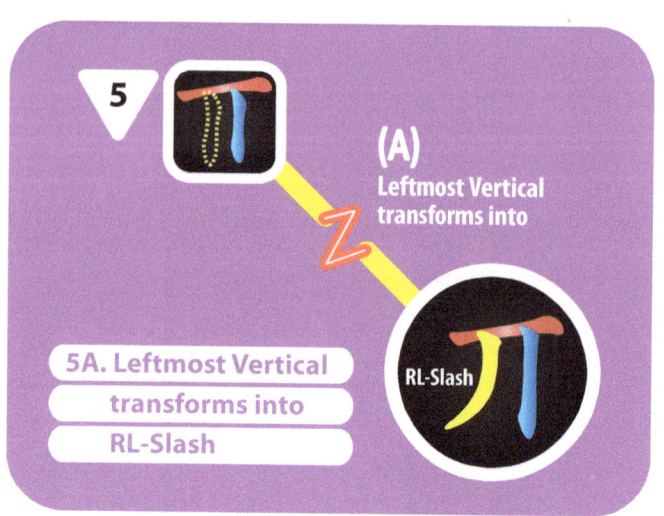

(A)
Leftmost Vertical transforms into

5A. Leftmost Vertical transforms into RL-Slash

RL-Slash

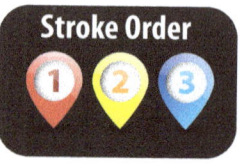

Stroke Order
1 2 3

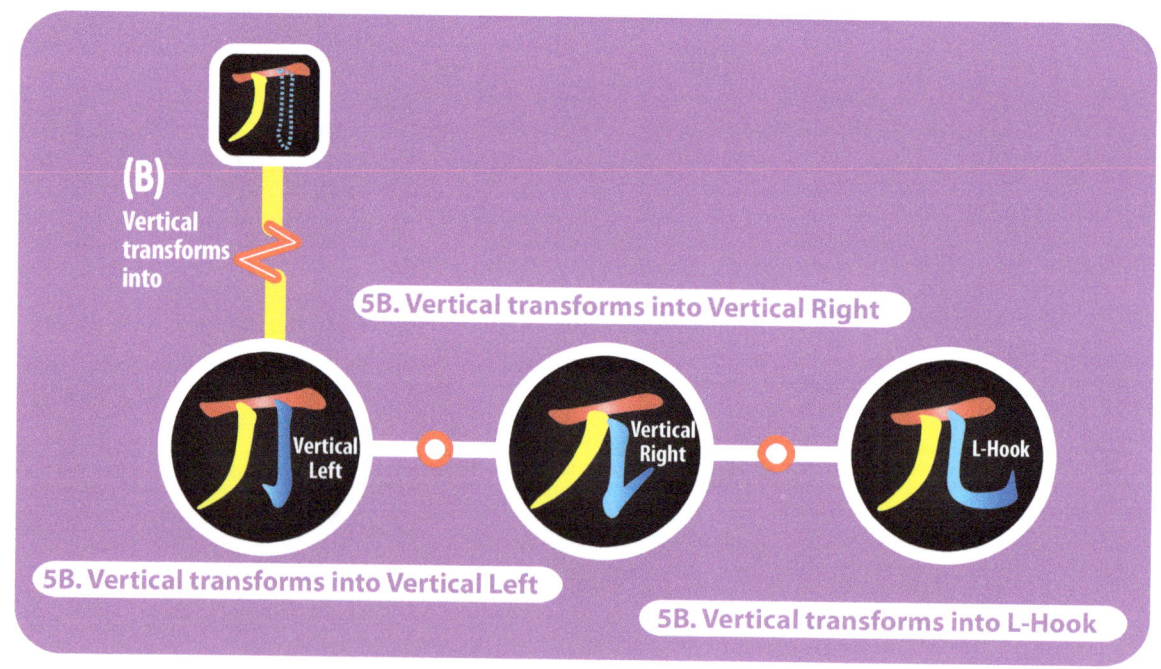

(B)
Vertical transforms into

5B. Vertical transforms into Vertical Right

Vertical Left

Vertical Right

L-Hook

5B. Vertical transforms into Vertical Left

5B. Vertical transforms into L-Hook

Activity 54B

顽 鼻 延
庆 楚 元
皮 越 亦

Shifts left

1. Horizontal

2. _____

Activity 55

Match the basic qTRAILS (around the clock) to their respective variations (in the middle) by writing the number of the basic qTRAIL in the given frames. See example.

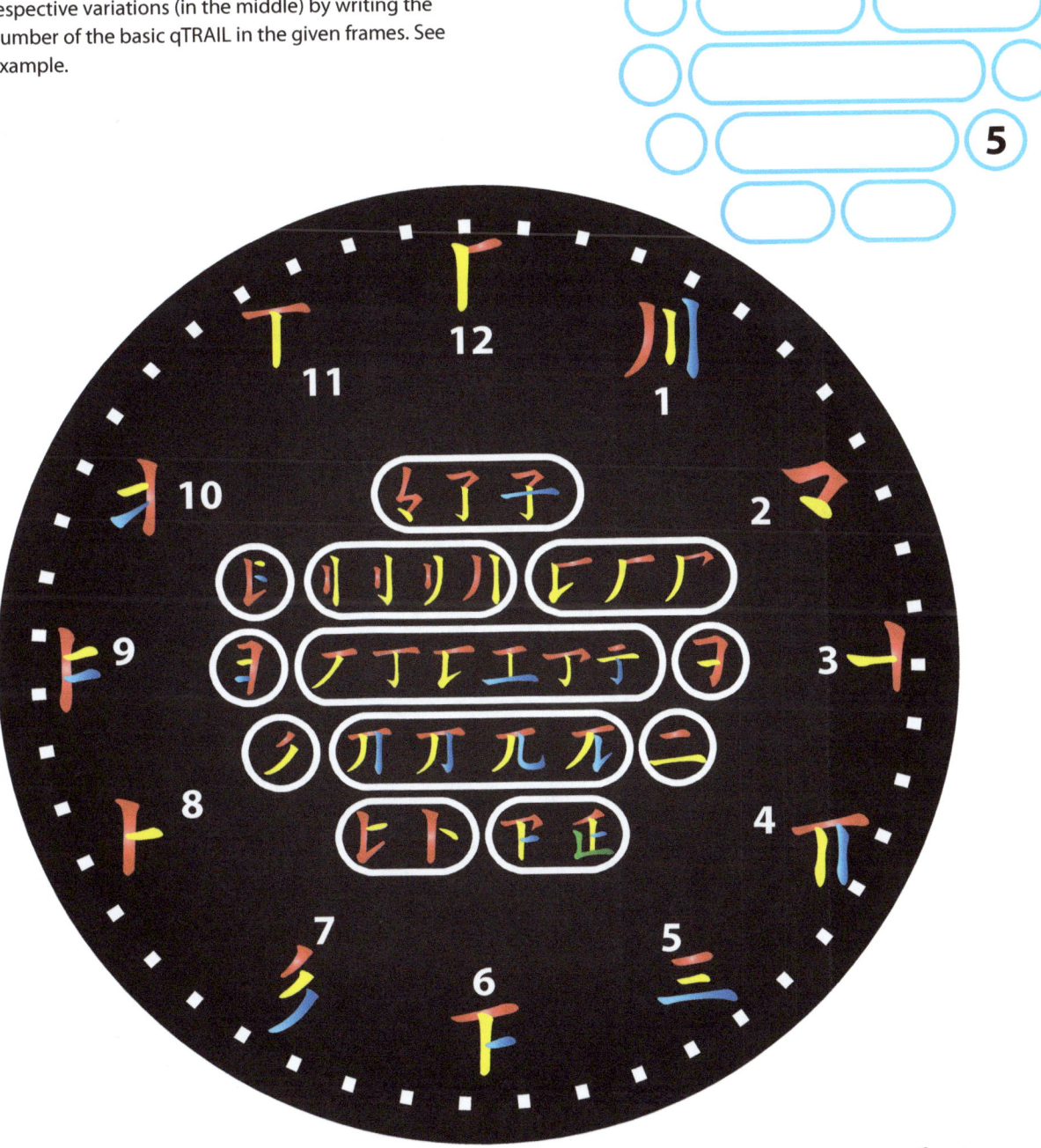

5

Intersections (Single Leg)

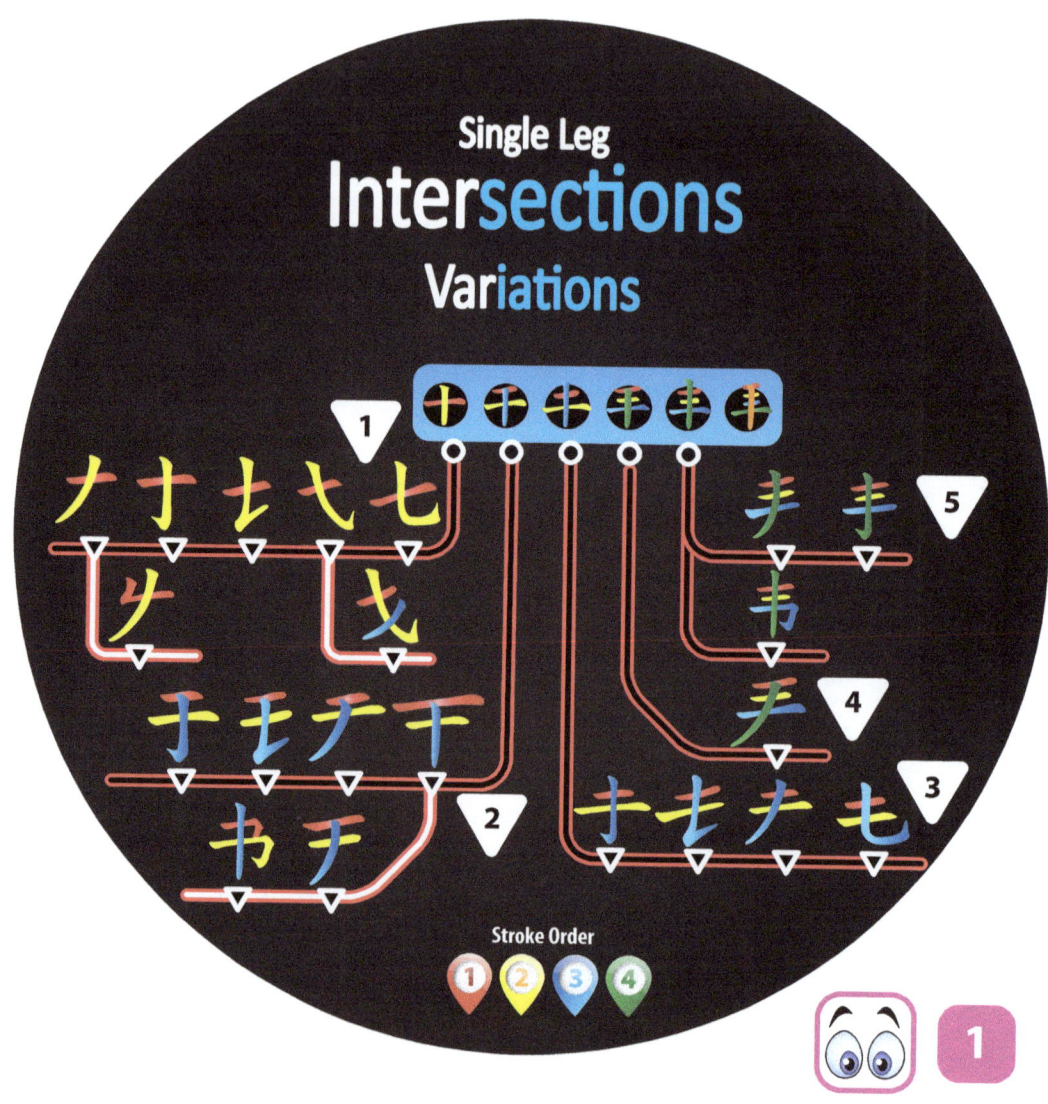

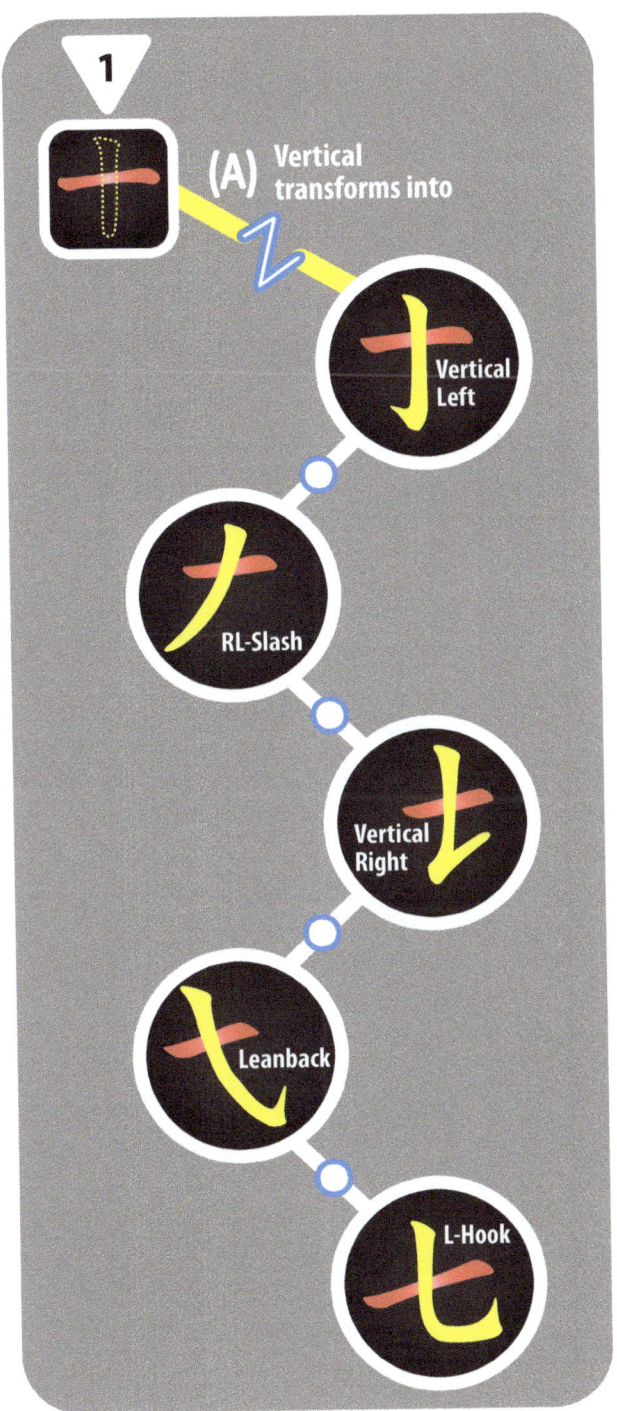

1

(A) Vertical transforms into

Vertical Left

RL-Slash

Vertical Right

Leanback

L-Hook

Stroke Order
1 2 3

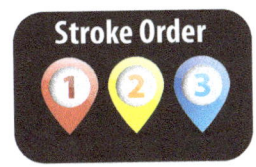

2

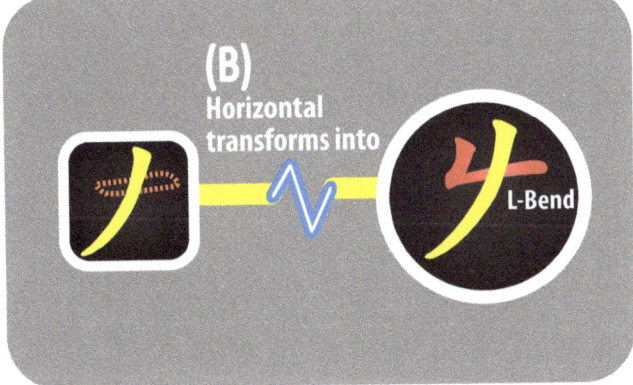

(B) Horizontal transforms into

L-Bend

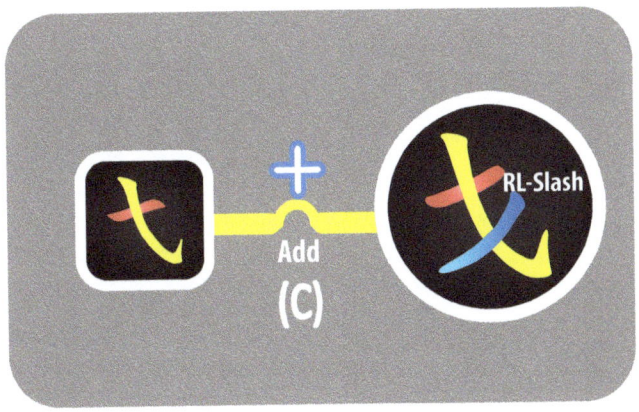

(C) Add

RL-Slash

Activity 56A

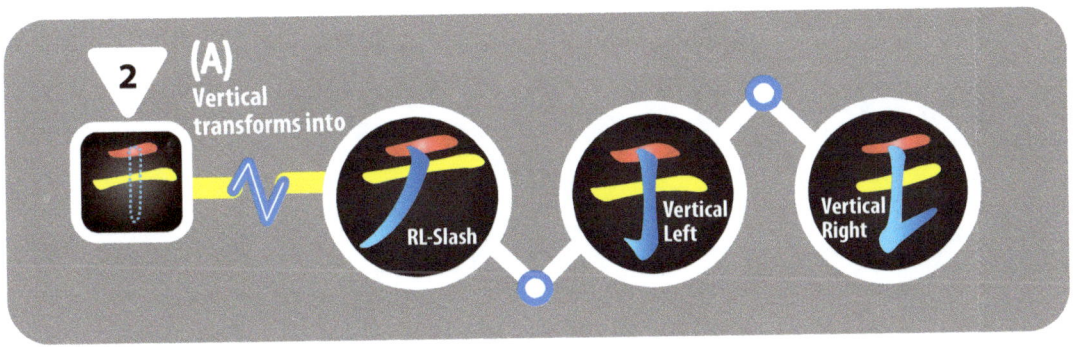

2 **(A)** Vertical transforms into

RL-Slash · Vertical Left · Vertical Right

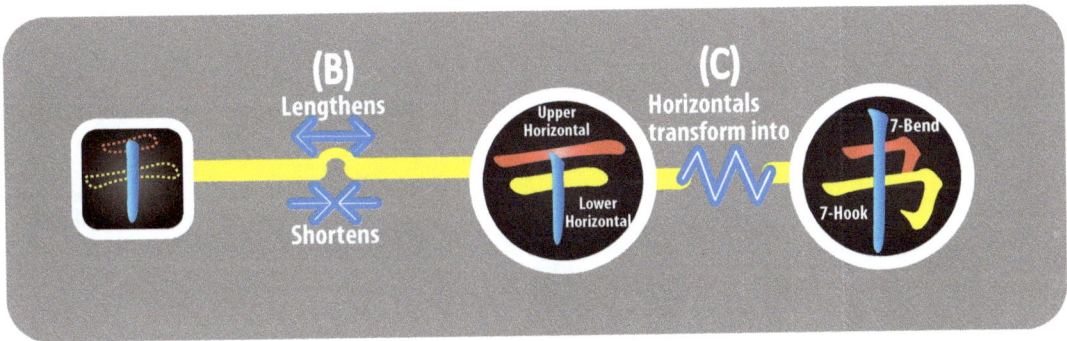

(B) Lengthens / Shortens

Upper Horizontal · Lower Horizontal

(C) Horizontals transform into

7-Bend · 7-Hook

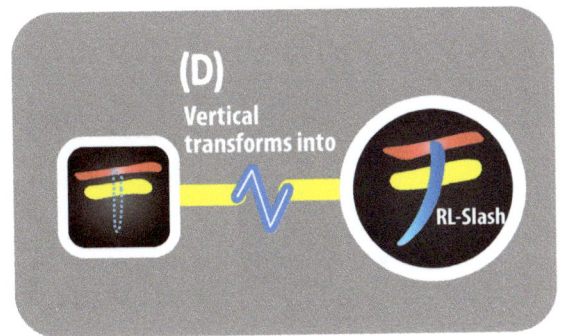

(D) Vertical transforms into

RL-Slash

Stroke Order
1 2 3

 2

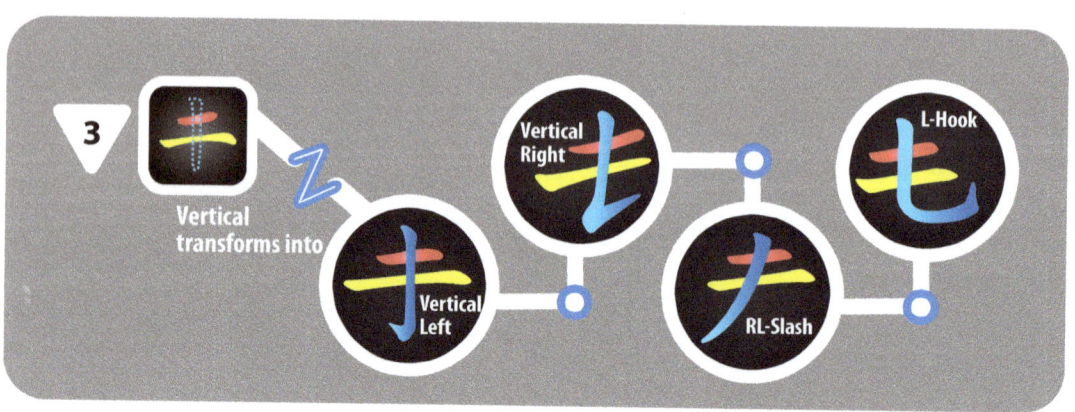

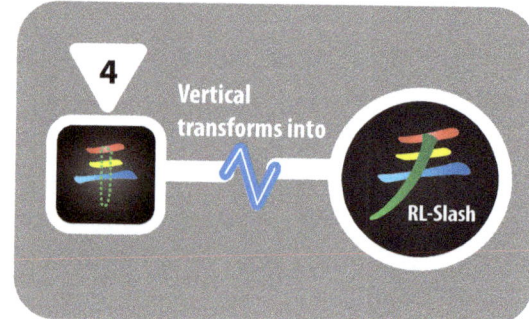

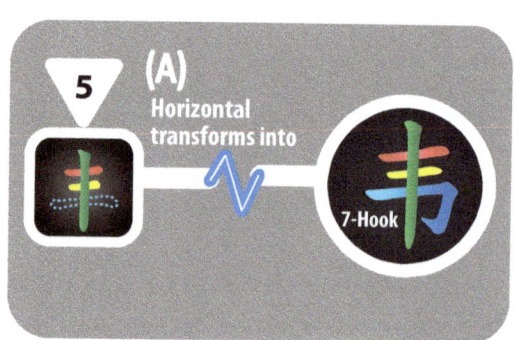

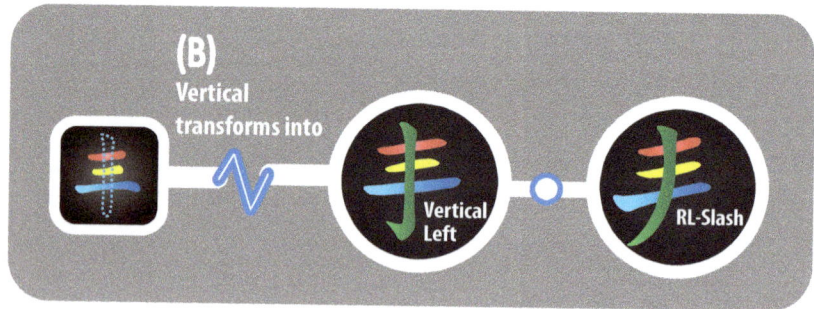

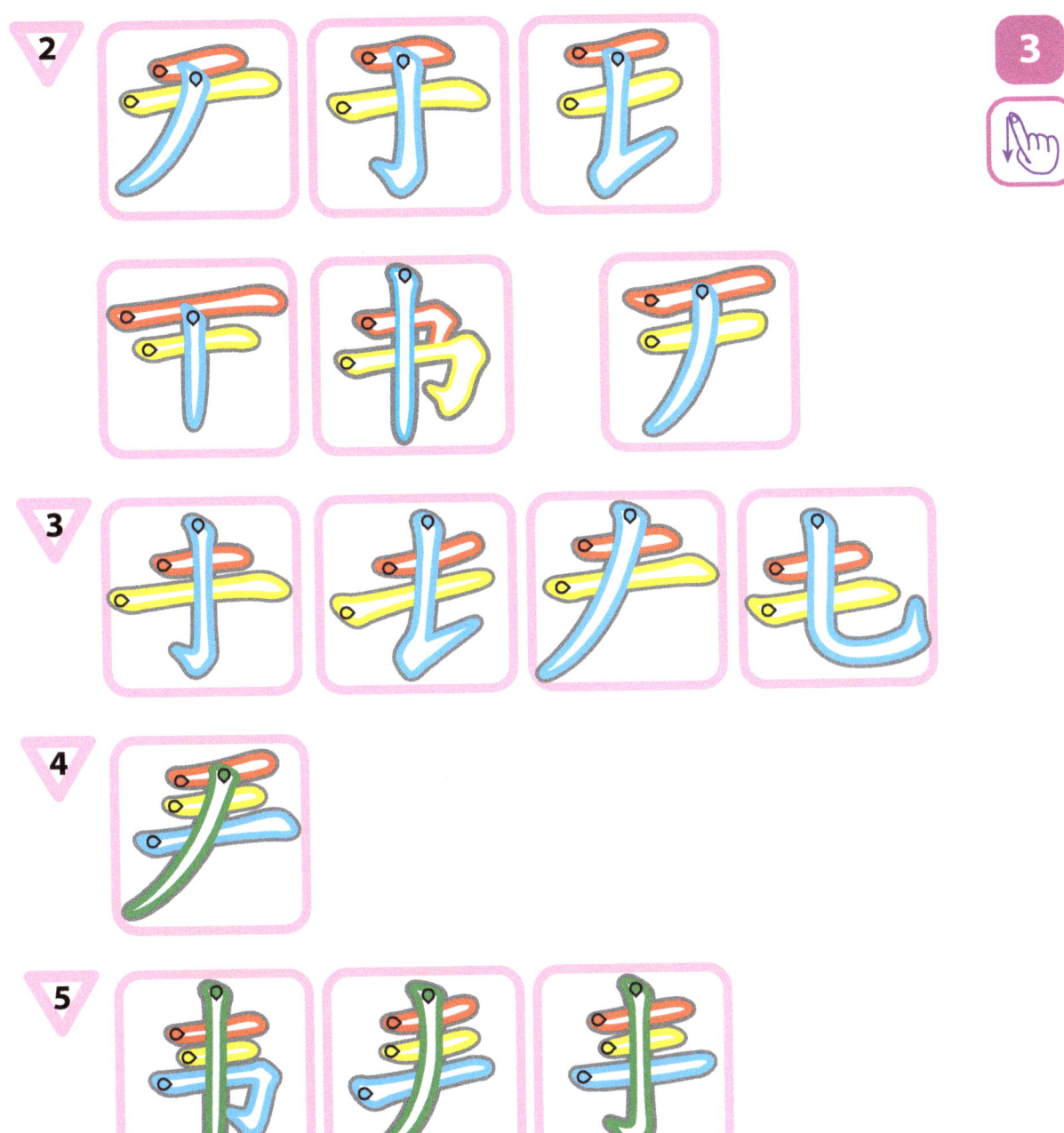

Activity 56B

手　毛　围　着　撬
辨　援　承　甩　翔
看　宇　余　帮　钉　4

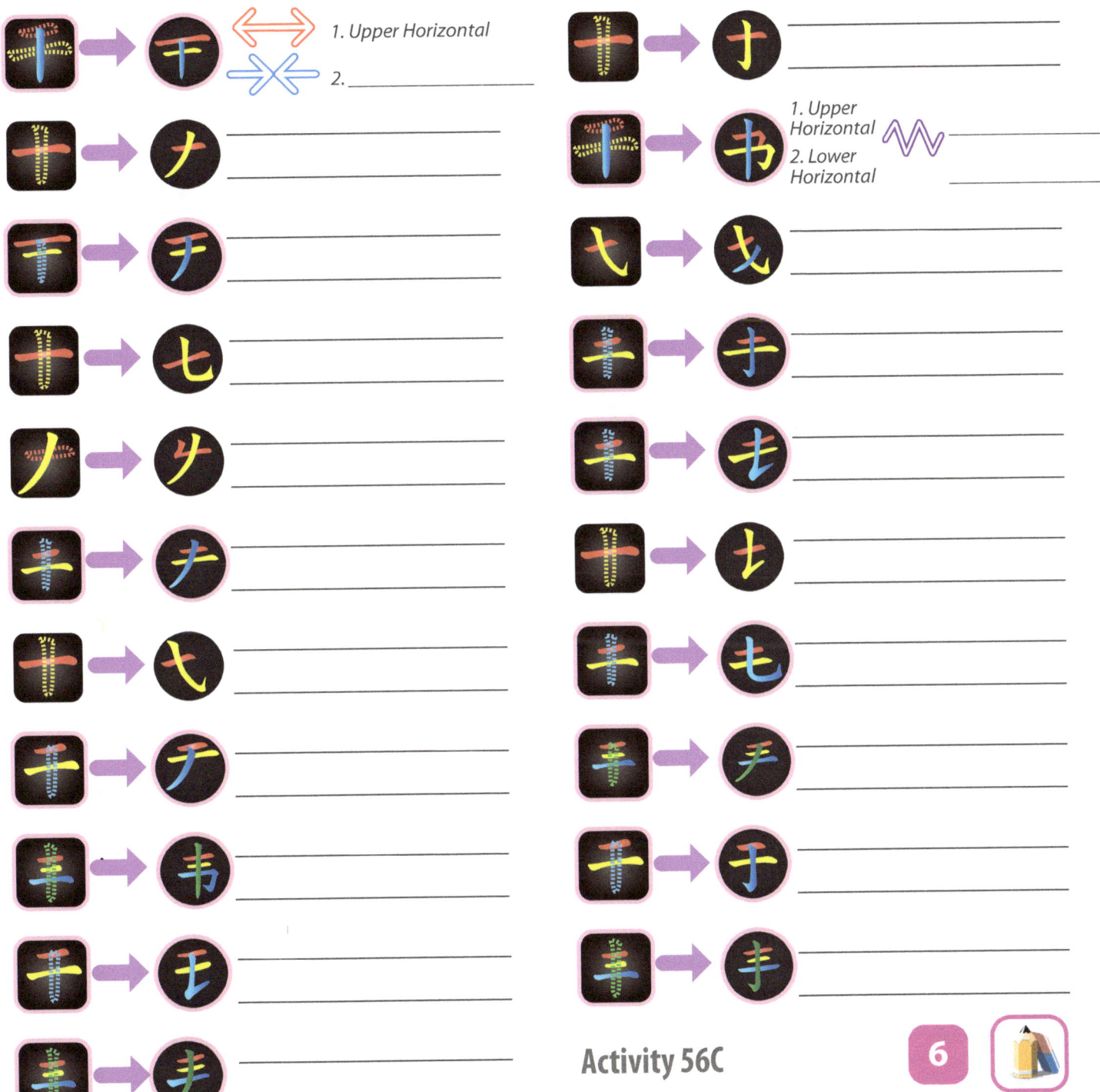

1. Upper Horizontal
2. _____

1. Upper Horizontal
2. Lower Horizontal

⑥ Intersections (Multiple Legs)

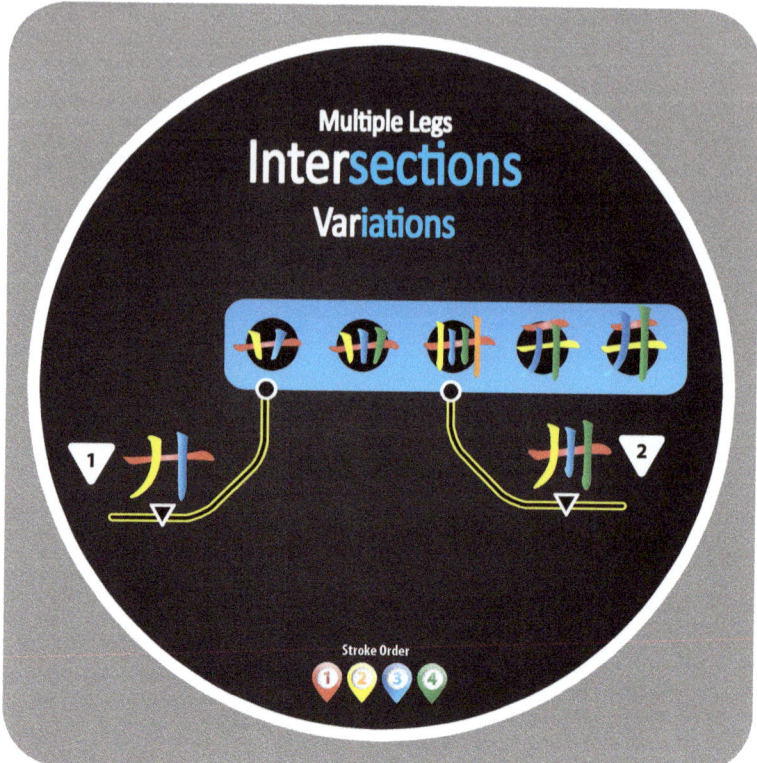

Multiple Legs
Intersections
Variations

Stroke Order
① ② ③ ④

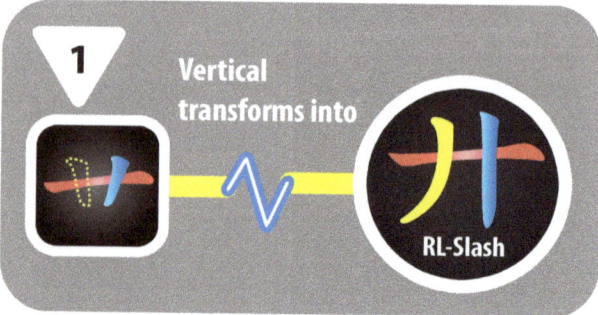

1 Vertical transforms into

RL-Slash

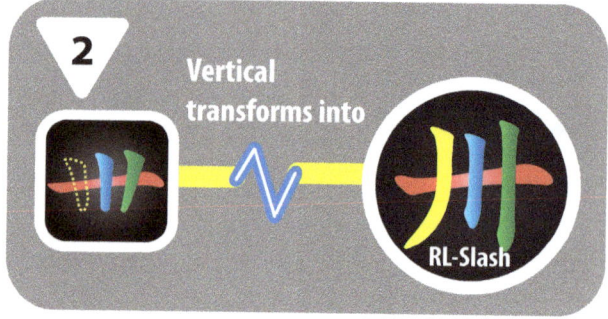

2 Vertical transforms into

RL-Slash

Activity 57A

1

 **3**

 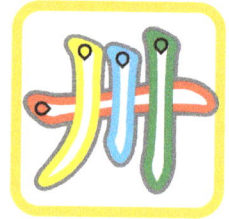

 **4**

⑦ Intersections (Flat Bottom)

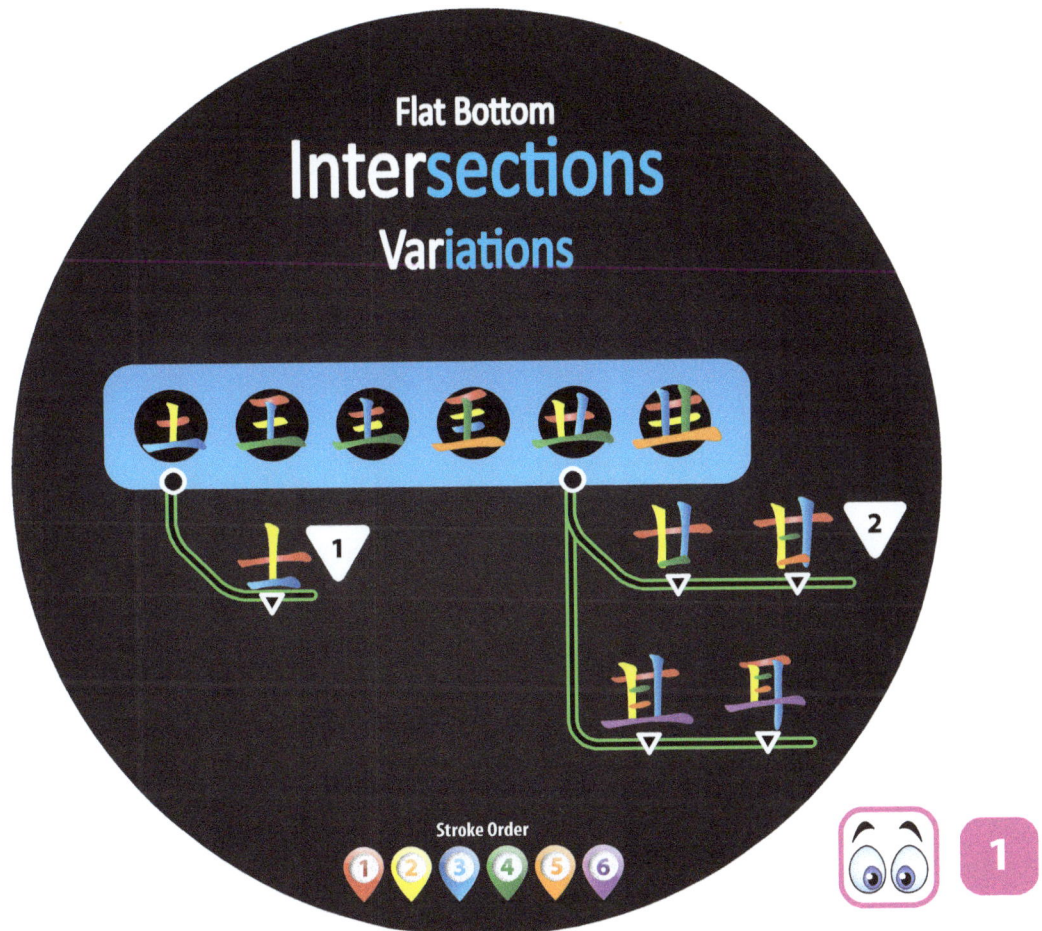

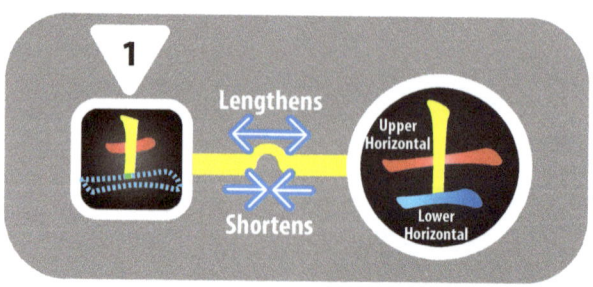

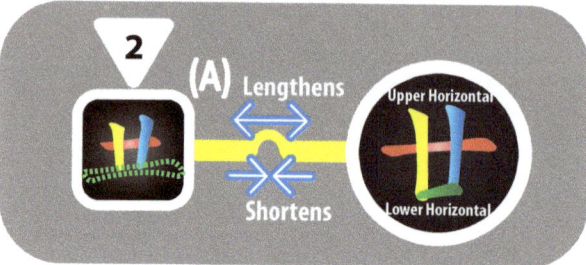

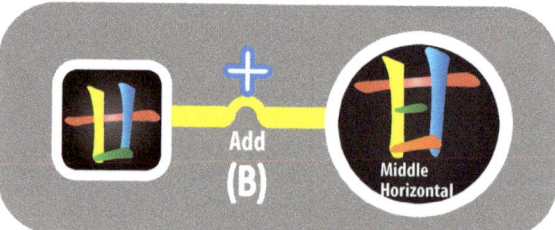

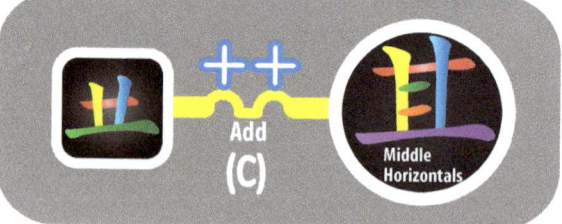

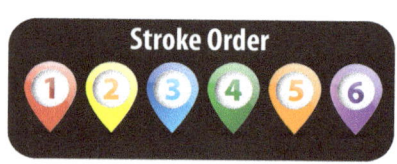

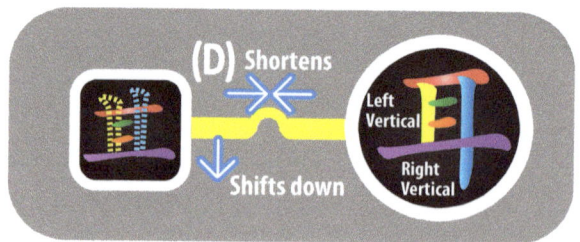

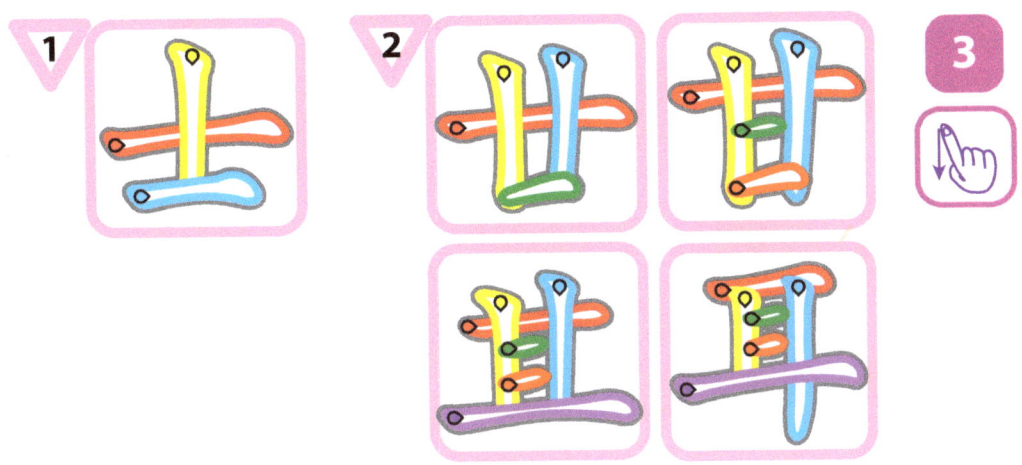

Activity 57B

Activity 57C

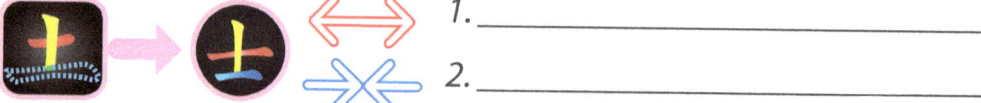

1. _____
2. _____

_____

_____

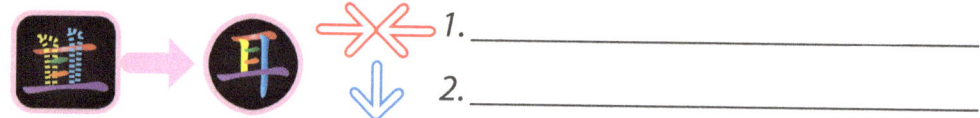

1. _____
2. _____

_____

_____

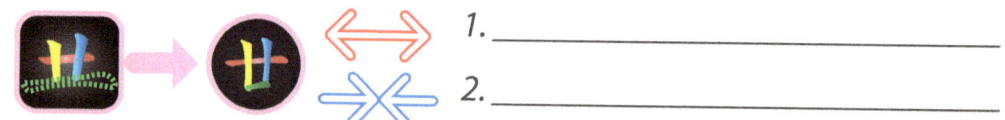

1. _____
2. _____

Activity 58

Write/draw the basic qTRAIL that these variations are transformed from.

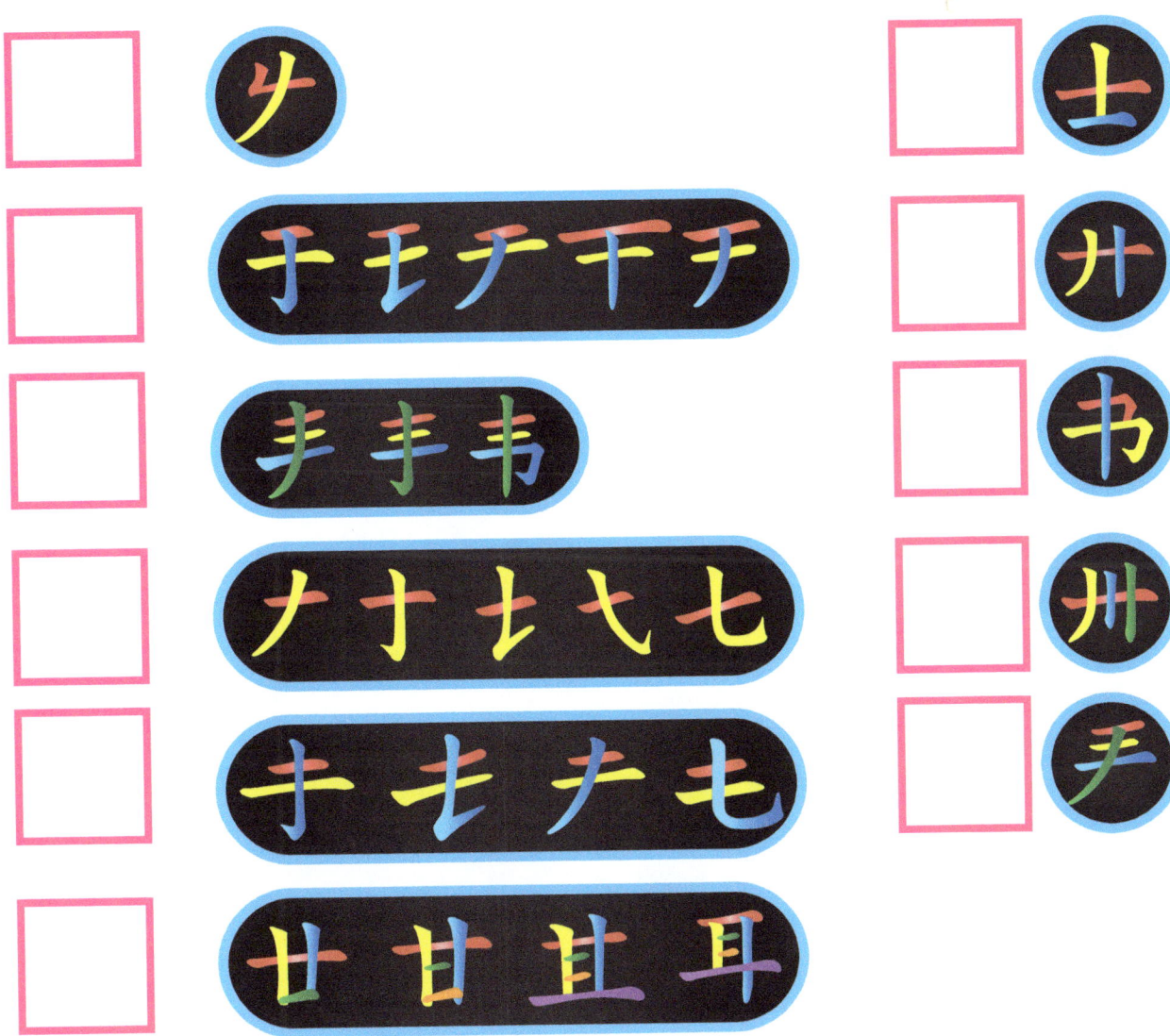

⑧ Split (Simple)

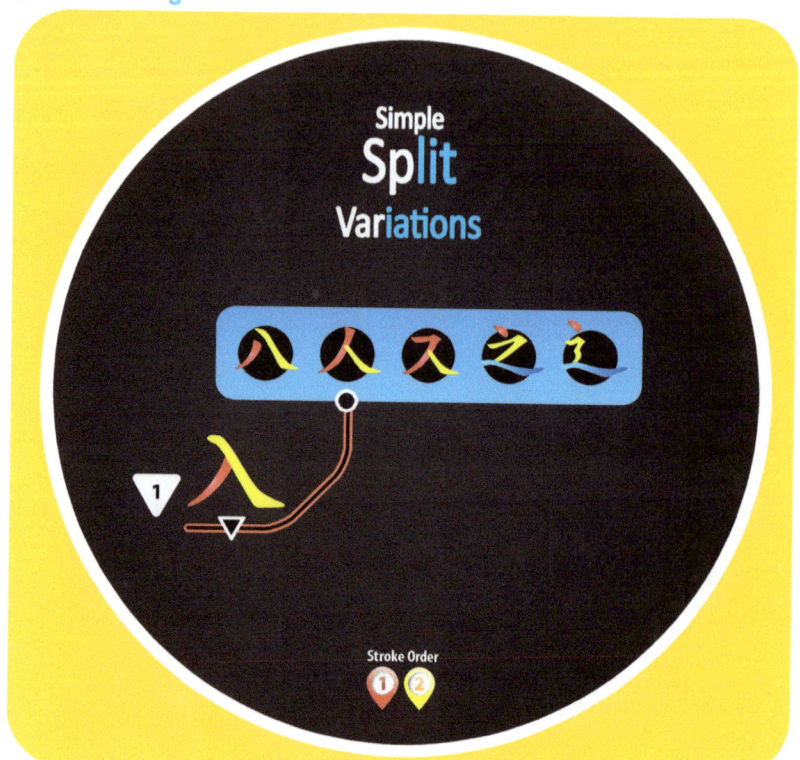

Simple
Split
Variations

Stroke Order
1 2

1

3

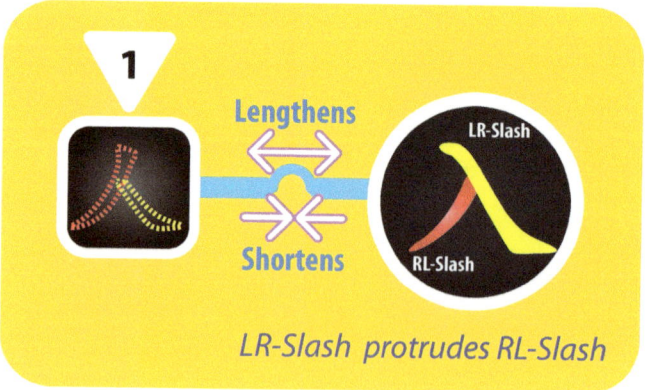

1

Lengthens

Shortens

LR-Slash

RL-Slash

LR-Slash protrudes RL-Slash

2

9 Split (with Vertical or Horizontal)

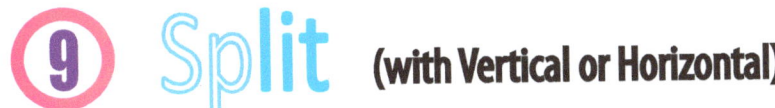

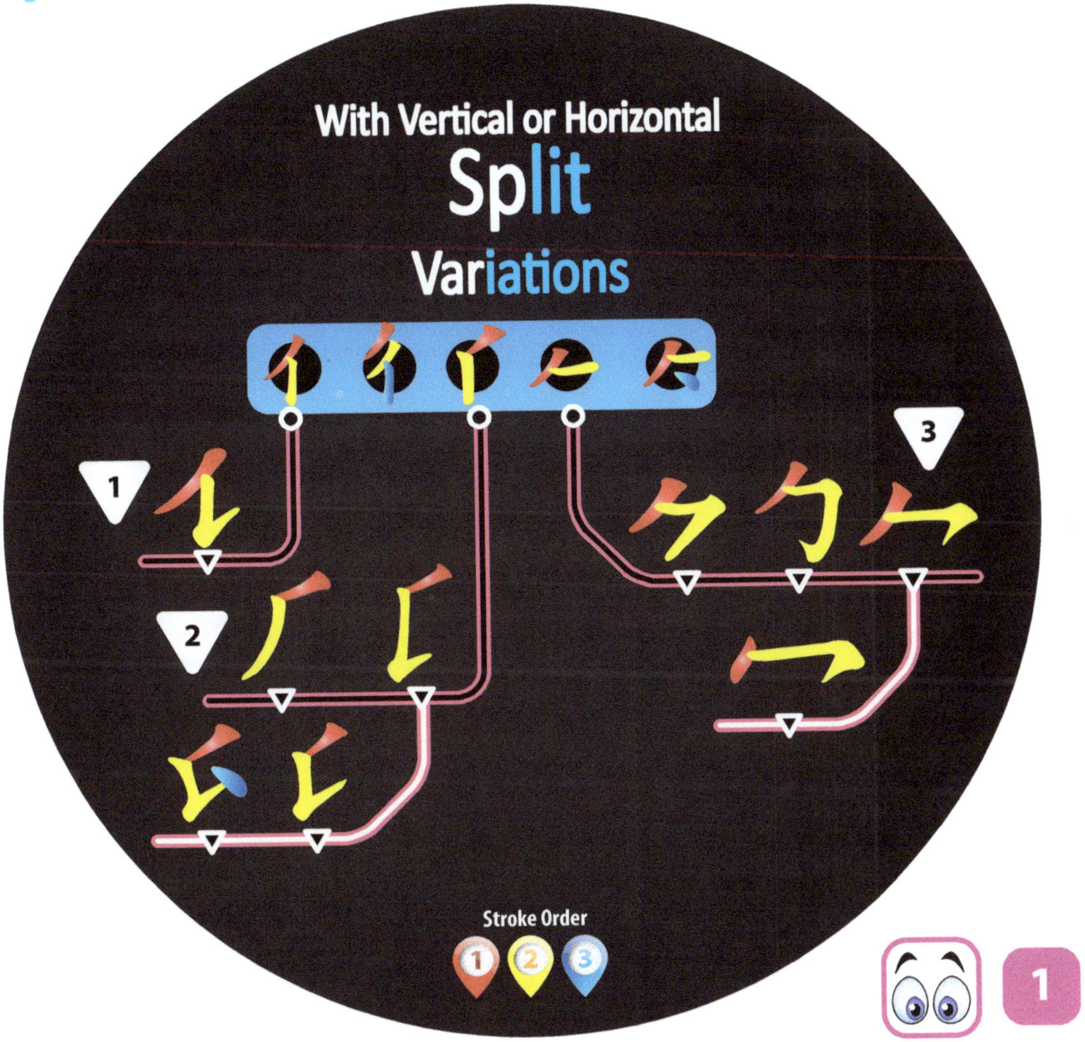

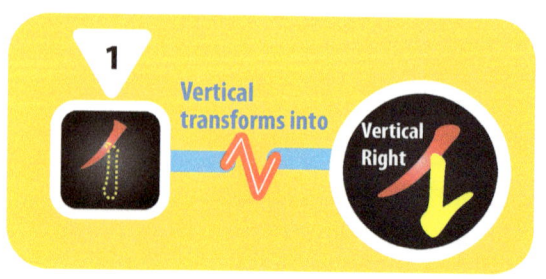

1 Vertical transforms into → Vertical Right

Stroke Order
1 2 3

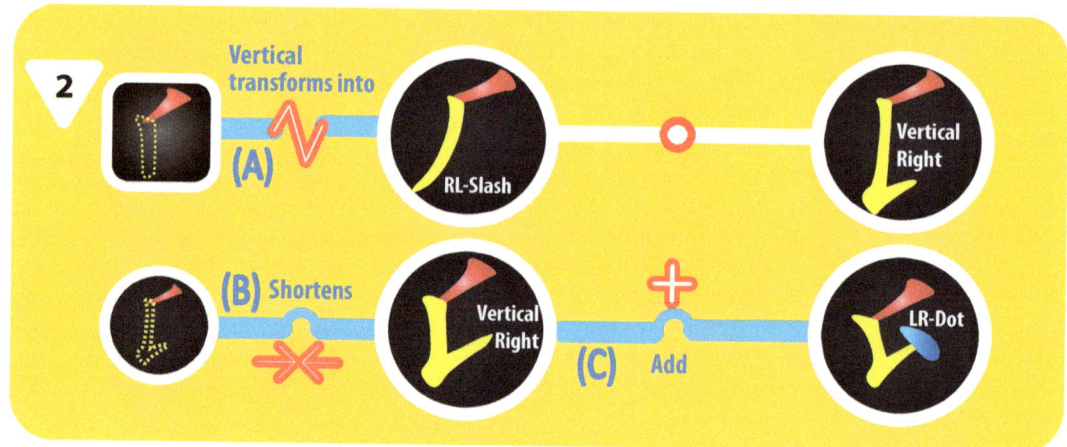

2 Vertical transforms into

(A) → RL-Slash ○ Vertical Right

(B) Shortens → Vertical Right **(C)** + Add → LR-Dot

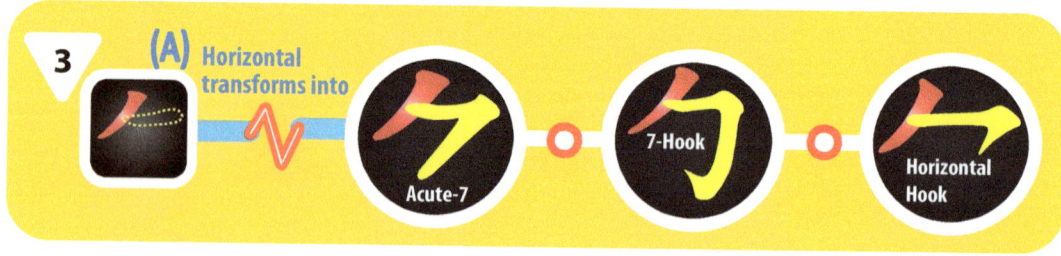

3 **(A)** Horizontal transforms into → Acute-7 ○ 7-Hook ○ Horizontal Hook

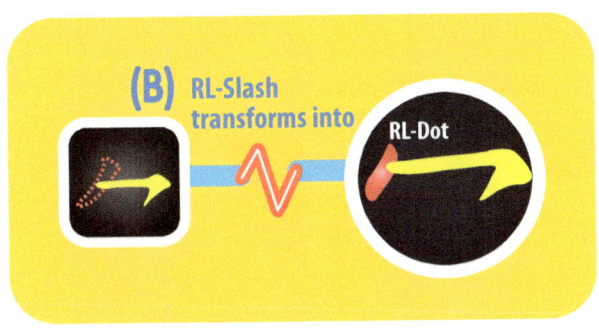

(B) RL-Slash transforms into RL-Dot

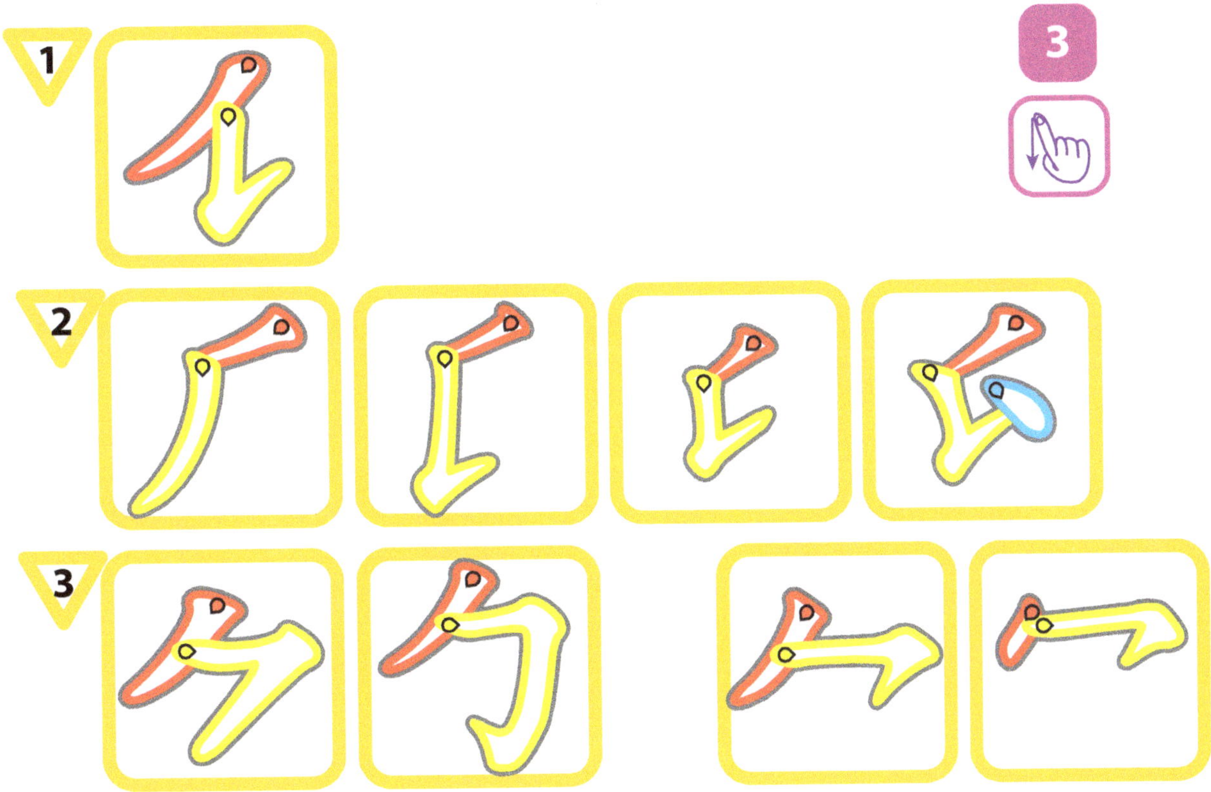

1

3

2

3

Activity 59A

表　贸　留　深　衣　鱼
纸　实　次　迎　句　印

Activity 59B

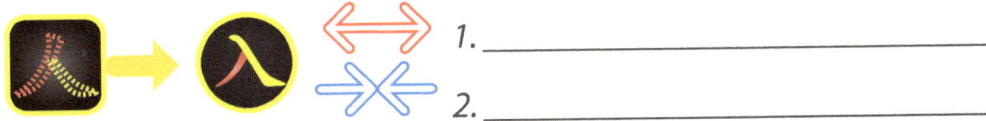

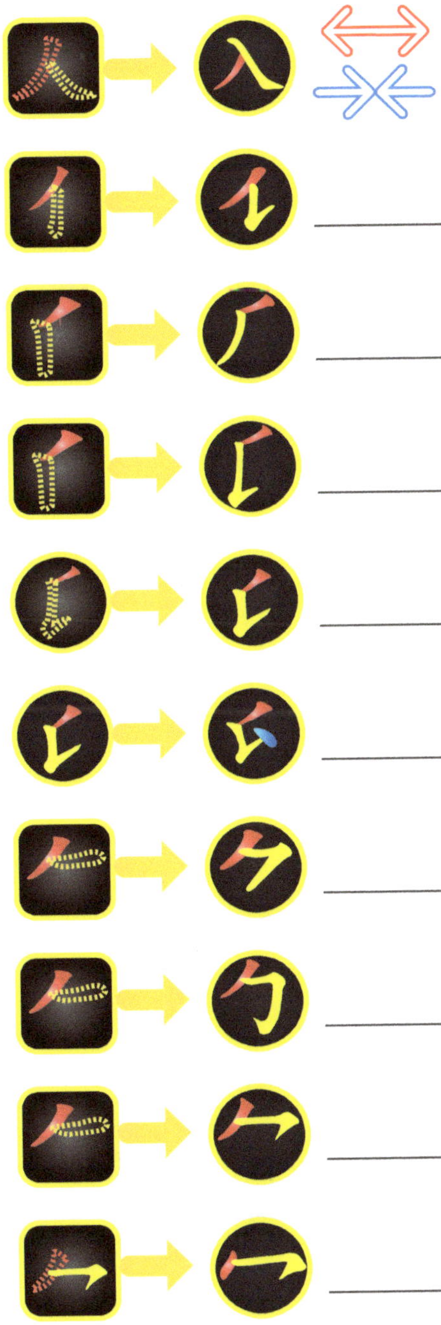

1. _____

2. _____

_____

_____

_____

_____

_____

_____

_____

_____

_____

⑩ Slide

7-Hook Slide Variations

Stroke Order

1

3

2

RL-Slash transforms into

Acute-7

Activity 60

4

祭 察

L-Hook / 7L-Hook
Split & Cross
Variations

Stroke Order
① ②

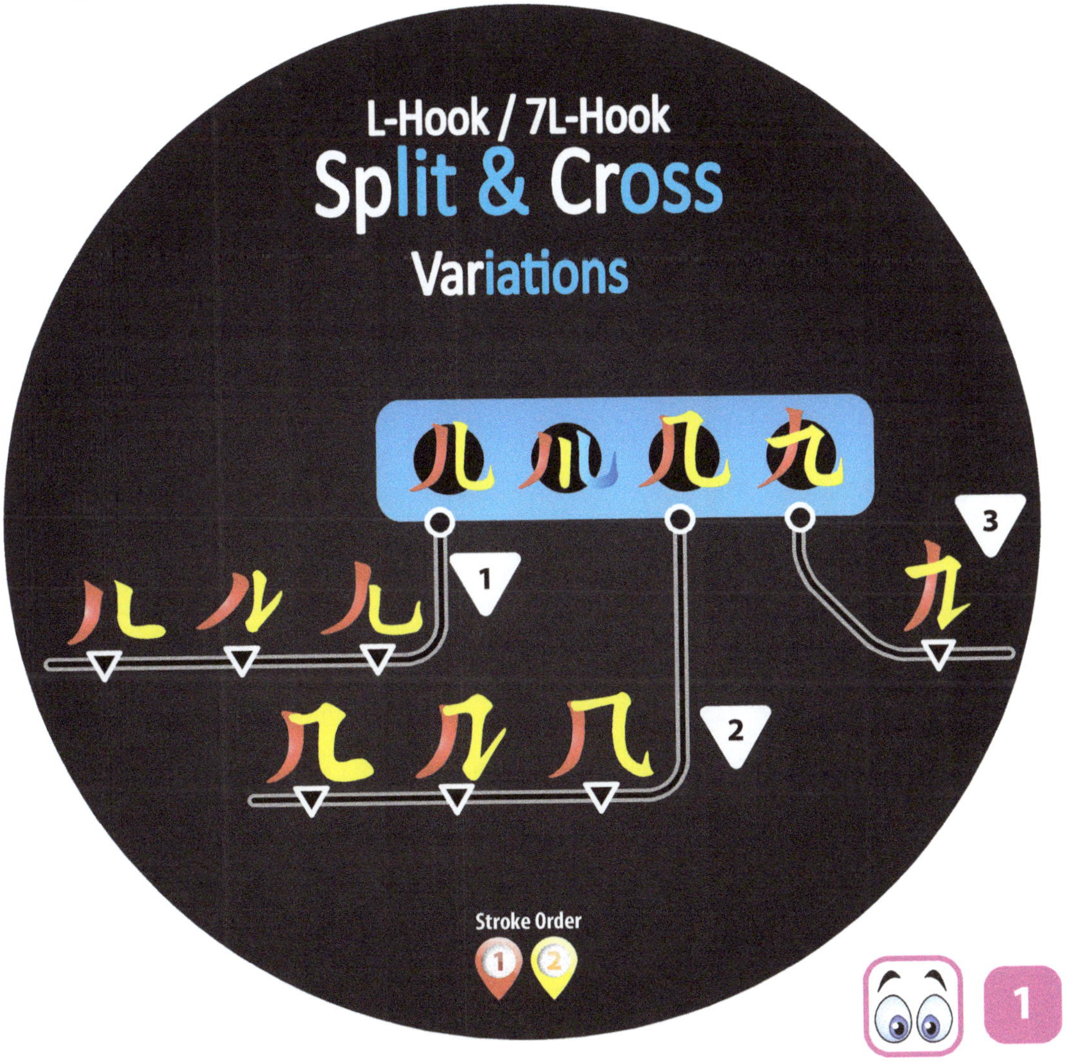

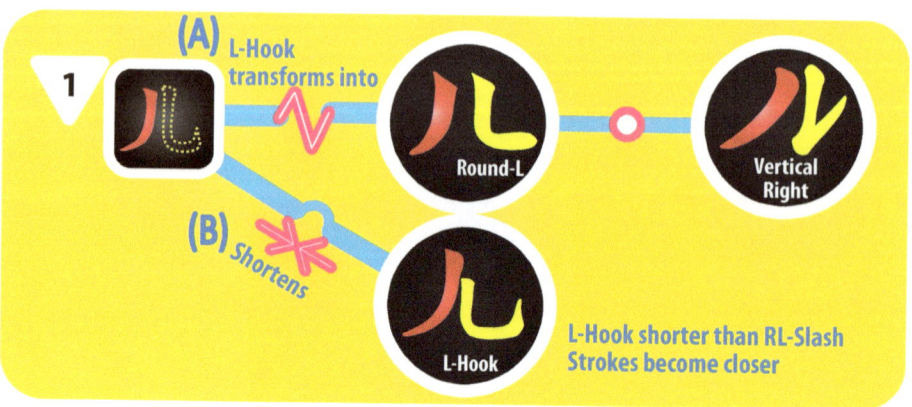

1

(A) L-Hook transforms into

Round-L

Vertical Right

(B) Shortens

L-Hook

L-Hook shorter than RL-Slash
Strokes become closer

2

7L-Hook transforms into

7-Leanback

Round-7L

7-Backkick

3

7L-Hook transforms into

7-Back kick

Stroke Order

1 2

2

Activity 61A

见	兢	没
四	凤	颓
微	鸠	沿

Activity 61B

 _____

  _____
Strokes become closer

 _____

 _____

 _____

 _____

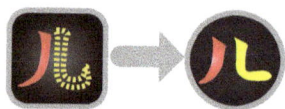 _____

 _____

Activity 62

Match the basic qTRAIL Alphabets (in the triangle) to their respective variations (in the rhombus) by writing the basic qTRAIL Alphabet in the given frames.

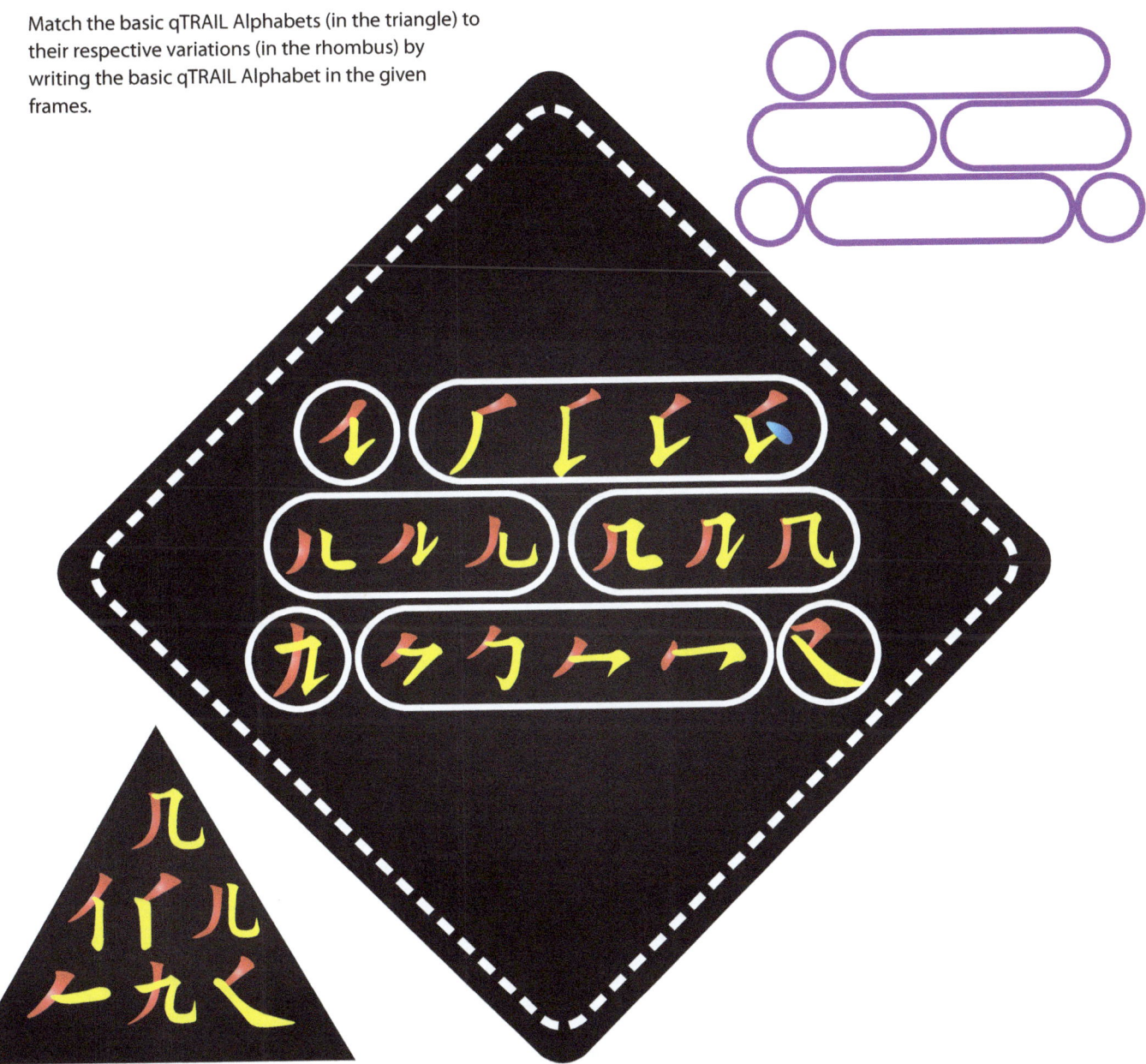

 **Flag** (7-Hook)

1

3

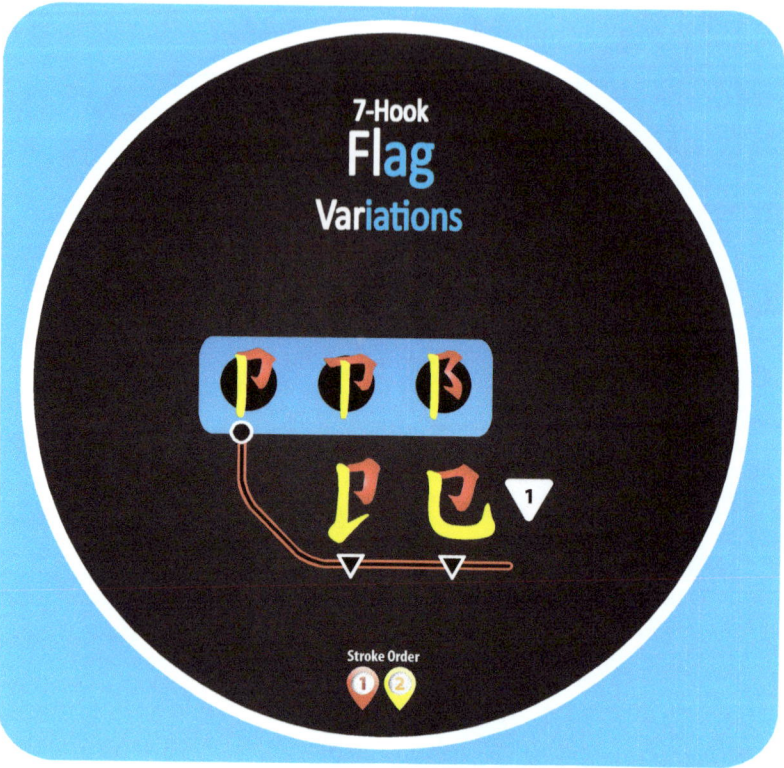

7-Hook
Flag
Variations

Stroke Order

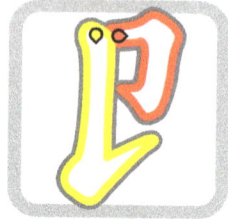 

Activity 63

 顾　 危

 卷　 仓　
4

2

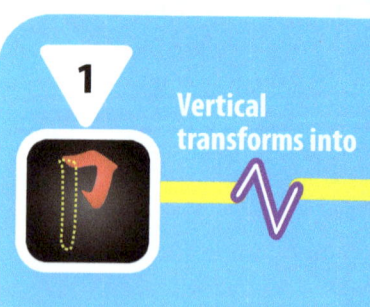
1

Vertical
transforms into

**Vertical
Right**

L-Hook

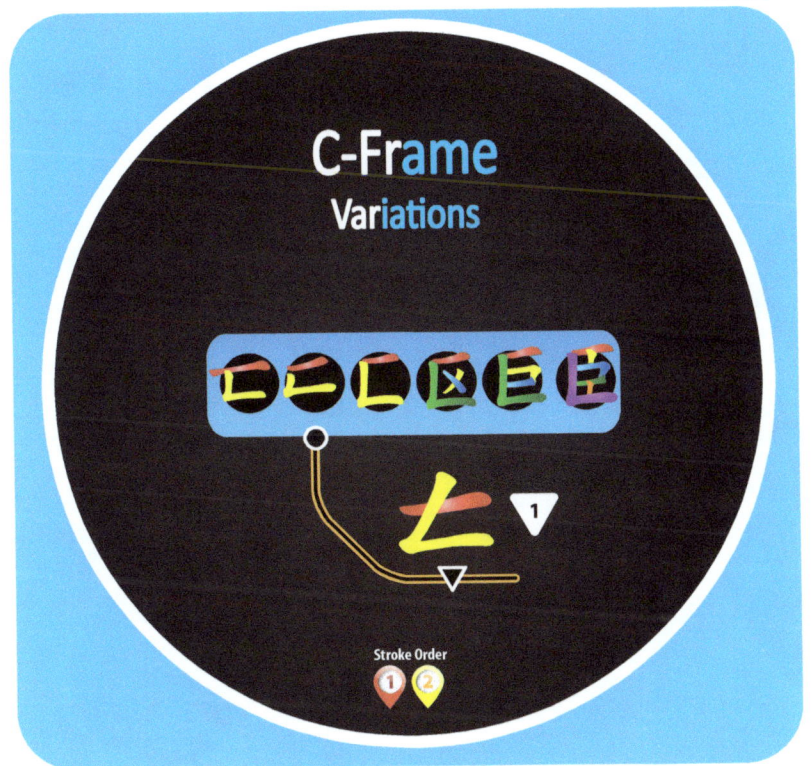

C-Frame
Variations

Stroke Order
1 2

1

L-Bend
transforms into

Acute-L

L-Bend
intersects horizontal

Activity 64

车 连
军 转

 4

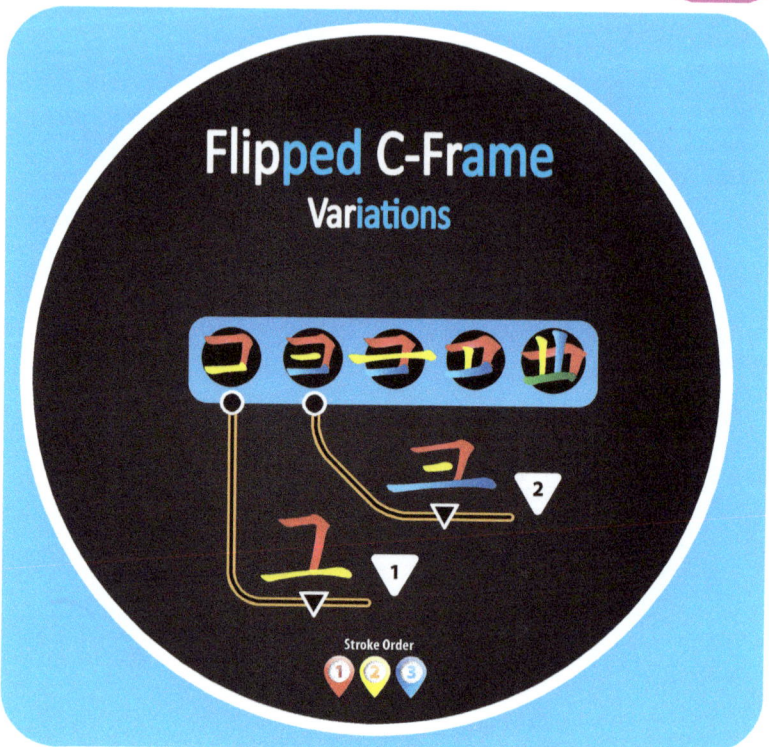

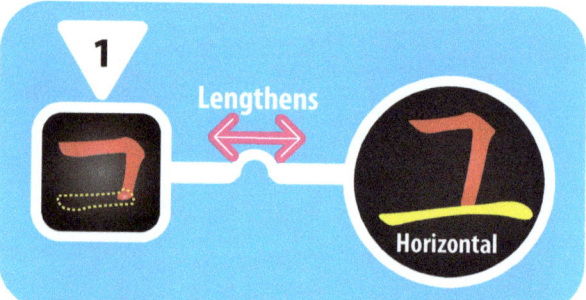

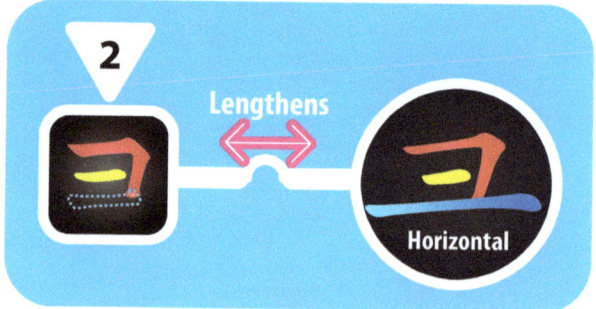

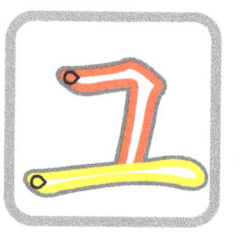
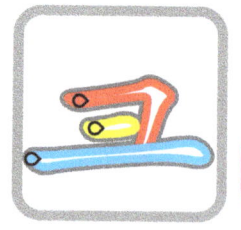

Activity 65

⑮ L7-Hook

 1

 3

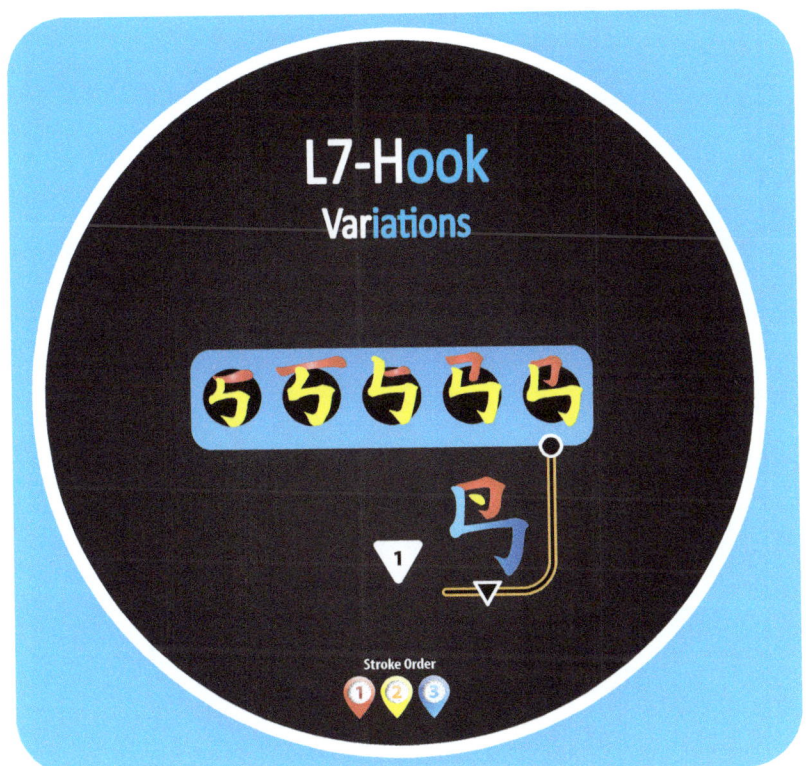

L7-Hook
Variations

马

Stroke Order

2

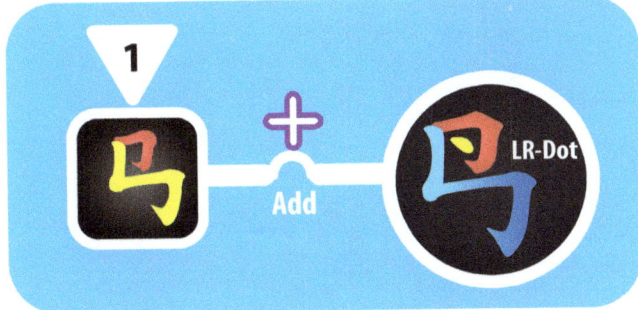

1

马 + 马 LR-Dot

Add

Activity 66 4

 鸣  鸟  枭

16 7-Hook Frame

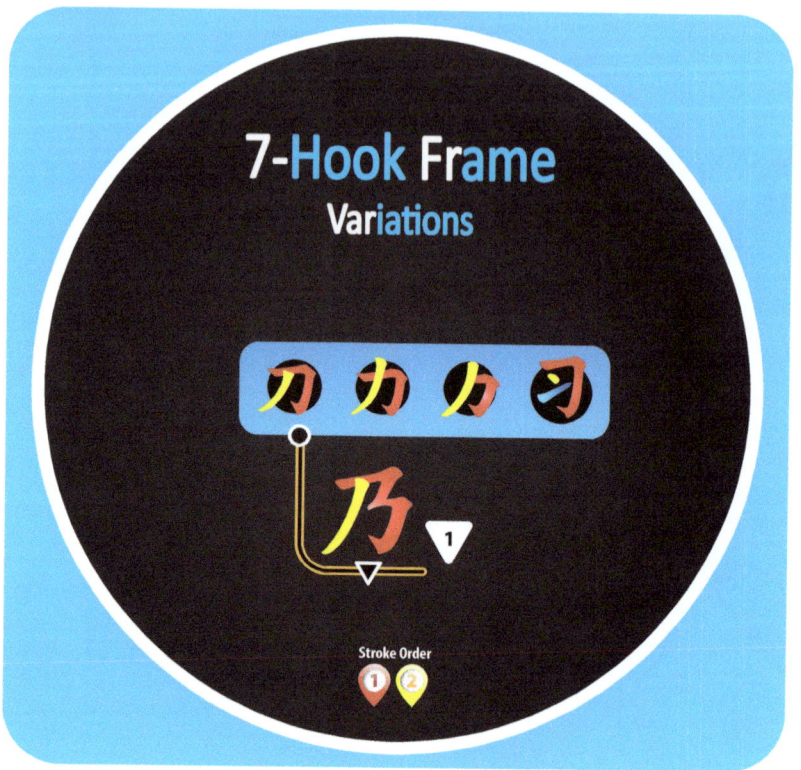

7-Hook Frame
Variations

Stroke Order
1 2

1

3

Activity 67

4

2
1
7-Hook transforms into
Double-7 Hook

Frame Variations Revision

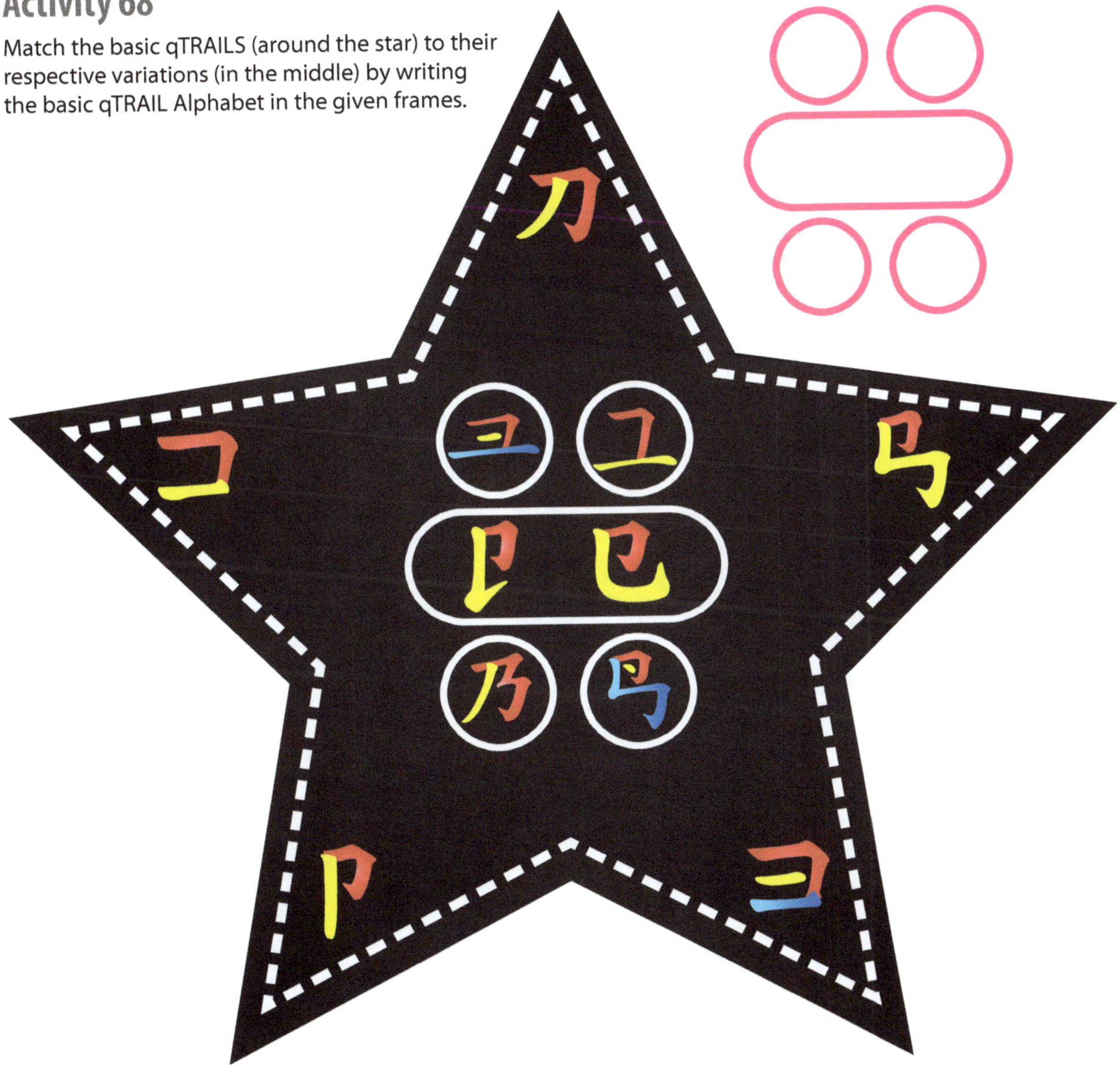

Activity 68

Match the basic qTRAILS (around the star) to their respective variations (in the middle) by writing the basic qTRAIL Alphabet in the given frames.

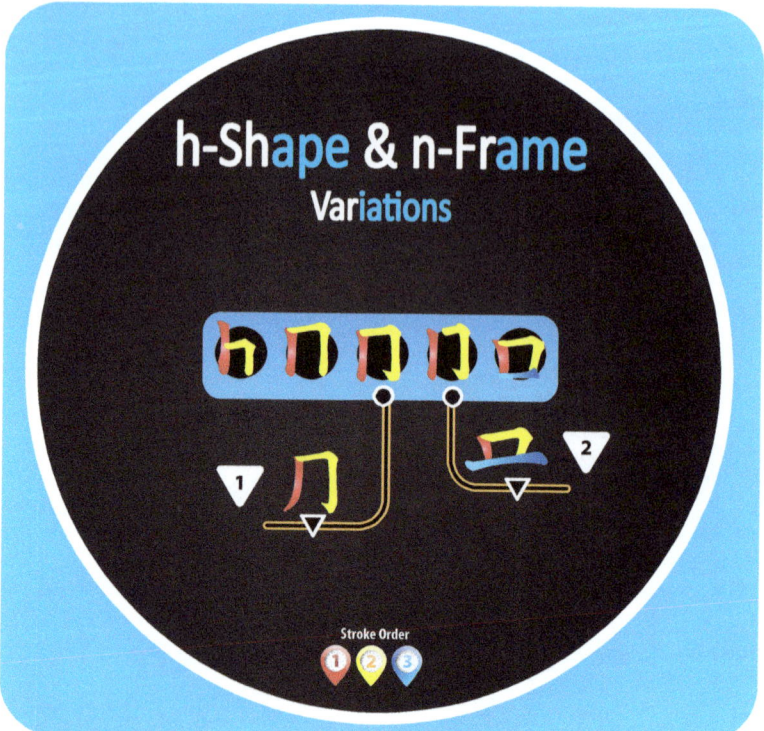

h-Shape & n-Frame
Variations

Stroke Order
① ② ③

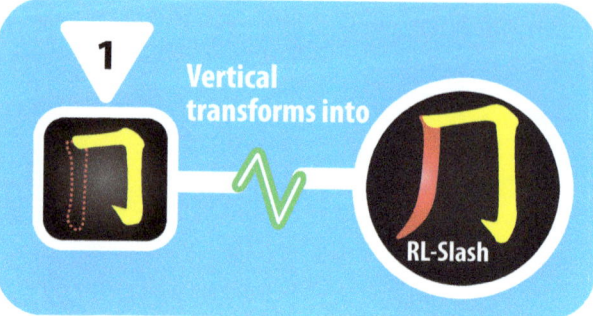

1 Vertical transforms into
RL-Slash

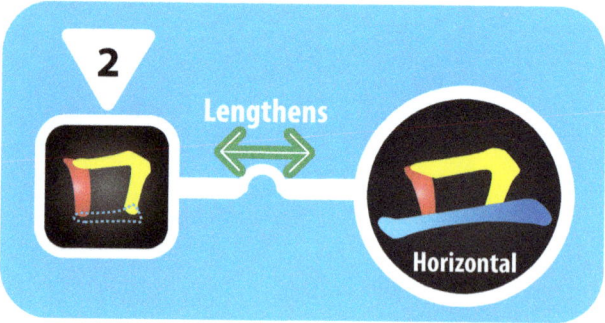

2 Lengthens
Horizontal

3

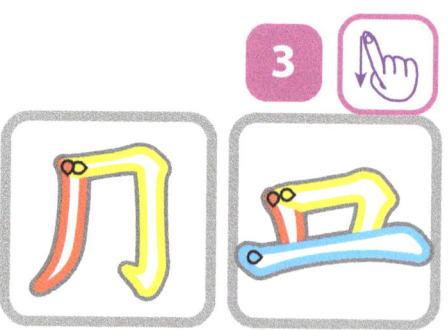

Activity 69

周 央

英 丹

4

2

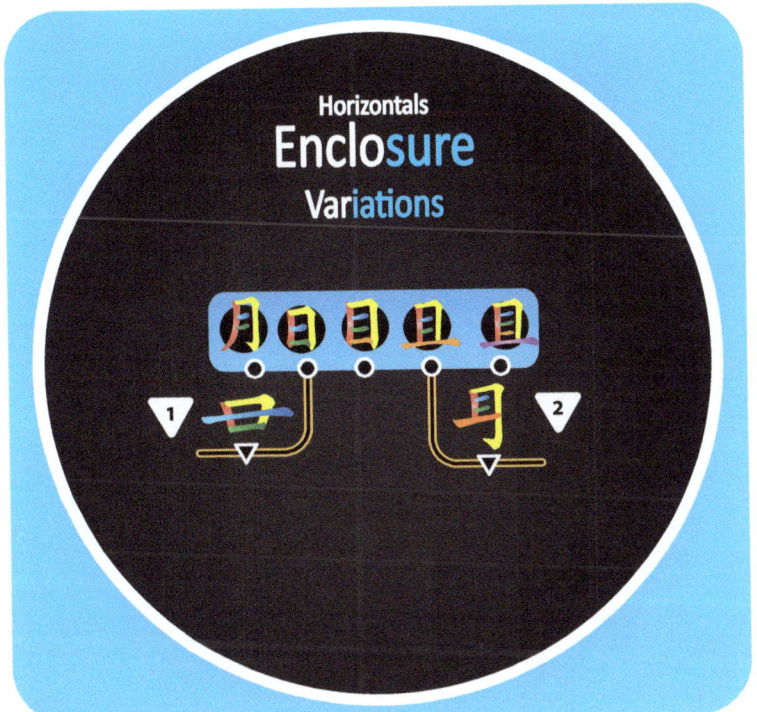

Horizontals
Enclosure
Variations

1

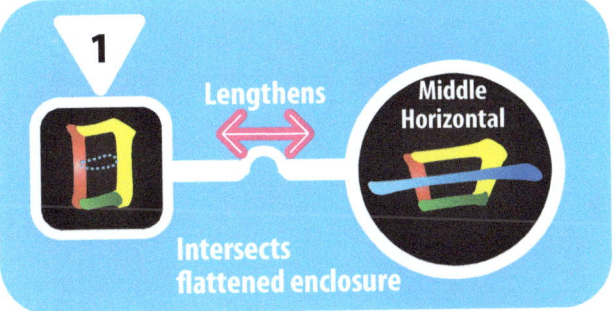

1

Lengthens

Middle
Horizontal

Intersects
flattened enclosure

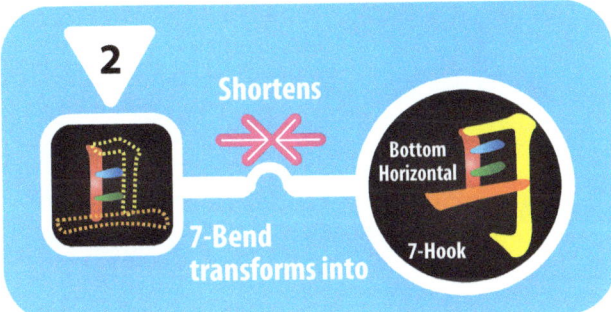

2

Shortens

Bottom
Horizontal

7-Bend
transforms into

7-Hook

1

3

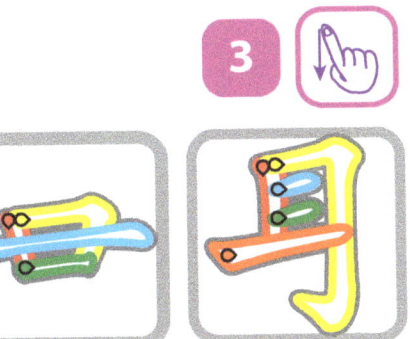

Activity 70

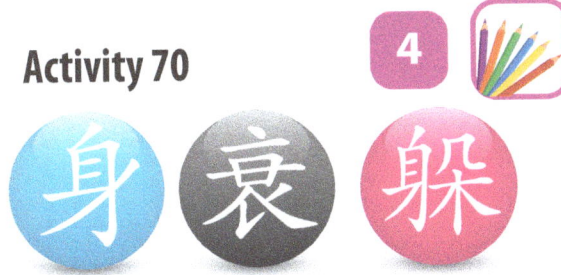

4

身 衰 躬

㉙ Enclosure (Intersections)

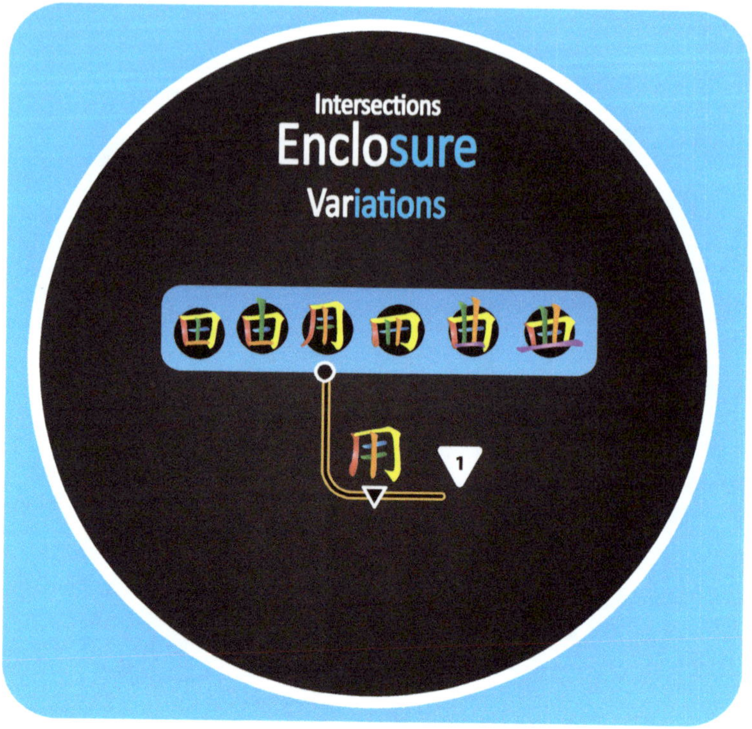

Intersections
Enclosure
Variations

田 由 用 冊 曲 曲

用 ▽①

1 👀

2 😬

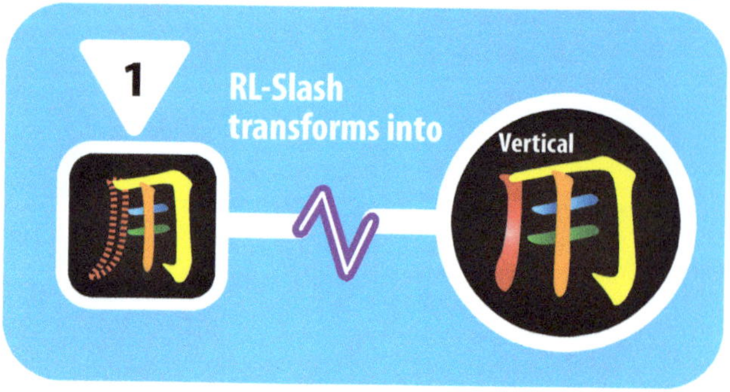

▽**1**   **RL-Slash transforms into**   **Vertical**

冊 〰 用

3 👆

用

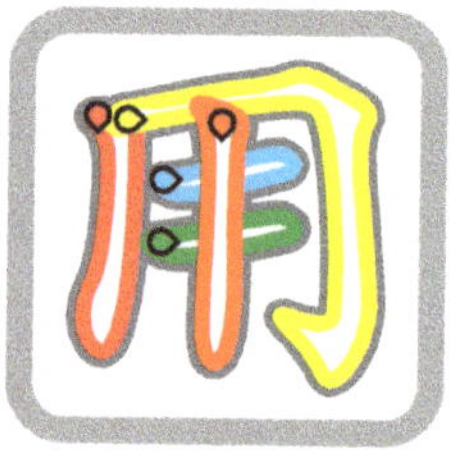

Activity 71A

甬 通
痛

4 ✏️

 _____

 _____

 _____

 _____

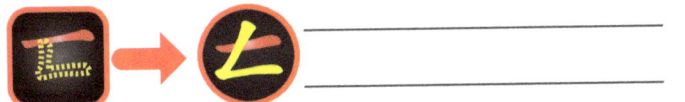 _____

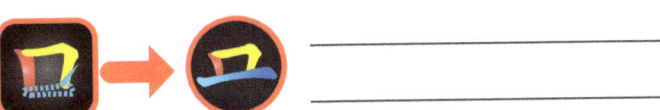 _____

 _____

 _____

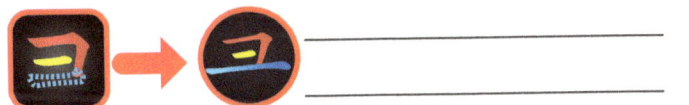 _____

 _____

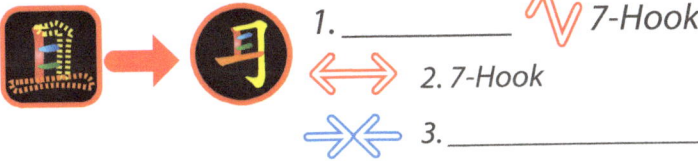

1. _____ ⋀ 7-Hook

2. 7-Hook

3. _____

 _____

Horizontal intersects Enclosure

Activity 72

Match the basic qTRAILS (around the hexagon) to their respective variations (in the middle) by writing the basic qTRAIL Alphabet in the given frames.

Activity 73

Transform the vertical in these *basic qTRAILS Alphabets* into RL-Slash and write the varied Alphabets in the boxes. See example.

Example:

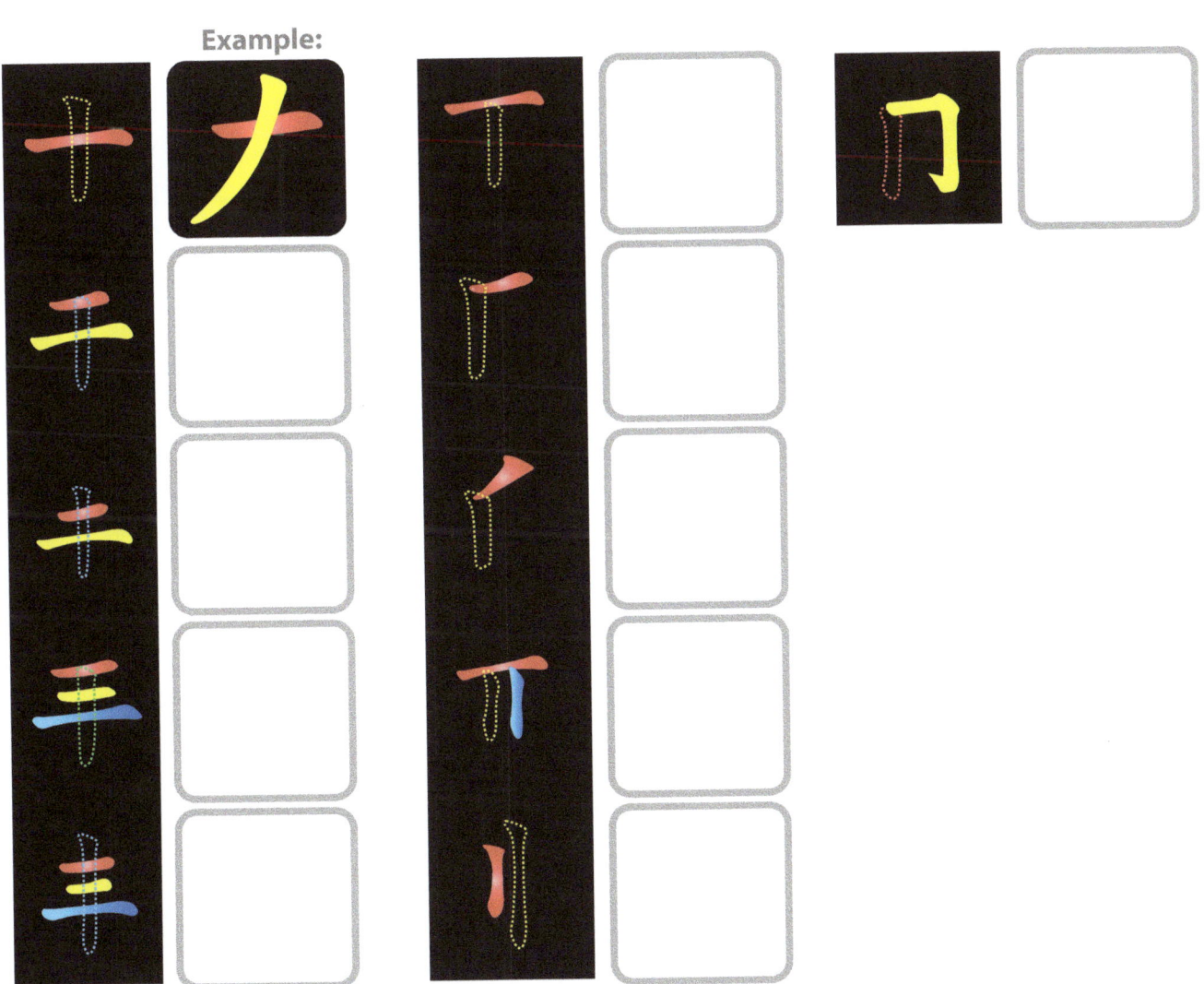

Activity 74

Transform the vertical in these *basic qTRAILS Alphabets* into Vertical Left and write the varied Alphabets in the boxes.

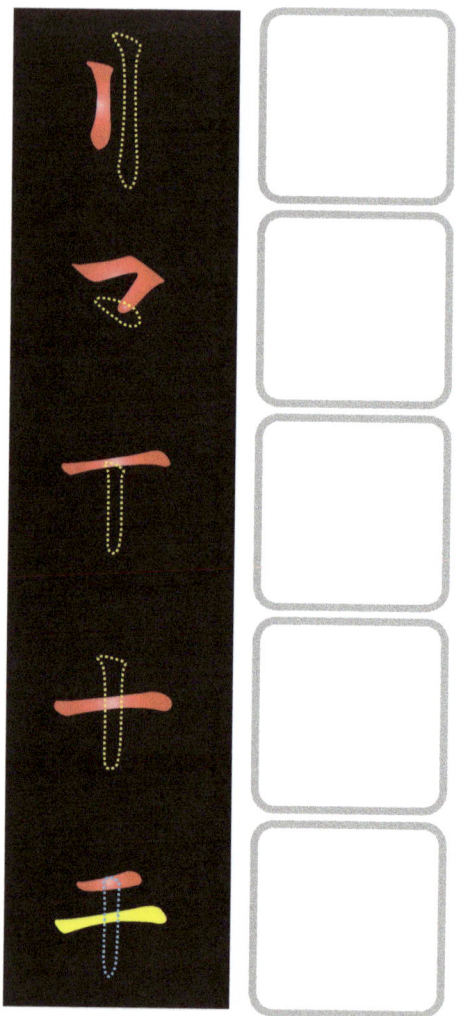

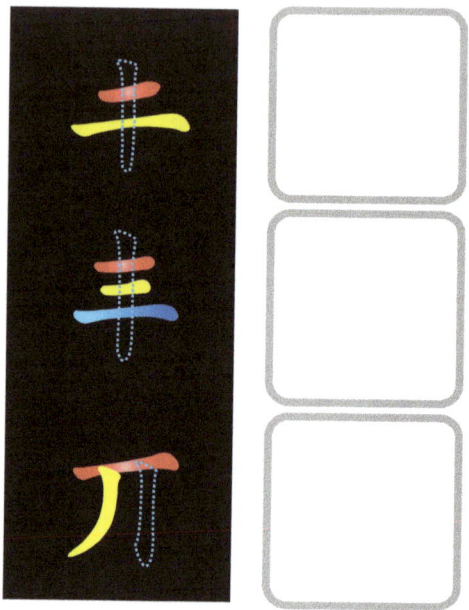

Activity 75

Transform the vertical in these *basic qTRAILS Alphabets* into Vertical Right and write the varied Alphabets in the boxes.

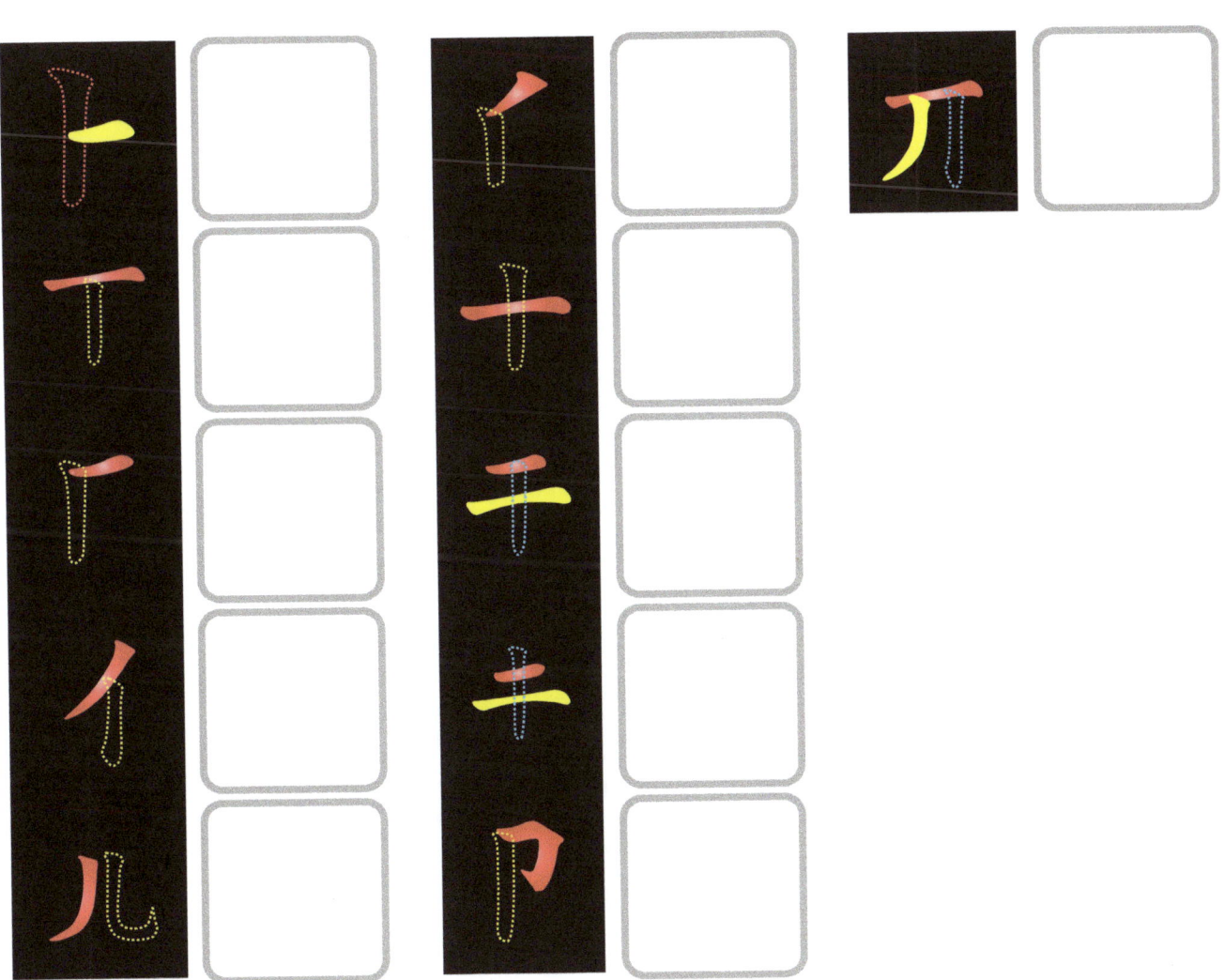

Activity 76

Transform the vertical in these *basic qTRAILS Alphabets* into L-Hook and write the varied Alphabets in the boxes.

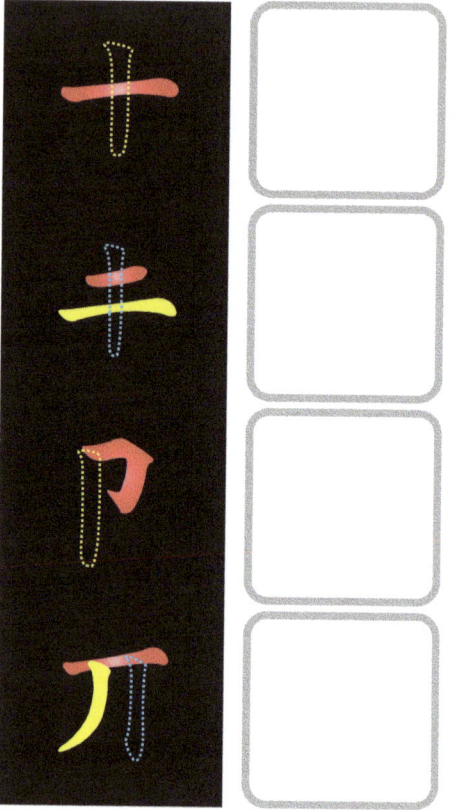

Transform the horizontal in these *basic qTRAILS Alphabets* into 7-Hook and write the varied Alphabets in the boxes.

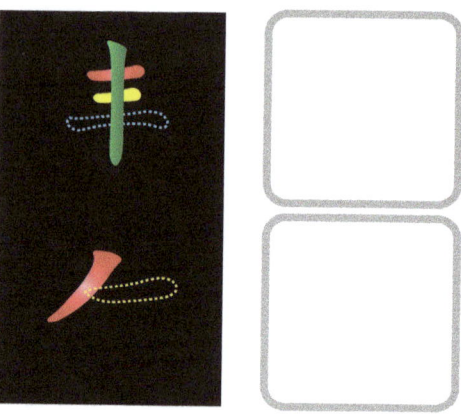

Transform the 7L-Hook in these *basic qTRAILS Alphabets* into 7-Backkick and write the varied Alphabets in the boxes.

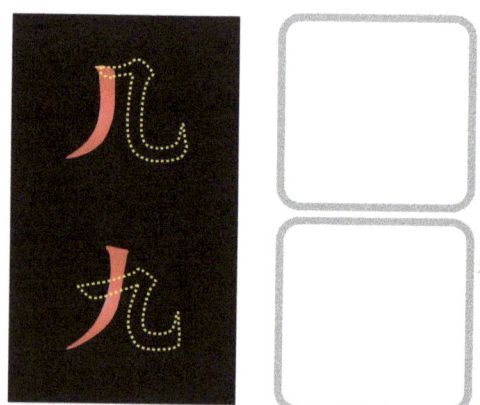

Activity 77

Transform the dotted stroke in the *basic qTRAILS Alphabets* into Acute-L and write the varied Alphabets in the boxes.

Transform the dotted stroke in the *basic qTRAILS Alphabets* into Double 7 Hook and write the varied Alphabets in the boxes.

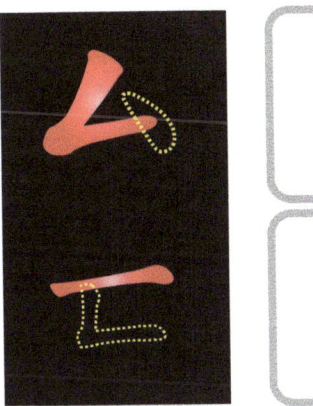
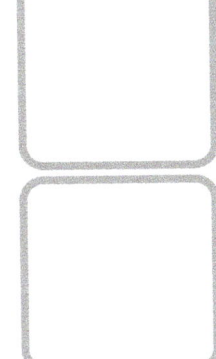

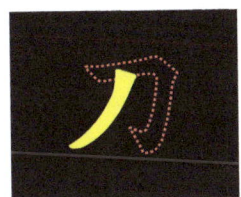

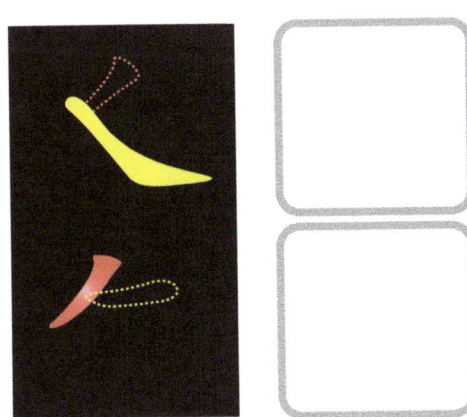

Activity 78

Add a stroke

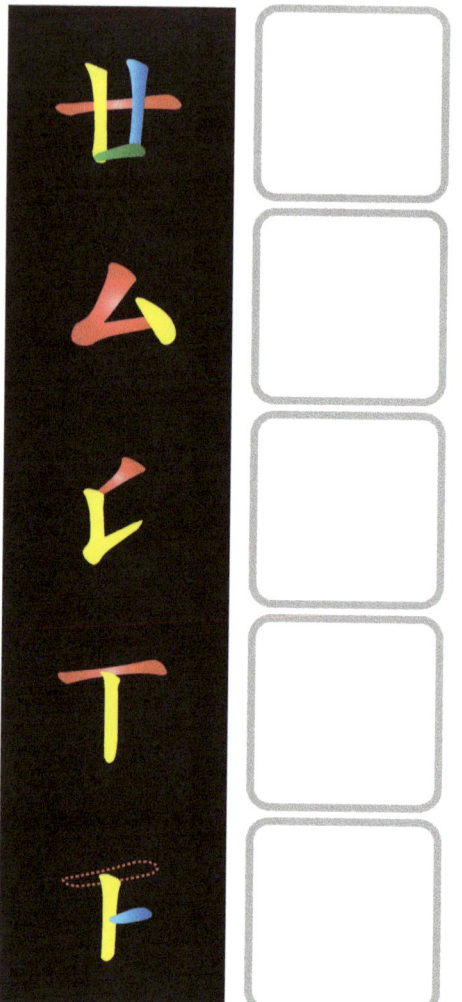

Add two strokes

Activity 79

Extend or shorten the dotted stroke(s) to form a variation of the *basic qTRAILS Alphabet.*

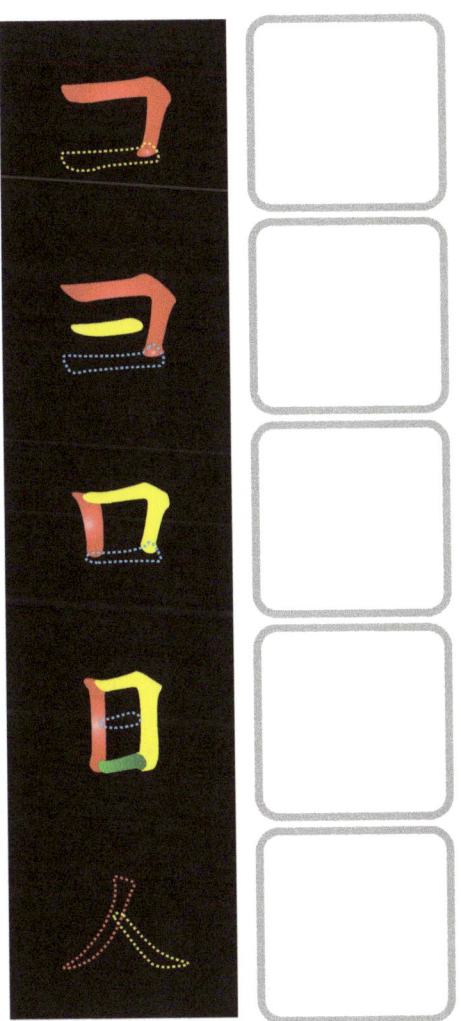

Activity 80

These **basic qTRAILS Alphabets** were transformed twice. Trace back how these parts were transformed. See examples.

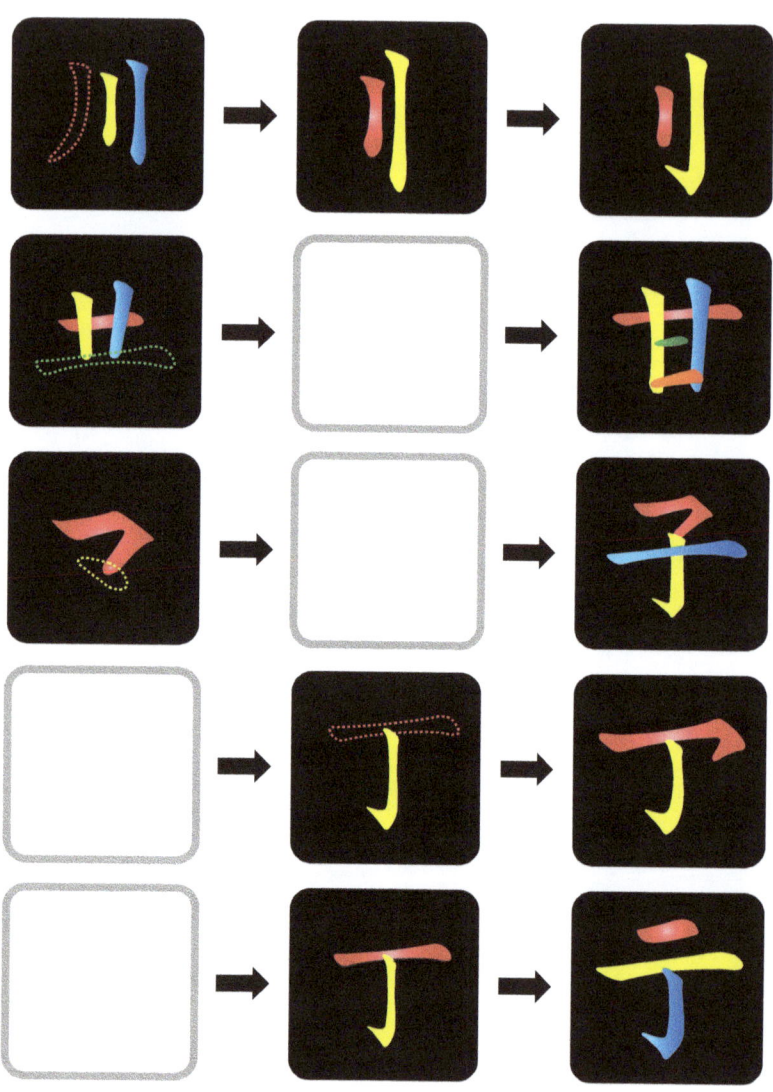

Activity 81

These **basic qTRAILS Alphabets** were transformed twice. Trace back how these parts were transformed.

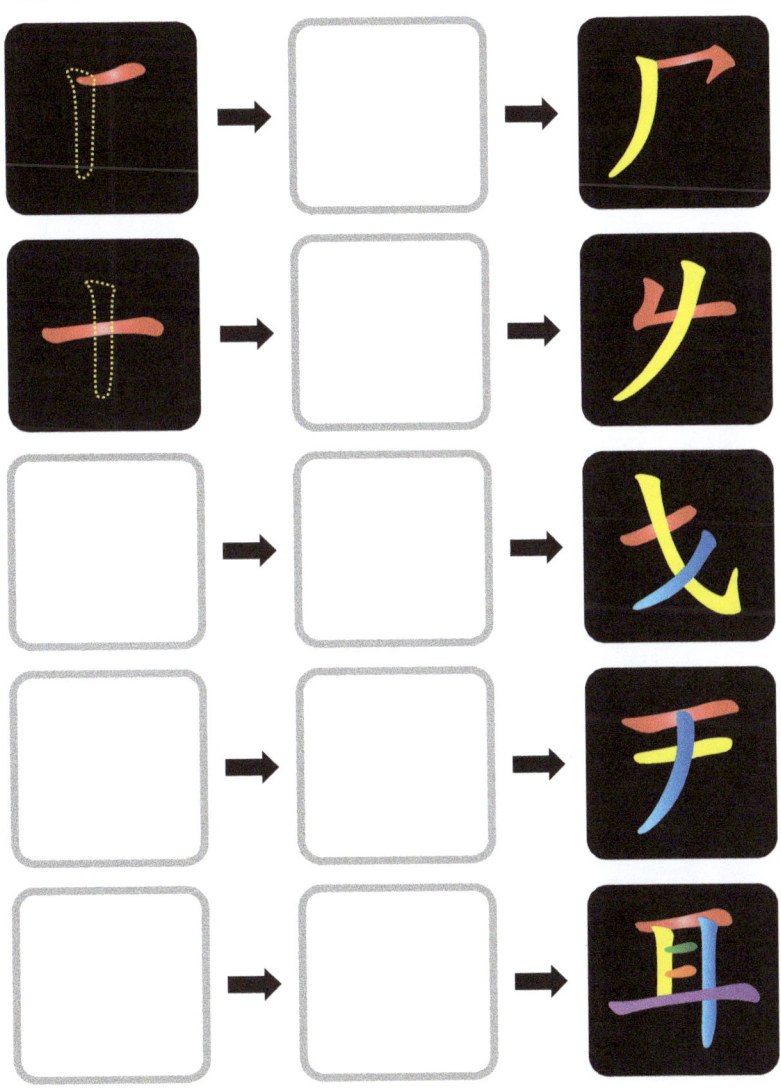

Activity 82

These **basic qTRAILS Alphabets** were transformed twice. Trace back how these Alphabets were transformed.

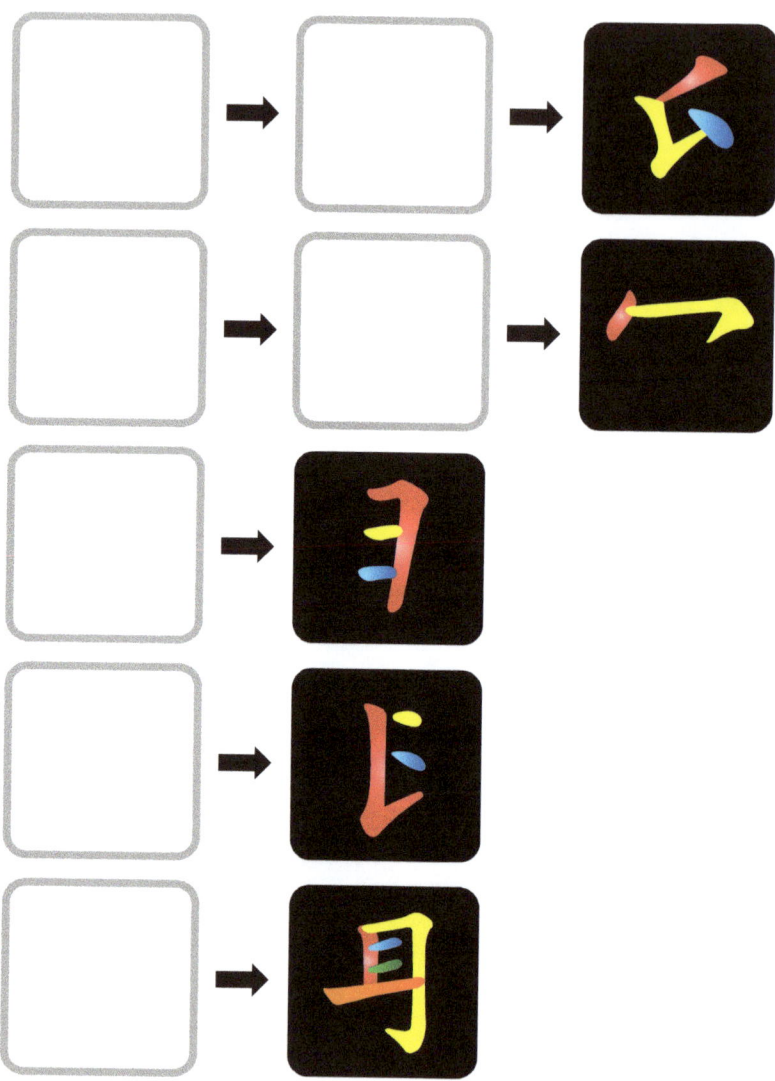

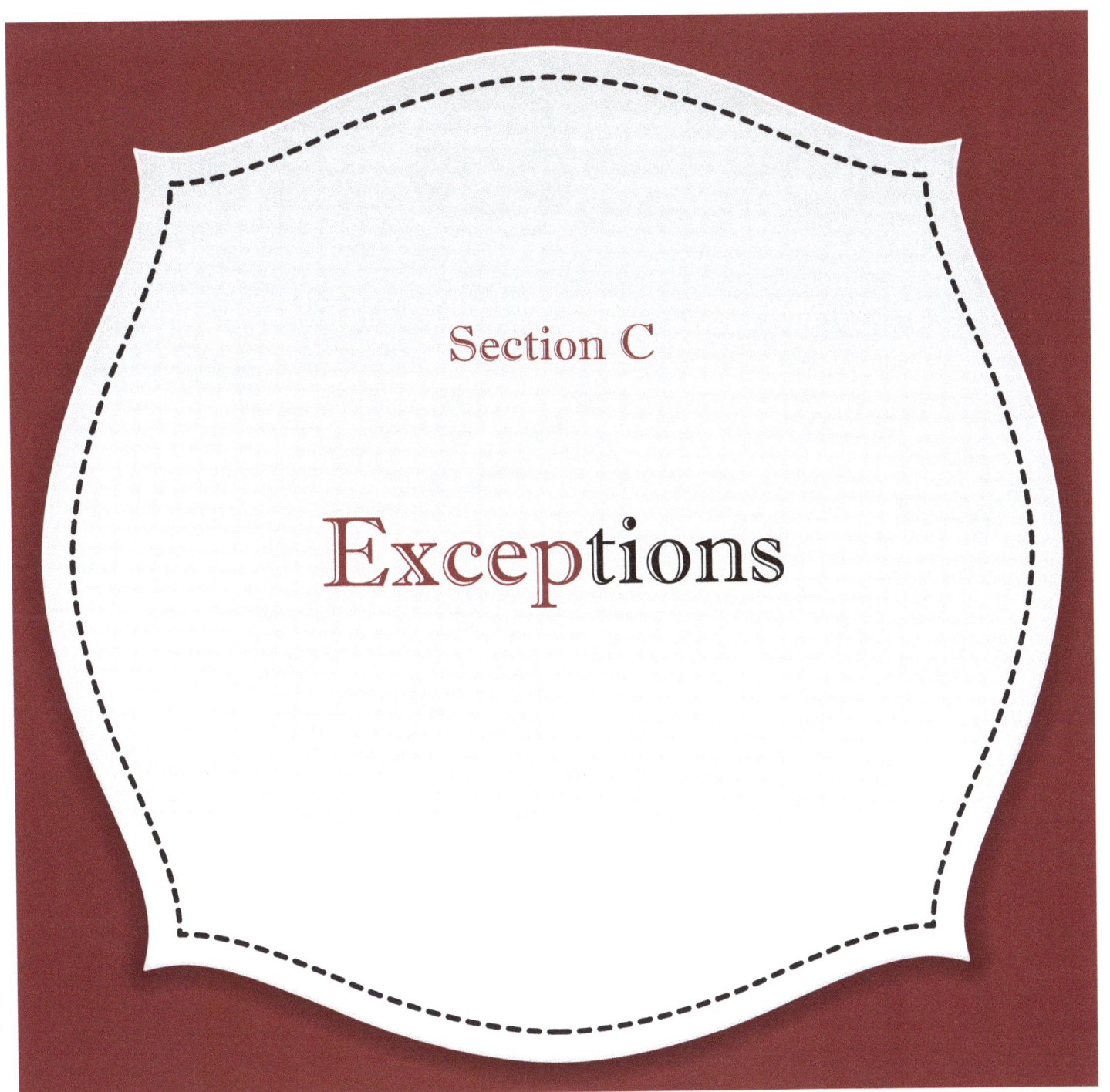

Section C

Exceptions

Exceptions

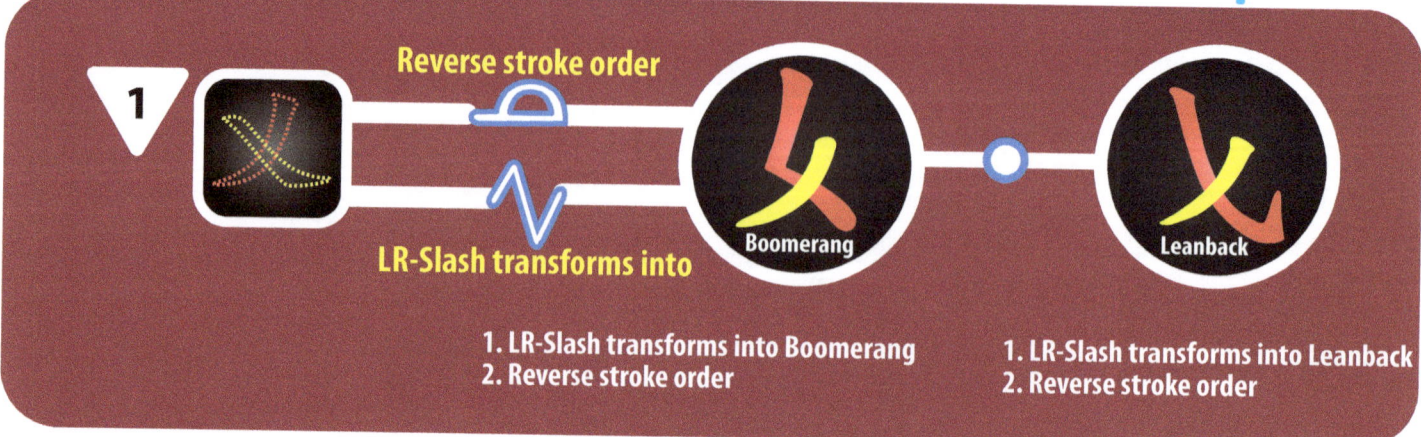

Reverse stroke order

LR-Slash transforms into

Boomerang

Leanback

1. LR-Slash transforms into Boomerang
2. Reverse stroke order

1. LR-Slash transforms into Leanback
2. Reverse stroke order

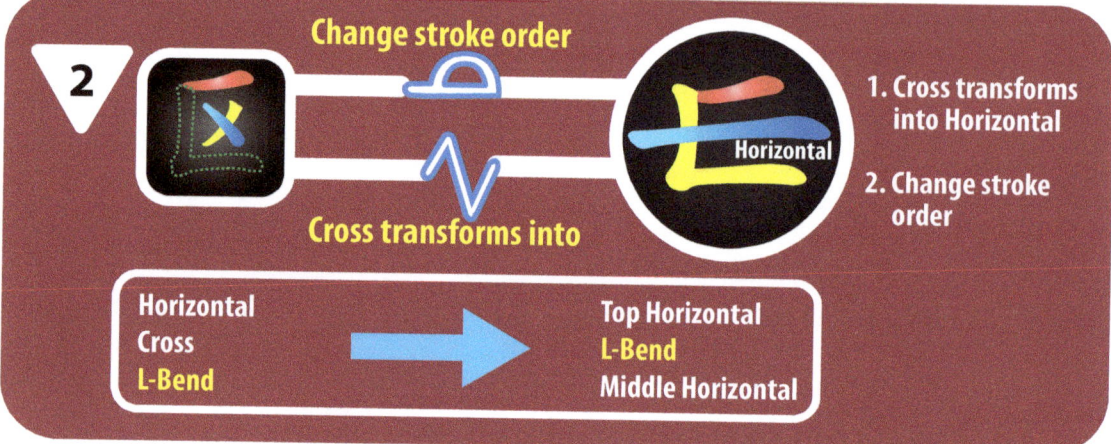

Change stroke order

Cross transforms into

Horizontal

1. Cross transforms into Horizontal

2. Change stroke order

Horizontal		Top Horizontal
Cross	→	L-Bend
L-Bend		Middle Horizontal

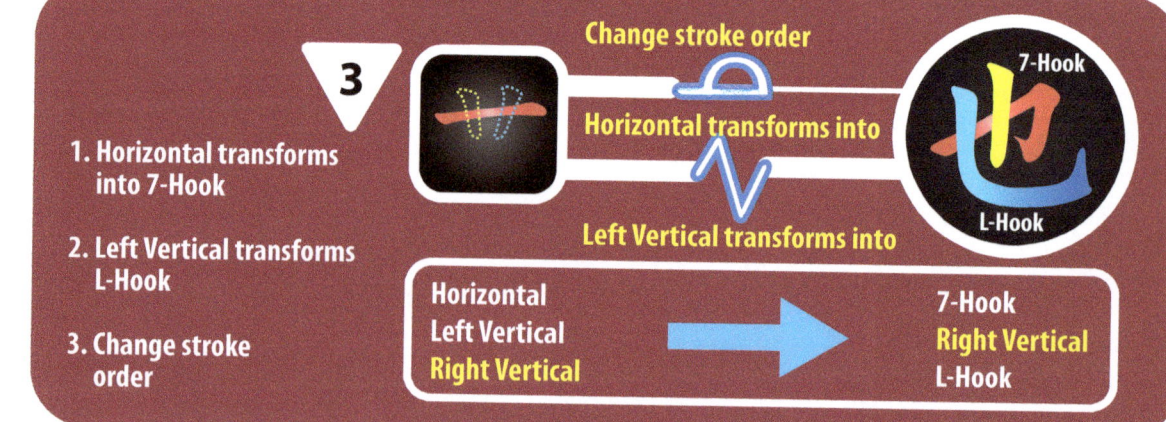

Change stroke order

7-Hook

Horizontal transforms into

Left Vertical transforms into

L-Hook

1. Horizontal transforms into 7-Hook

2. Left Vertical transforms L-Hook

3. Change stroke order

Horizontal		7-Hook
Left Vertical	→	Right Vertical
Right Vertical		L-Hook

3

1

2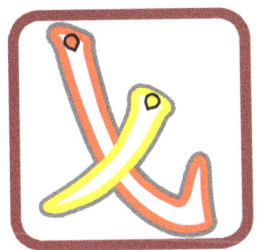

3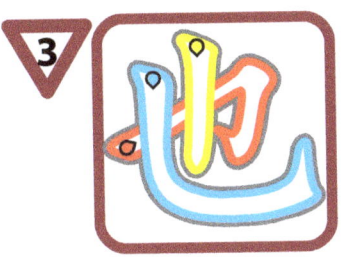

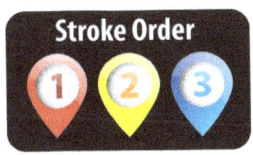
Stroke Order
1 2 3

4

 池  女  虐  如

他 成 或 威

我 疟 施 安

Activity 83

qTRAILS Variations & Exceptions

1. List the **qTRAILS**

    a) with at least one variation/exception

    b) with the MOST variations and exceptions

2. List the **Varied qTRAILS Alphabets**

    a) with the stroke RL-Slash

Create your own sketchbook! Add clippings. Doodle,
Make Notes, Summarise . . .

My Questions:
Write down your own questions.

Overall Revision

Activity 84
Symmetrical qTRAILS Alphabets

Draw the remaining parts of these symmetrical **qTRAILS Alphabets** along the lines of symmetry.

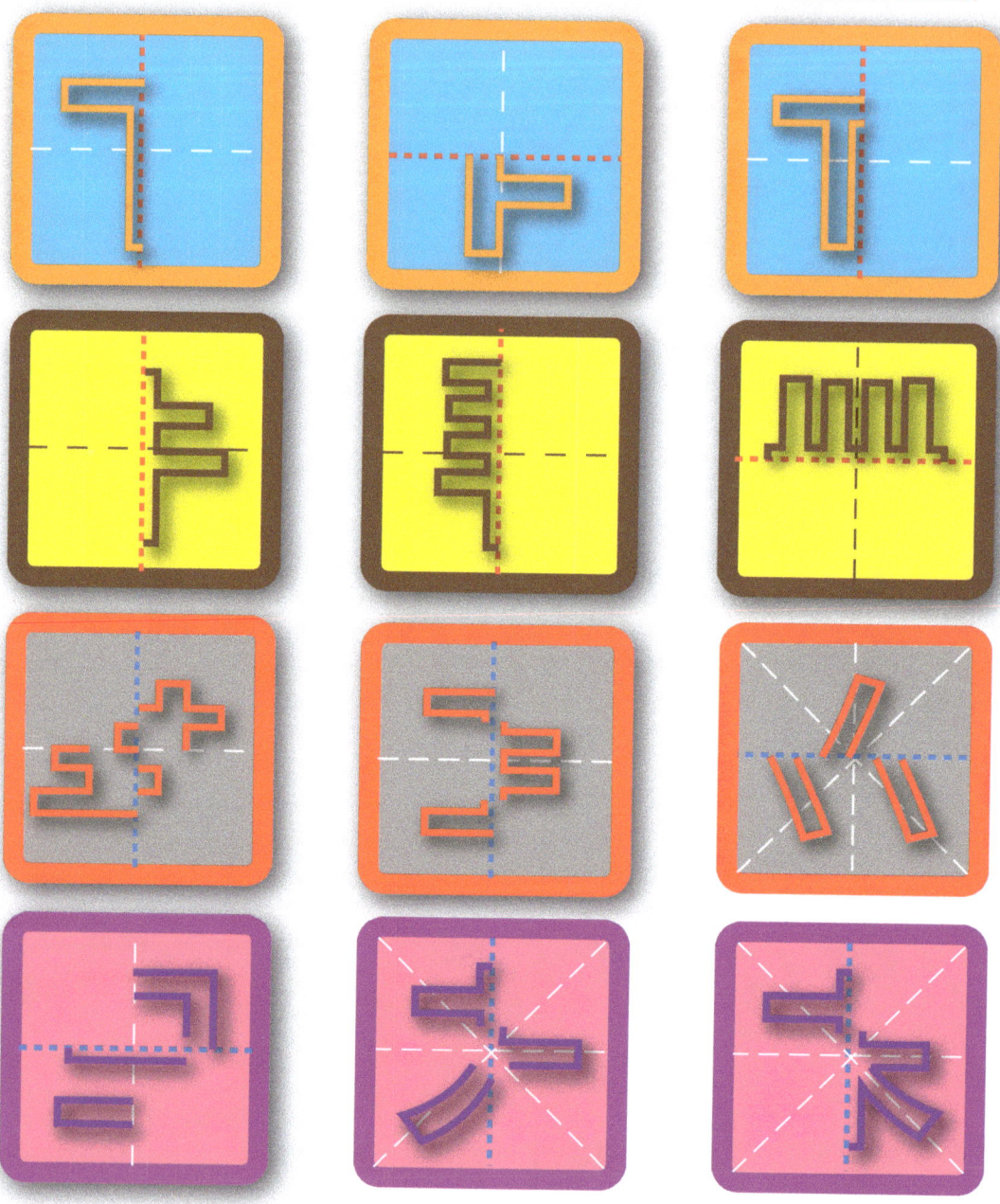

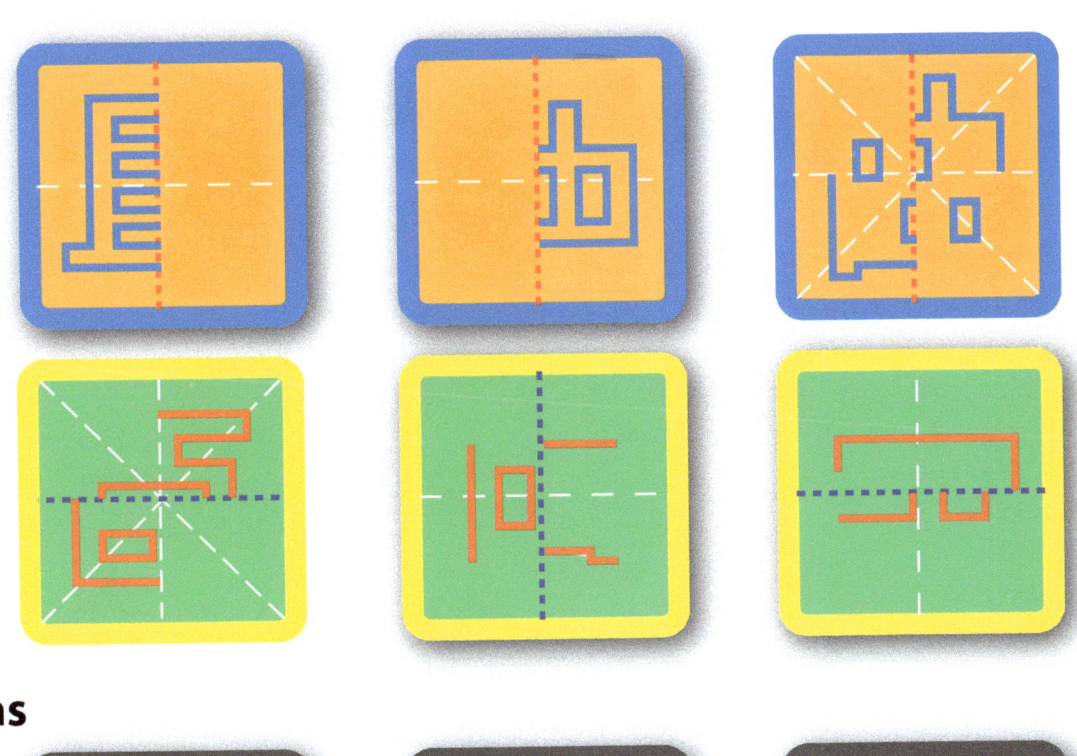

Variations

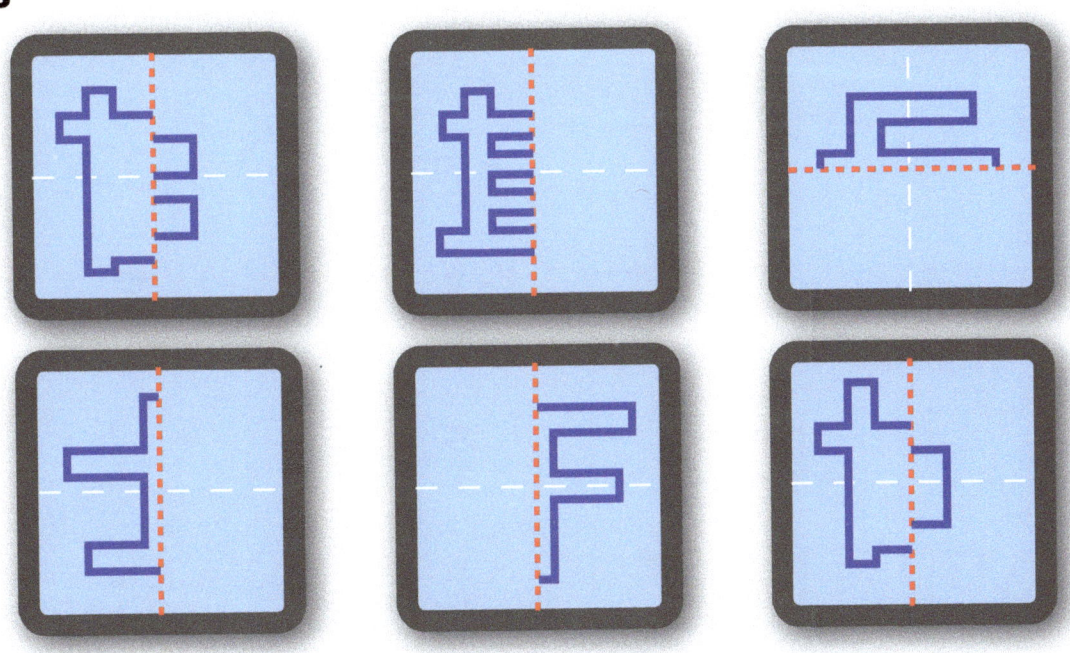

Activity 85 Put These Strokes Together 1

Put these strokes together **in order** to form qTRAILS Alphabets. Use at least one or more of the **Bond Points / Cross Points (BP/CP)** but there should <u>NOT</u> be more than 2 unused BP/CP.

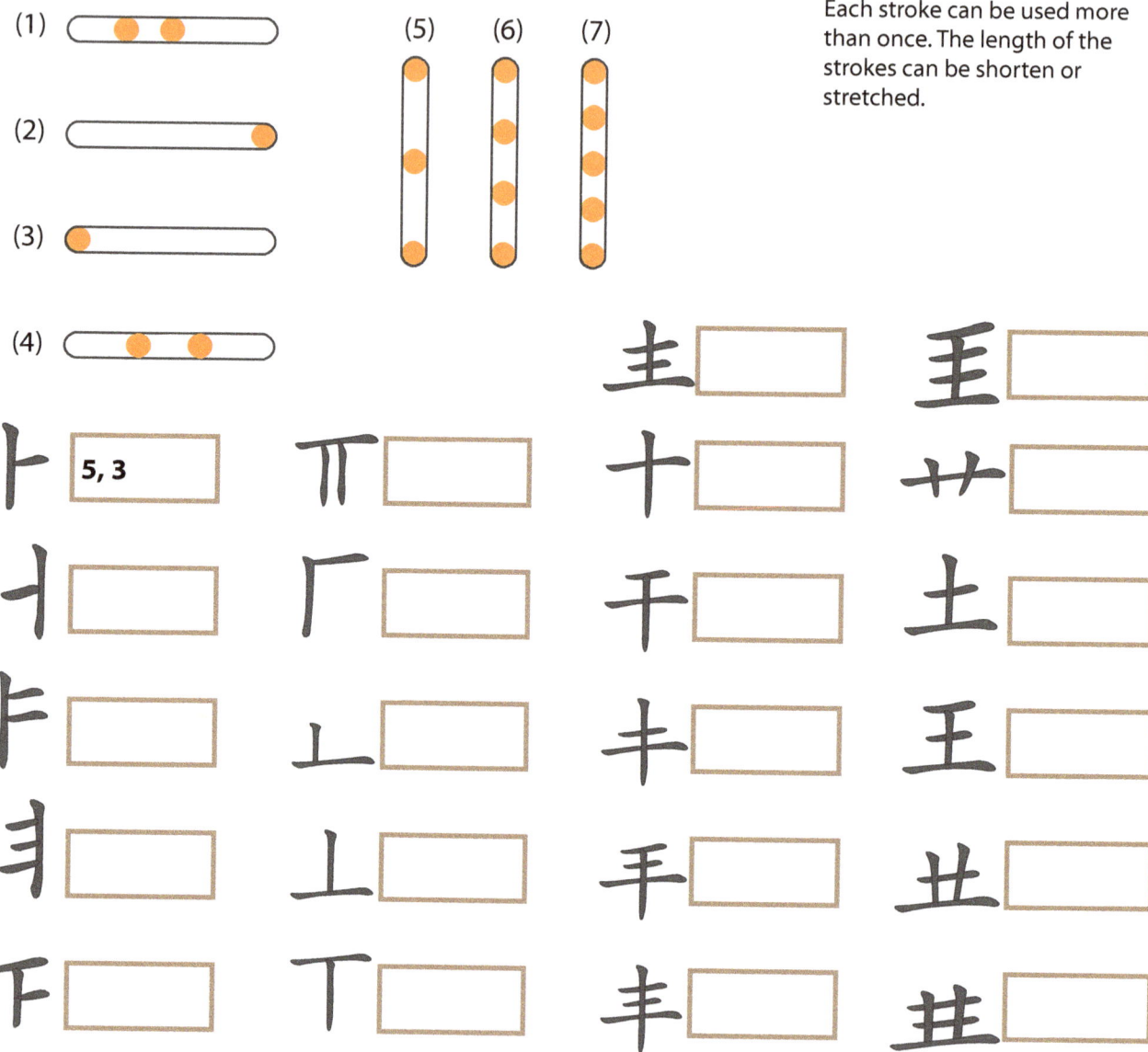

Each stroke can be used more than once. The length of the strokes can be shorten or stretched.

Activity 86

Put these strokes together **in correct order** to form qTRAILS Alphabets. Use at least one or more of the **Bond Points / Cross Points (BP/CP)**.

Each stroke can be used more than once. The length of the strokes can be shorten or stretched.

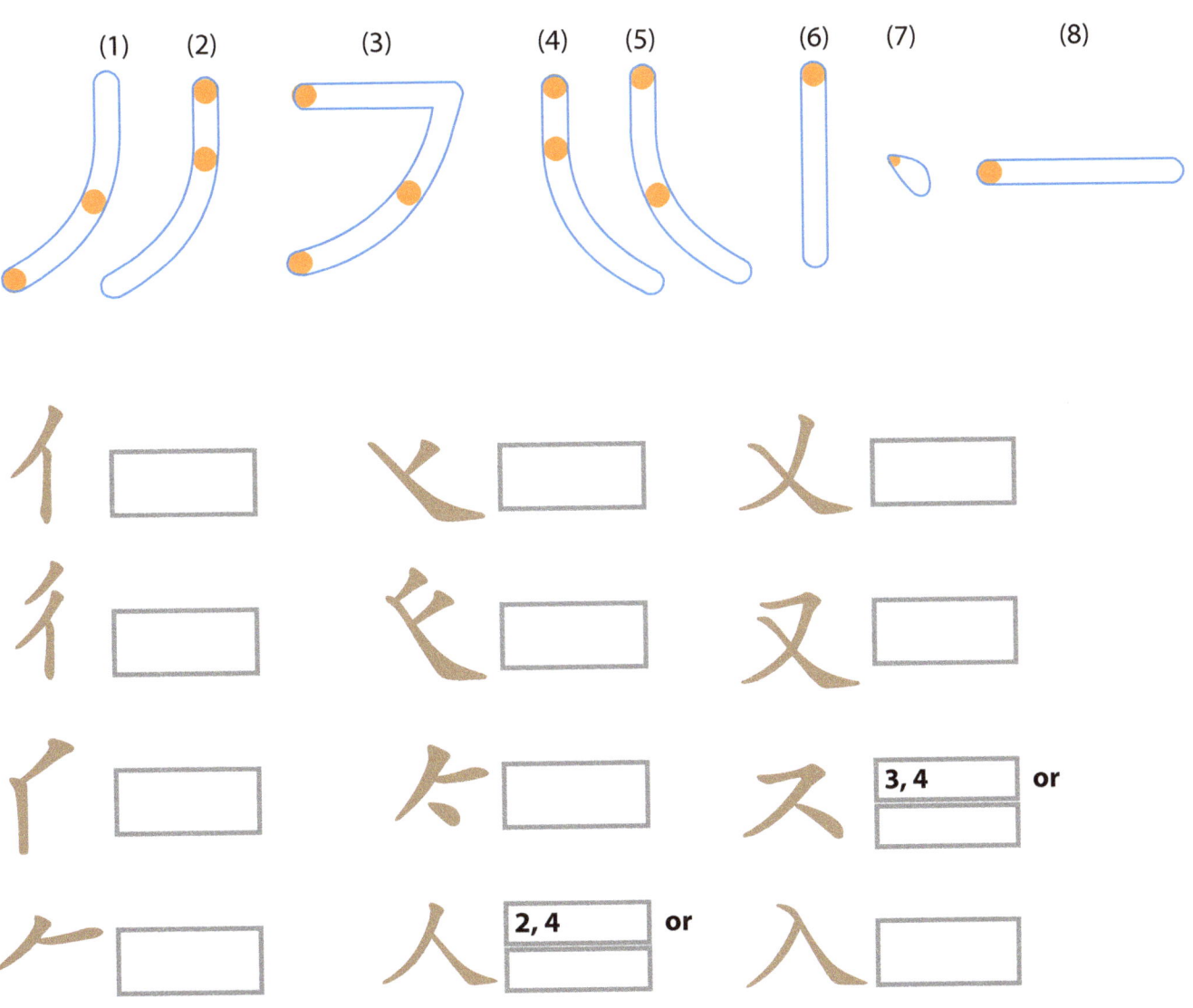

Match the description of the transformation (from basic qTRAILS Alphabet to varied Alphabet) by writing the number in the bracket and fill in the transformed stroke. See examples.

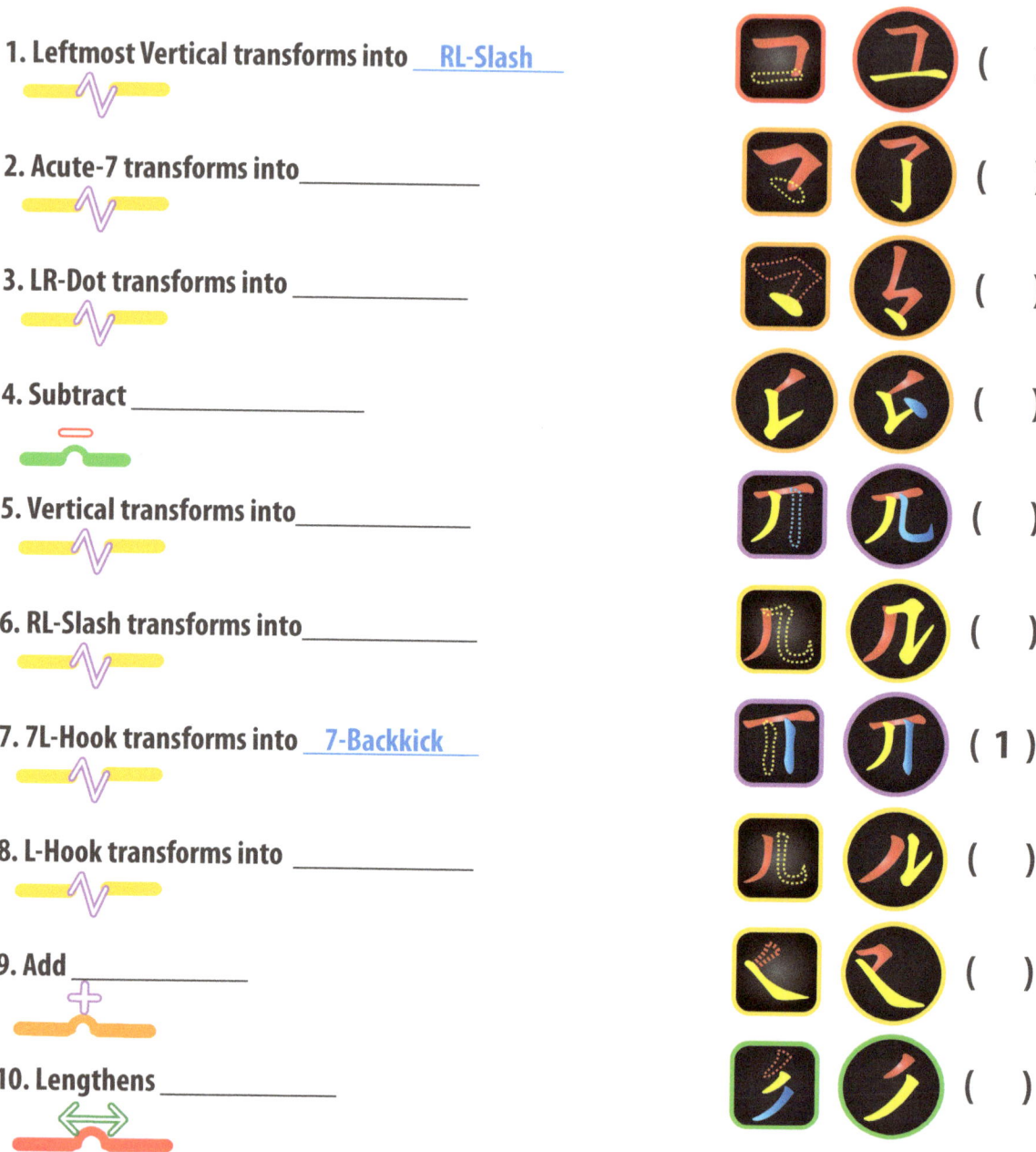

1. Leftmost Vertical transforms into _RL-Slash_ ( )

2. Acute-7 transforms into_____ ( )

3. LR-Dot transforms into_____ ( )

4. Subtract_____ ( )

5. Vertical transforms into_____ ( )

6. RL-Slash transforms into_____ ( )

7. 7L-Hook transforms into _7-Backkick_ (1)

8. L-Hook transforms into_____ ( )

9. Add_____ ( )

10. Lengthens_____ ( )

Activity 88

Match the description of the transformation (from basic qTRAILS Alphabet to varied Alphabet) by writing the number in the bracket and fill in the transformed stroke.

1. Shortens _____
   _____ shifts down ( )

2. Add _____ ( )

3. Lengthens _____
   Shortens _____ ( )

4. Upper Horizontal transforms into _____ and
   Lower Horizontal transforms into _____ ( )

5. Vertical transforms into _____
   Tick transforms into _____ ( )

6. Vertical transforms into _____
   Horizontals transform into _____ ( )

7. Shortens _____
   7-Bend transforms into _____ and lengthens ( )

8. L-Bend transforms into _____
   L-Bend intersects with _____ ( )

9. Lengthens _____
   which intersects flattened enclosure ( )

Classify these alphabets into the right boxes by drawing an arrow from an alphabet to a box. See example.

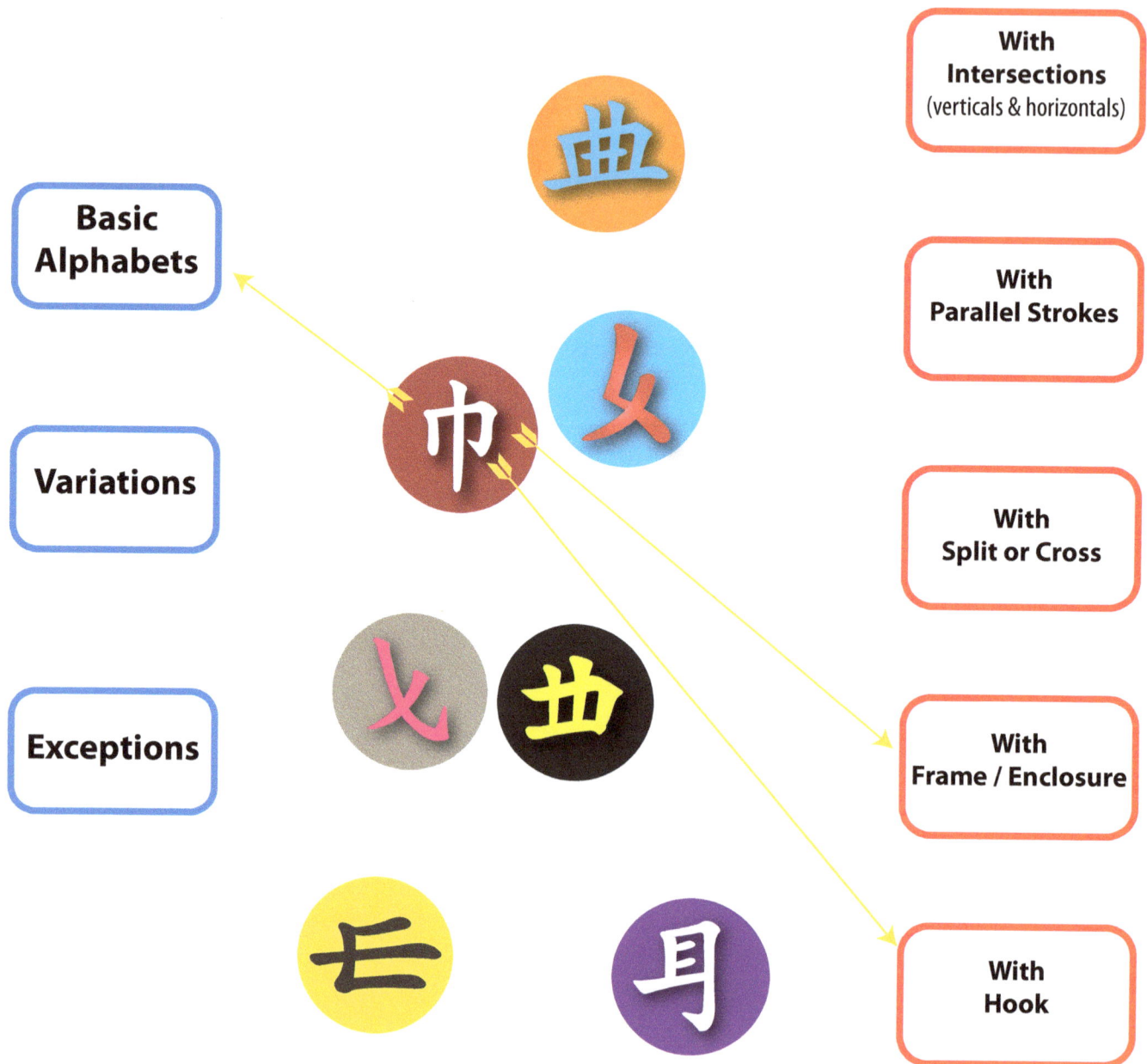

With Intersections
(verticals & horizontals)

With Parallel Strokes

With Split or Cross

With Frame / Enclosure

With Hook

Basic Alphabets

Variations

Exceptions

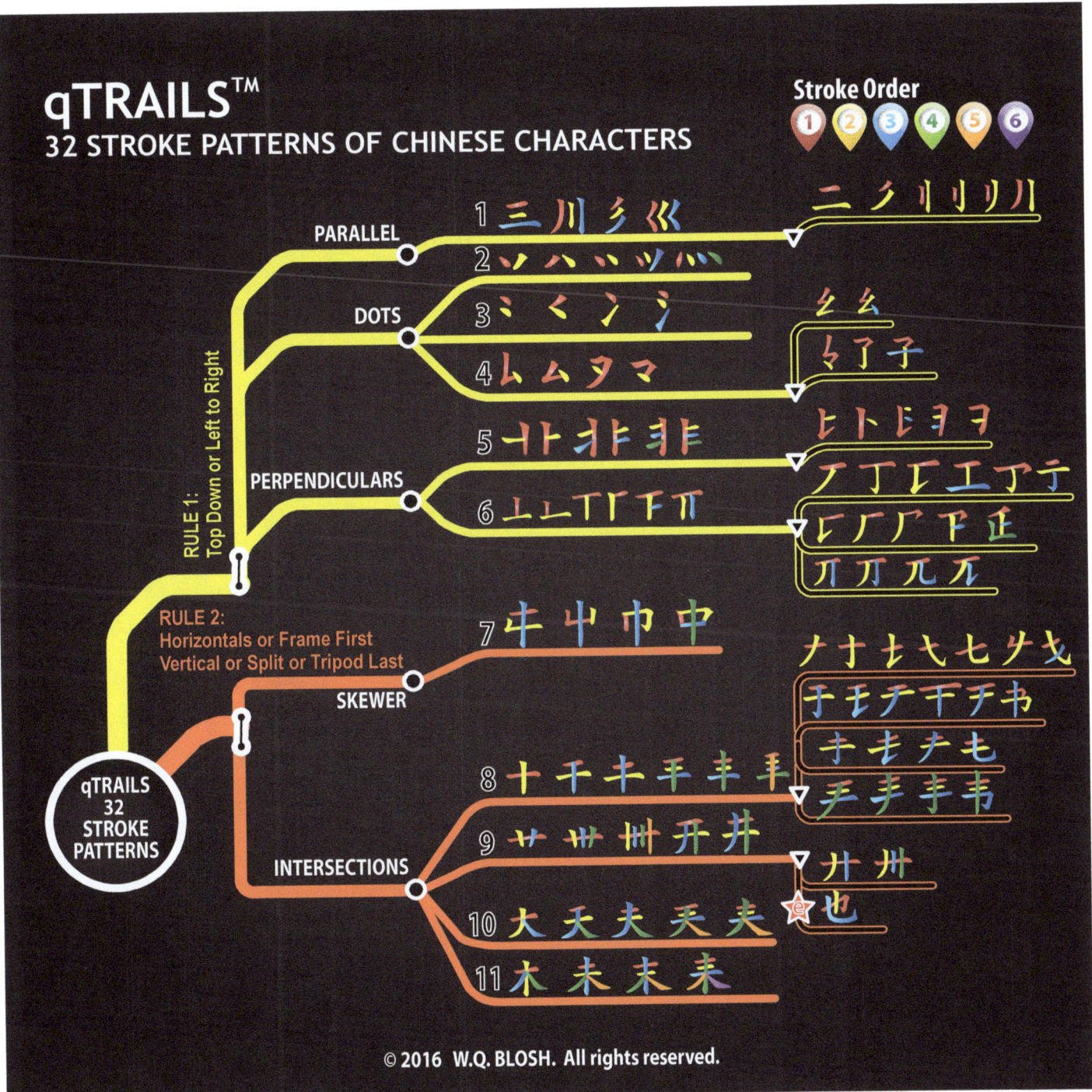

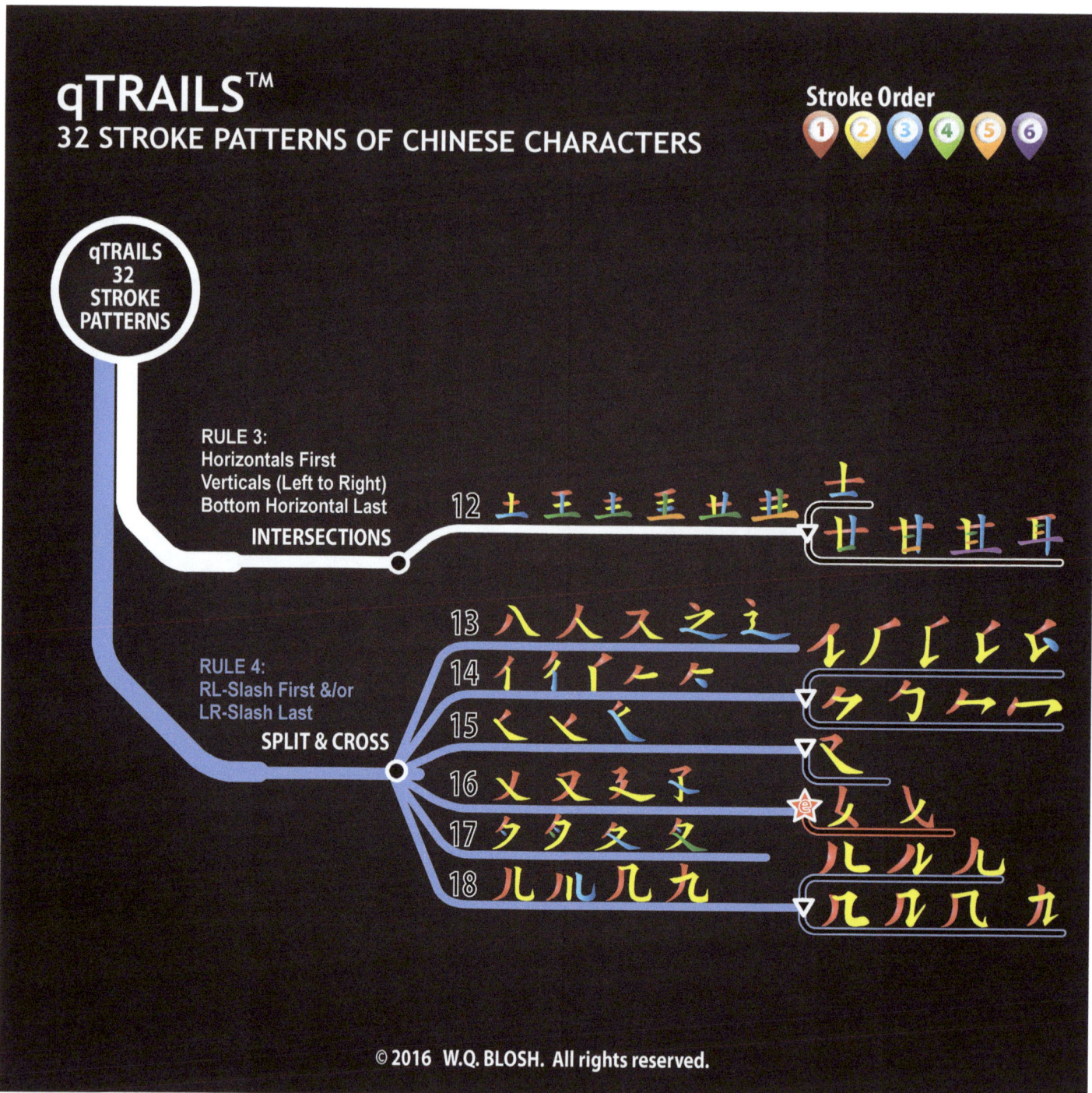

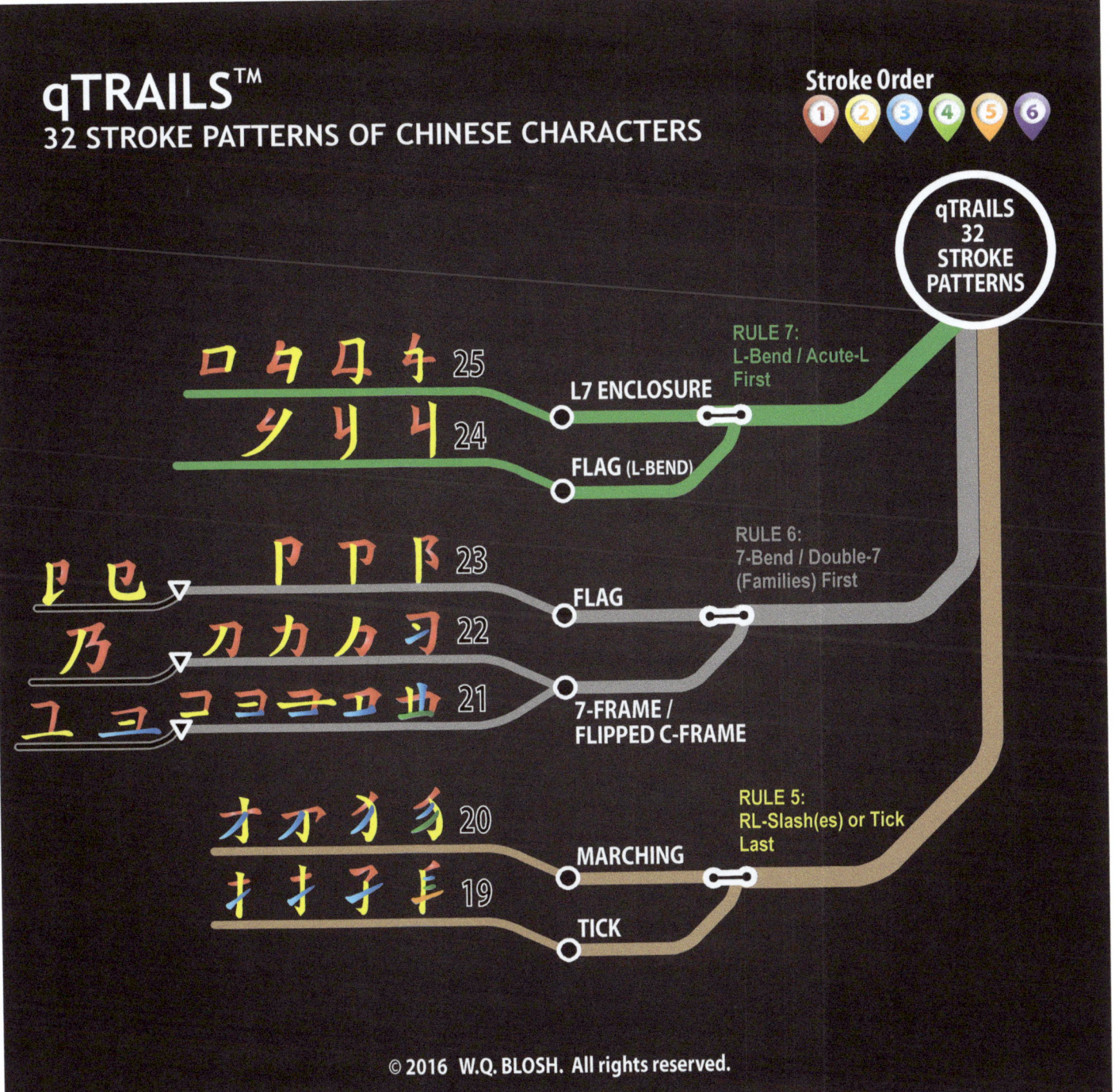

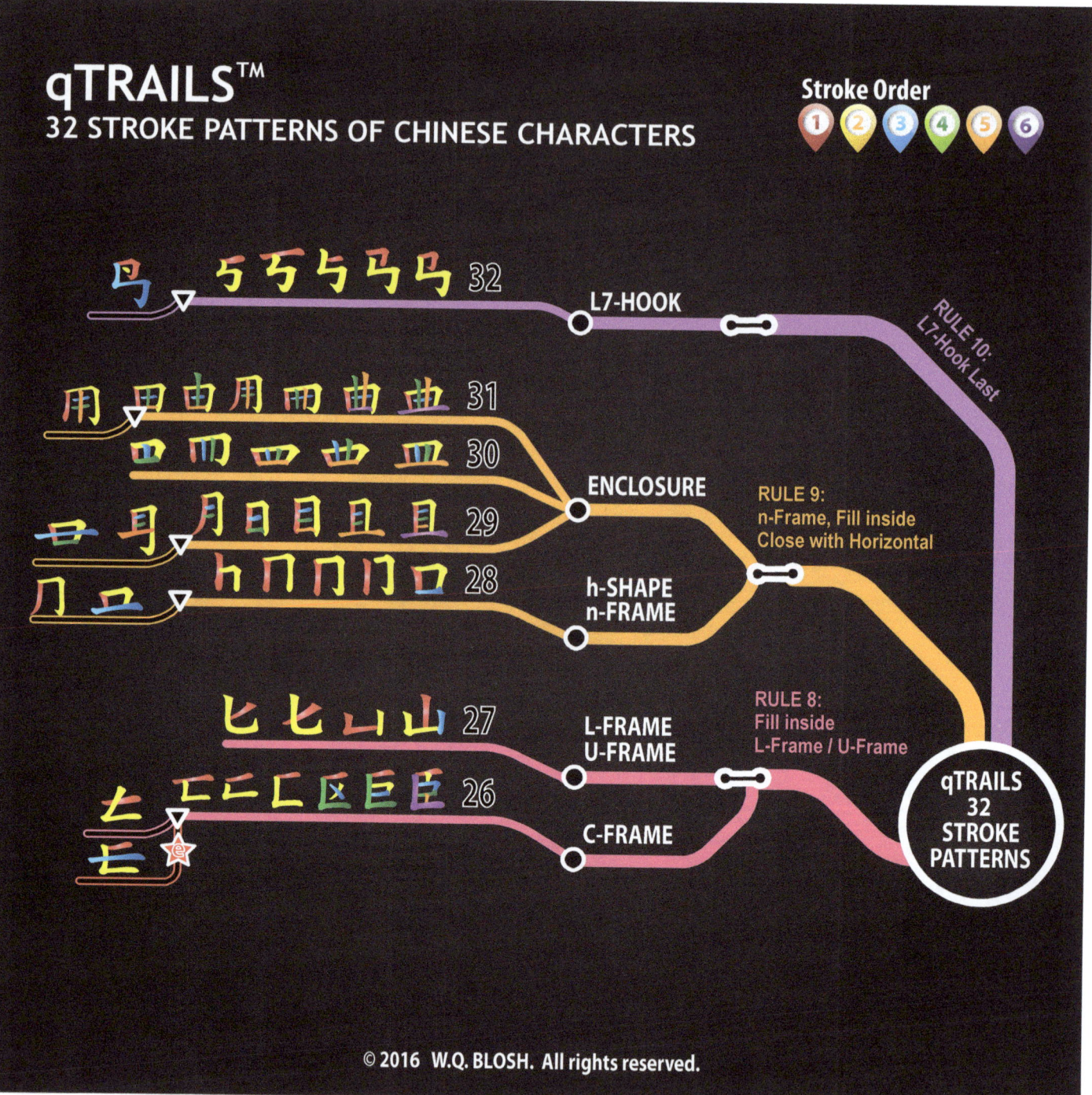

Answers

35 Strokes Poster

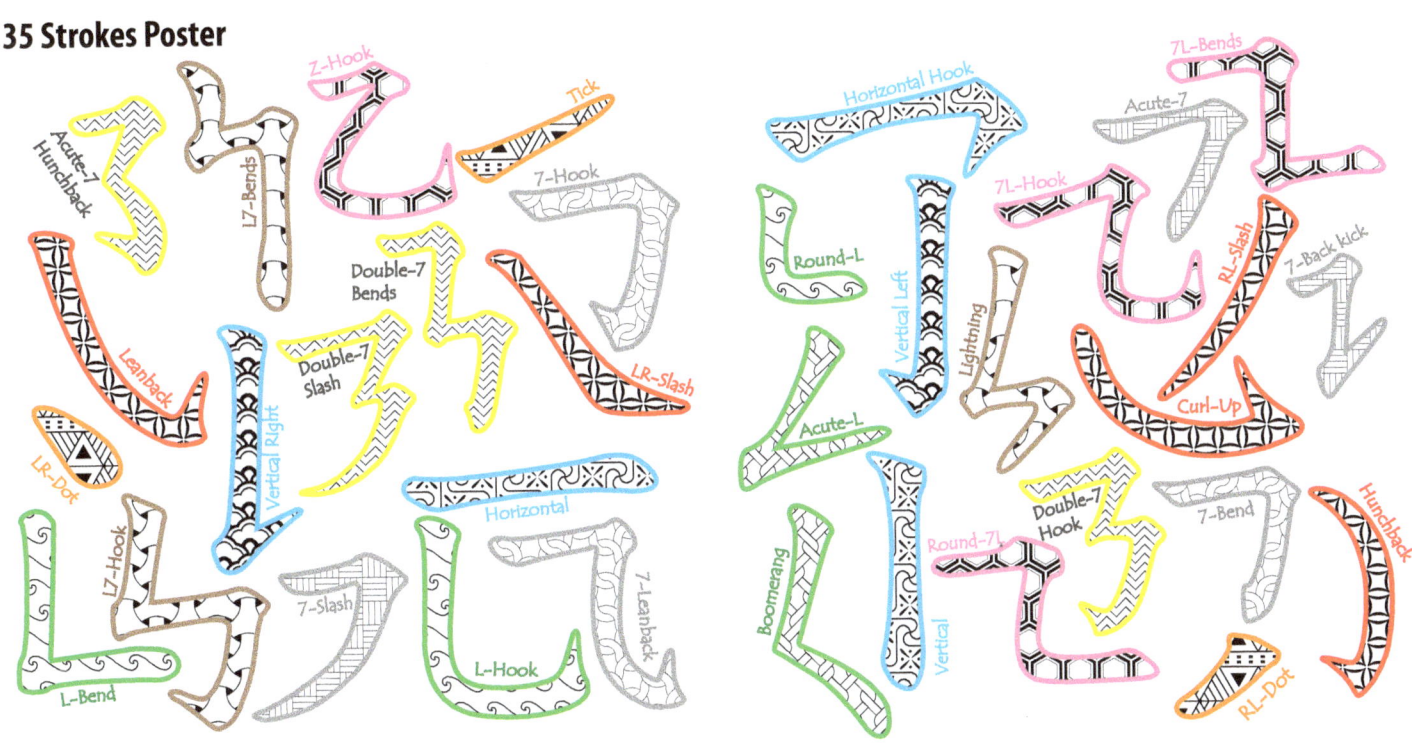

Activity 1

Example: 参

形	顺	训
须	缪	仁	巢
彦	叁	鼠	巡

Activity 2

羔	兴	总	忝
交	光	金	学
豆	黑	乐	办

Activity 3

江	头	衫	冬
衬	河	病	飞
尽	球	洗	妆

Activity 4

公	予	去	瓜
柔	令	么	癸
登	至	孤	郎

Activity 5

上	半	乍	叔
非	桌	北	面
齿	乘	排	走

Activity 6

正	步	片	斤
套	是	五	亚
虫	变	斥	企

Activity 7

车	午	斗	卖
岸	拜	害	牛
夆	用	举	羊

Activity 8

花	讲	贡
草	带	舞
廾	进	刑

Activity 9

春	矢	扶
太	天	失
养	关	哭

Activity 10

| 本 | 朱 | 耕 | 米 |
| 桌 | 禾 | 茉 | 耘 |

Activity 11

| 焦 | 青 | 生 | 塞 |
| 玉 | 在 | 先 | 共 |

Activity 12

卜 卮 下 丌
主 手 卅
丑 壬 丄 井

Activity 13

Activity 15

Stroke Order Rules

qTRAILS

1. Horizontal(s) First Vertical(s) Last
2. Dot Last
3. Horizontal(s) First Tripod Last
4. Top down or Left to right
5. Left to right
6. Horizontal(s) First Split Last
7. Vertical First Horizontal(s) Last
8. Top down
9. Top Horizontal(s) First Vertical(s) Bottommost Horizontal Last

三 川 彡 巛
ソ ハ ぃ ツ 灬
彡 く ノ 氵
厶 厶 夕 マ
卜 北 非 非
工 L T F F T
十 十 十 手 丰 丰
廾 卅 卅 开 井
大 天 夫 夭 夫
木 未 末 耒
土 王 主 玍 丗 丗

Activity 14

1. ― ｜   十 丁 广
2. ― ｜ ―   土 下
3. ― ｜ ｜   廾 Ⅱ
4. ― ｜ ｜ ｜   卅
5. ― ｜ ｜ ―   丗
6. ― ｜ ｜ ｜ ｜   卅
7. ― ― ｜ ―   王 主
8. ― ― ― ｜ ｜ ―   丗

9. ― ― ノ ｜   开 井
10. ― ― ― ― ｜   丰 丰
11. ― ― ― ｜ ―   玍
12. ― ― ― ― ｜   丰
13. ｜ ―   上 L 卜
14. ｜ ― ―   扌 ト
15. ｜ ― ― ―   非
16. ノ ｜ ｜   川

Activity 16

火 个 丙
穴 芝 过
边 分 久

Activity 17

华 蓝 丘 行
作 吃 街 笑

Activity 18

水 衣 家 橙

Activity 19

友 延 义
凶 廷 交

Activity 20

歹 条 多
然 夜 夏

Activity 21

允 凡 丸
旭 流 说

Activity 22

义 乀 儿 夕 几
乚 人 子 乀
之 亻 八 夂
儿 九 乚 又 辶
夂 乁 亻 夕 又

Activity 23

八 | 夊夊义 八人乀乀乀
冂八 | 夊又乙之夊
乃八 | 又之
刀乚 | 儿几
刀一 | 亻亻亻儿川开 井木耒耒耒
刀フ | 夕夕夊夊
丶フ | 歹夕夕夊
刀一 | 乧仒开井 大天夫夭夫 木未耒耒

Activity 24

象 材 狗 孑

Activity 25

打 牡
段 孔

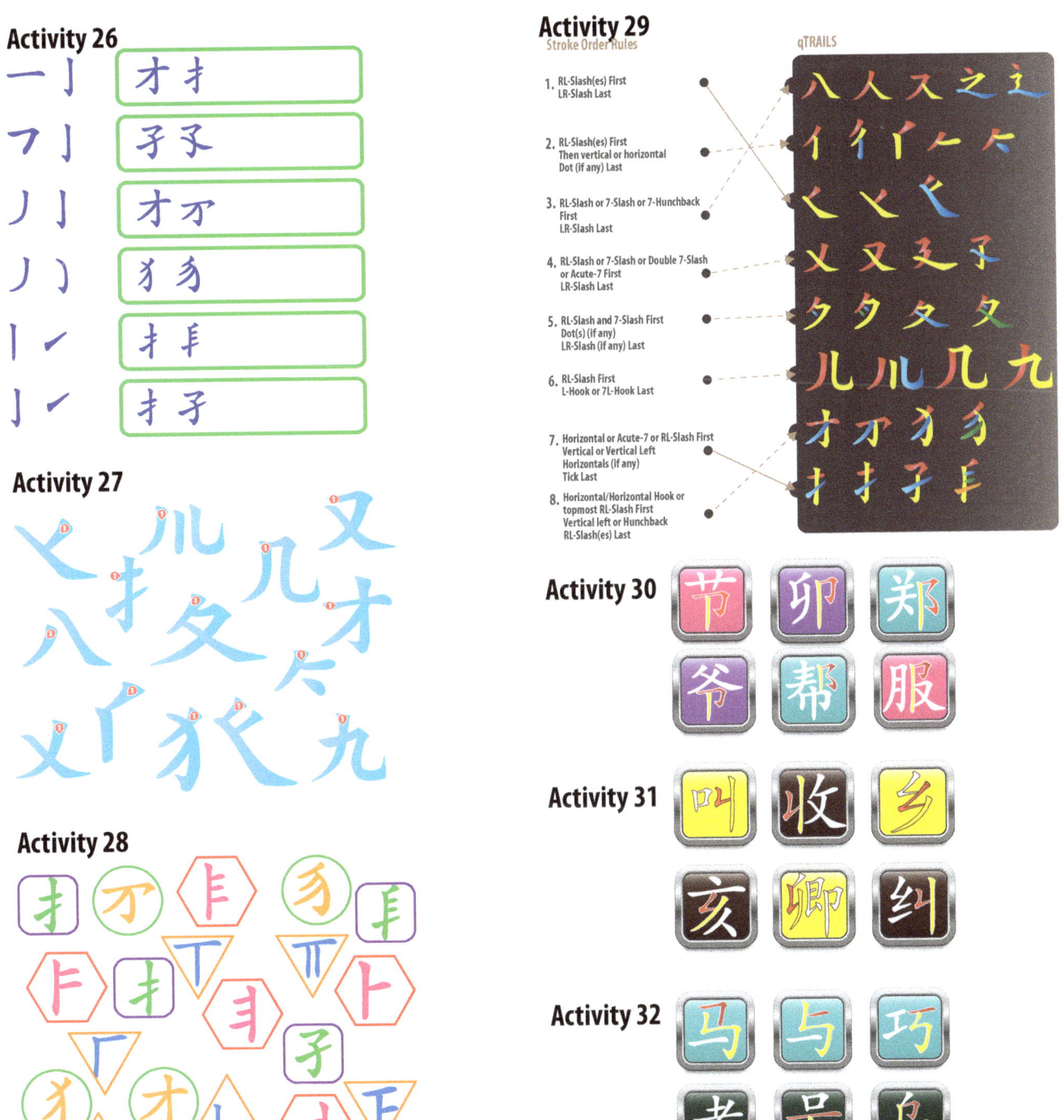

Activity 33

万 切 方 劳
别 厉 扇 剪

Activity 34

它 岸 北 画
化 讪 出 龙

Activity 35

呕 牙 亡
汇 距

Activity 36

事 扫 弓 声
弟 鹿 争 很

Activity 37

门 贝 只 同 内
问 园 丽 启 鼎

Activity 38

出 串 布
束 舜 末

Activity 39

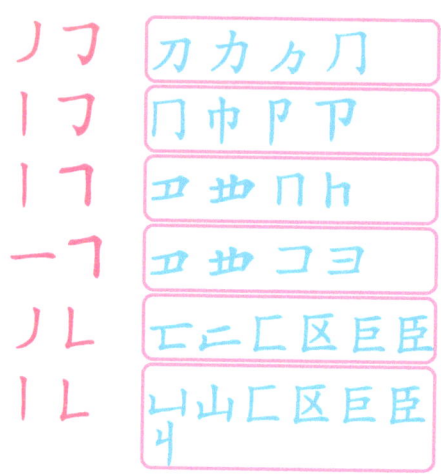

丿 刀
丿 刁 丁
丿 亅 门
一 乛 刁
乚 儿
乚

刀 力 勹 几
冂 巾 卩 阝
卫 凷 几 h
卫 凷 コ ヨ
匚 匸 匚 区 巨 臣
凵 山 匚 区 巨 臣

Activity 40

匕 卩 丩 山
牛 匚 巾 力
几 与 屮

Activity 41

Activity 42

白 日 晴
者 看 具

Activity 43

而 罪 血 要
盒 临 枭 耍

276   ANSWERS

Activity 44

Activity 45

Activity 46

Activity 47

Stroke Order Rules

1. L-Bend or Acute-L First
   RL-Slash or Vertical Last

2. L-Bend or Acute-L First
   7-Bend or Acute-7 or 7-Hook Last

3. Horizontal First
   Inside
   L-Bend Last

4. Horizontal or 7-Bend or 7-Hook First
   L7-Bends Last

5. 7-Hook First

6. 7-Hook or 7-Hunchback First
   Vertical Last

7. 7-Bend First
   Horizontal or Vertical(s)
   Bottommost Horizontal Last

8. Vertical First
   7-Bend or 7-Hook
   Horizontal (if any)

9. n-Frame First
   Horizontal(s) inside
   Bottommost horizontal Last

10. Inside First
    L-Frame or U-Frame Last

11. n-Frame First
    Intersections inside
    Horizontal Last

12. n-Frame First
    Vertical(s) inside
    Horizontal Last

13. C-Frame, U-Frame, n-Frame or Enclosure First
    Vertical Last

qTRAILS

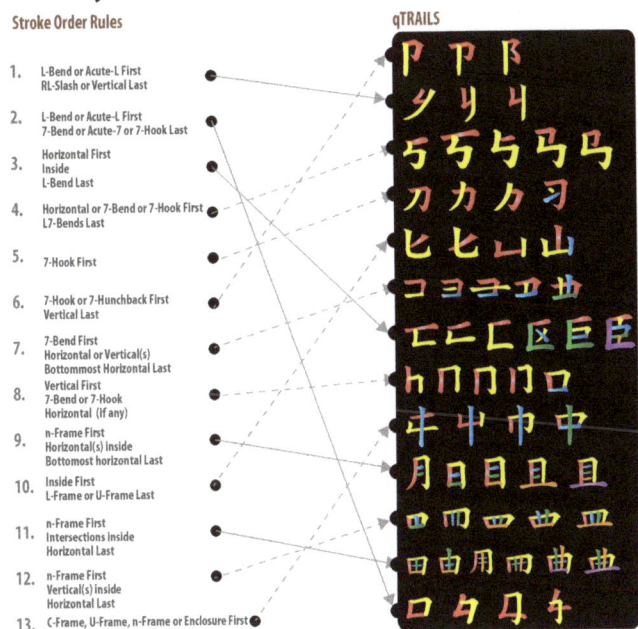

Activity 48

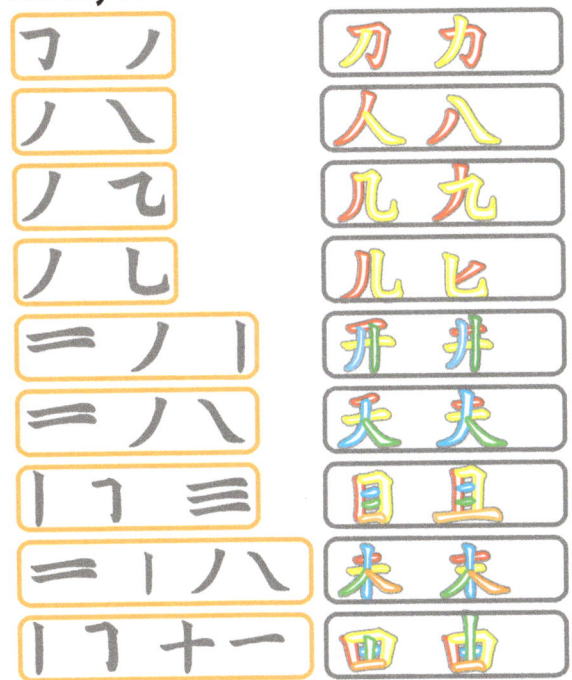

Activity 49

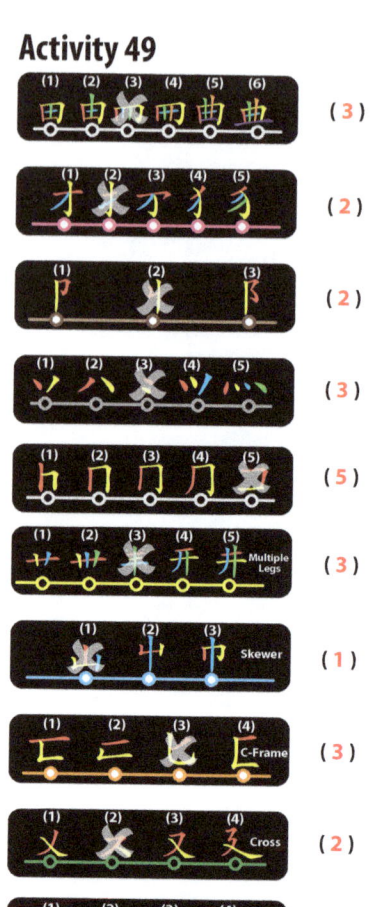

(3)
(2)
(2)
(3)
(5)
Multiple Legs (3)
Skewer (1)
C-Frame (3)
Cross (2)
Tick (4)

Activity 50

Activity 51A

Activity 51B

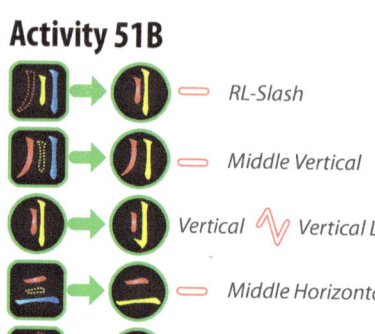

RL-Slash		
Middle Vertical		
Vertical	⟋	Vertical Left
Middle Horizontal		
Topmost RL-Slash		
Vertical	⟋	RL-Slash

Activity 52A

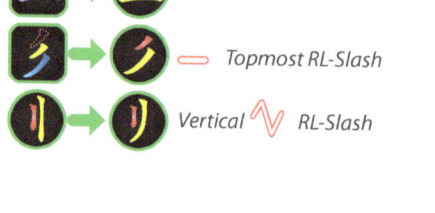
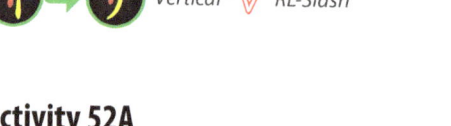

Activity 52B

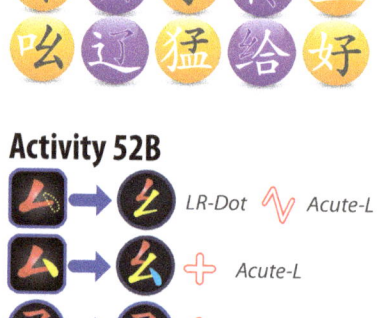

LR-Dot ⟋ Acute-L
Acute-L
Horizontal
LR-Dot ⟋ Vertical Left
Acute-7 ⟋ Lightning

Activity 53A

Activity 53B

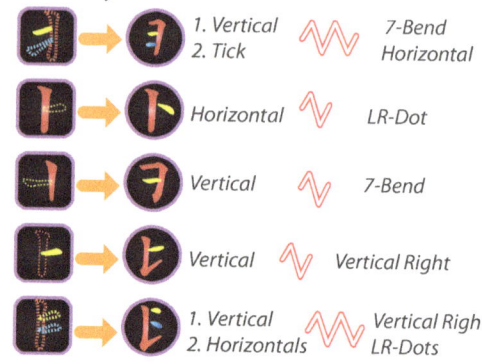

1. Vertical
2. Tick   7-Bend Horizontal
Horizontal   LR-Dot
Vertical   7-Bend
Vertical   Vertical Right
1. Vertical
2. Horizontals   Vertical Right LR-Dots

Activity 54A

Activity 54B

Activity 54C

- Leftmost Vertical / RL-Slash
- Horizontal / Horizontal Hook
- Vertical / RL-Slash
- Vertical / Vertical Left
- Horizontal / Horizontal Hook
- Vertical / Vertical Right
- Vertical / Vertical Right, Shifts left
- Vertical / Vertical Right
- Vertical / L-Hook
- Vertical / Vertical Left
- Vertical / Horizontal
- Vertical / RL-Slash
- Horizontal / Horizontal Hook
- Vertical / Bottom Horizontal
- 1. Horizontal / RL-Slash
- 2. L-Bend

Activity 56B

手　毛　围　着　撬
辨　援　承　甩　翔
看　字　余　帮　钉

Activity 55

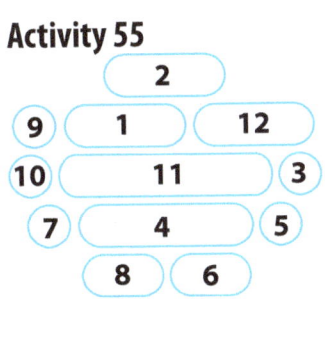

2
9　1　12
10　11　3
7　4　5
8　6

Activity 56A

切　代　找　氏
左　发　亲　毛
皂　杀　友　乎

Activity 56C

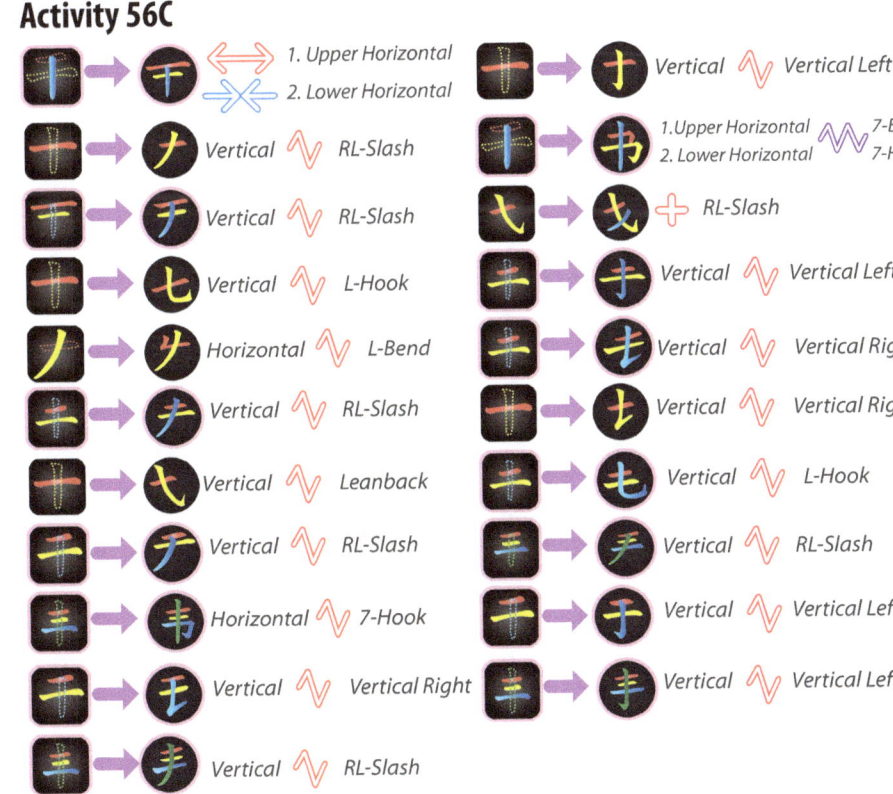

- 1. Upper Horizontal / 2. Lower Horizontal
- Vertical / RL-Slash
- Vertical / RL-Slash
- Vertical / L-Hook
- Horizontal / L-Bend
- Vertical / RL-Slash
- Vertical / Leanback
- Vertical / RL-Slash
- Horizontal / 7-Hook
- Vertical / Vertical Right
- Vertical / RL-Slash

- Vertical / Vertical Left
- 1. Upper Horizontal, 2. Lower Horizontal / 7-Bend 7-Hook
- RL-Slash
- Vertical / Vertical Left
- Vertical / Vertical Right
- Vertical / Vertical Right
- Vertical / L-Hook
- Vertical / RL-Slash
- Vertical / Vertical Left
- Vertical / Vertical Left

Activity 57A

Activity 57B

Activity 57C

 1. Upper Horizontal
2. Lower Horizontal

 Leftmost Vertical — RL-Slash

 Horizontal

 1. Left Vertical
2. Right Vertical

 Horizontals

 Vertical — RL-Slash

1. Top Horizontal
2. Bottom Horizontal

Activity 58

Activity 59A

Activity 59B

 1. LR-Slash
2. RL-Slash

 Vertical — Vertical Right

 Vertical — RL-Slash

 Vertical — Vertical Right

 Vertical Right

 LR-Dot

 Horizontal — Acute-7

 Horizontal — 7-Hook

 Horizontal — Horizontal Hook

 RL-Slash — LR-Dot

Activity 60

Activity 61A

Activity 61B

 7L-Hook — Round-7L

 L-Hook
Strokes become closer

 7L-Hook — 7-Leanback

 7L-Hook — 7-Backkick

 7L-Hook — 7-Backkick

 L-Hook — Vertical Right

L-Hook — Round-L

RL-Slash — Acute-7

Activity 62

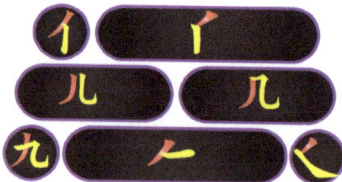

280   ANSWERS

Activity 63

Activity 64

Activity 65

Activity 66

Activity 67

Activity 68

Activity 69

Activity 70

Activity 71A

Activity 72
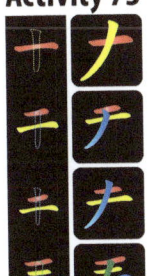

Activity 73
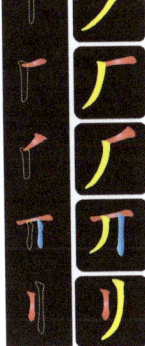 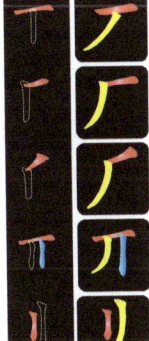

Activity 71B

  *Vertical* ~ *Vertical Right*

Vertical ~ *L-Hook*

L-Bend ~ *Acute-L*

<==> *Horizontal*

<==> *Bottom Horizontal*

1. *7-Bend* ~ *7-Hook*
2. *7-Hook*
3. *Bottom Horizontal*

 + *LR-Dot*

Vertical ~ *RL-Slash*

<==> *Horizontal*

RL-Slash ~ *Vertical*

7-Hook ~ *Double-7 Hook*

<==> *Middle Horizontal*
Horizontal intersects Enclosure

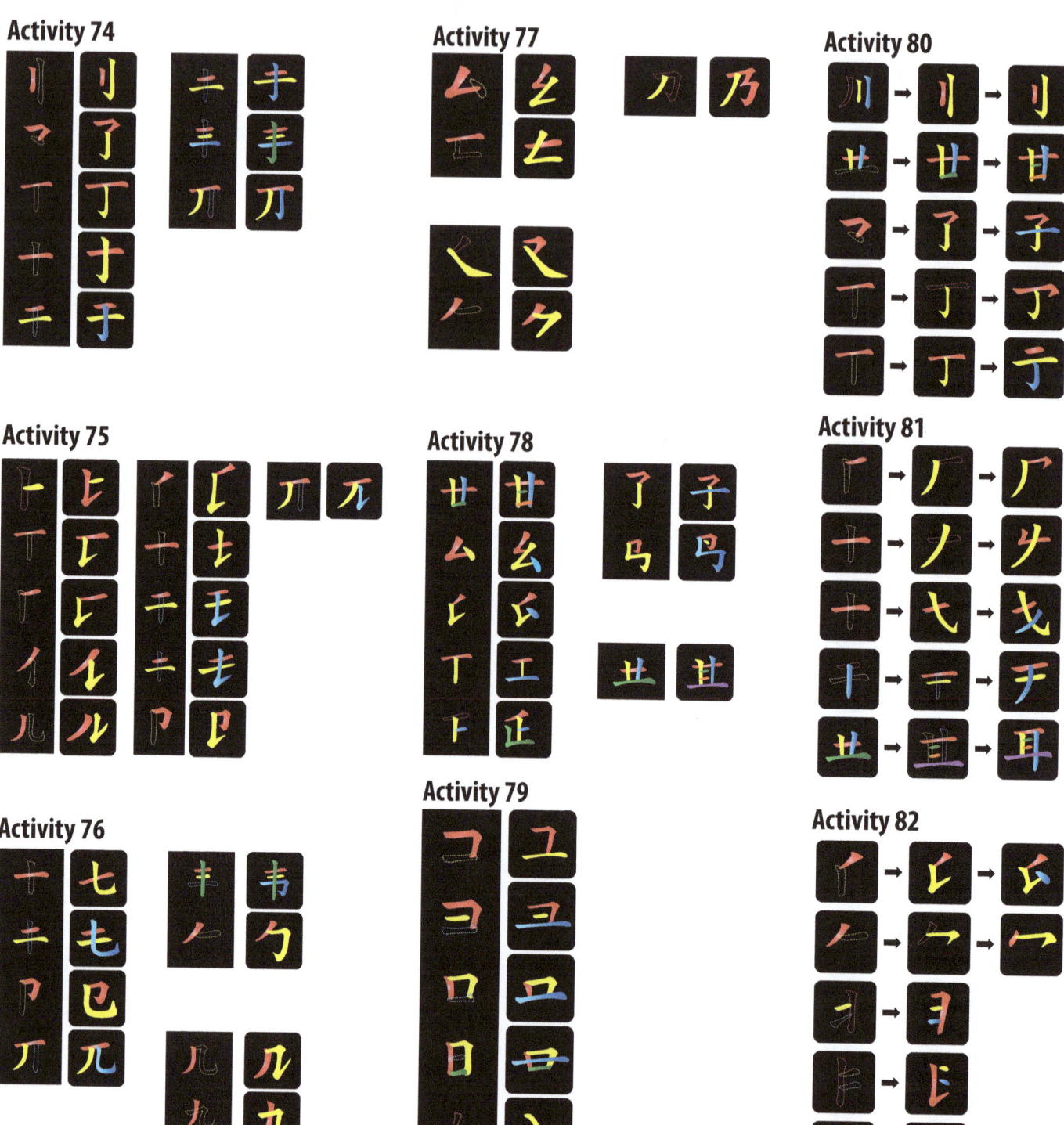

Activity 83

池 女 虐 如
他 成 或 威
我 疟 施 安

Activity 84

Activity 85

卜 [5, 3] 丌 [4, 5, 5] 十 [1, 5] 主 [1, 1, 7, 1] 王 [1, 1, 1, 6, 1]

丨 [5, 2] 厂 [3, 5] 干 [1, 1, 6] 廿 [4, 5, 5]

卜 [6, 3, 3] 𠃊 [5, 1] 丰 [1, 1, 6] 土 [1, 5, 1]

彐 [7, 2, 2, 2] 𠃊 [5, 1] 手 [1, 1, 1, 7] 王 [1, 1, 5, 1] or [1, 1, 7, 1]

下 [1, 5, 3] 丁 [1, 5] 丰 [1, 1, 1, 7] 卅 [4, 5, 5, 4]

丰 [1, 1, 1, 7] 卌 [4, 6, 6, 4]

Activity 86

亻 [1, 6] 乀 [1, 5] 乂 [1, 5]

彳 [1, 1, 6] 乀 [1, 1, 4] 又 [3, 5]

广 [1, 6] 夊 [1, 8, 7] 乄 [3, 4] or [3, 5]

乀 [1, 8] 人 [2, 4] or [2, 5] 入 [2, 4]

Activity 87

1. Leftmost Vertical transforms into ___RL-Slash___

2. Acute-7 transforms into ___Lightning___

3. LR-Dot transforms into ___Vertical Left___

4. Subtract ___topmost RL-Slash___

5. Vertical transforms into ___L-Hook___

6. RL-Slash transforms into ___Acute-7___

7. 7L-Hook transforms into ___7-Backkick___

8. L-Hook transforms into ___Vertical Right___

9. Add ___LR-Dot___

10. Lengthens ___Horizontal___

Activity 88

1. Shortens ___Left Vertical___
___Right Vertical___ shifts down

2. Add ___2 Middle Horiozntals___

3. Lengthens ___Upper Horizontal___
Shortens ___Lower Horizontal___

4. Upper Horizontal transforms into ___7-Bend___ and
Lower Horizontal transforms into ___7-Hook___

5. Vertical transforms into ___7-Bend___
Tick transforms into ___Tick___

6. Vertical transforms into ___Vertical Right___
Horizontals transform into ___LR-Dots___

7. Shortens ___bottom horizontal___
7-Bend transforms into ___7-Hook___ and lengthens

8. L-Bend transforms into ___Acute-L___
L-Bend intersects with ___horizontal___

9. Lengthens ___middle Horizontal___
which intersects flattened enclosure

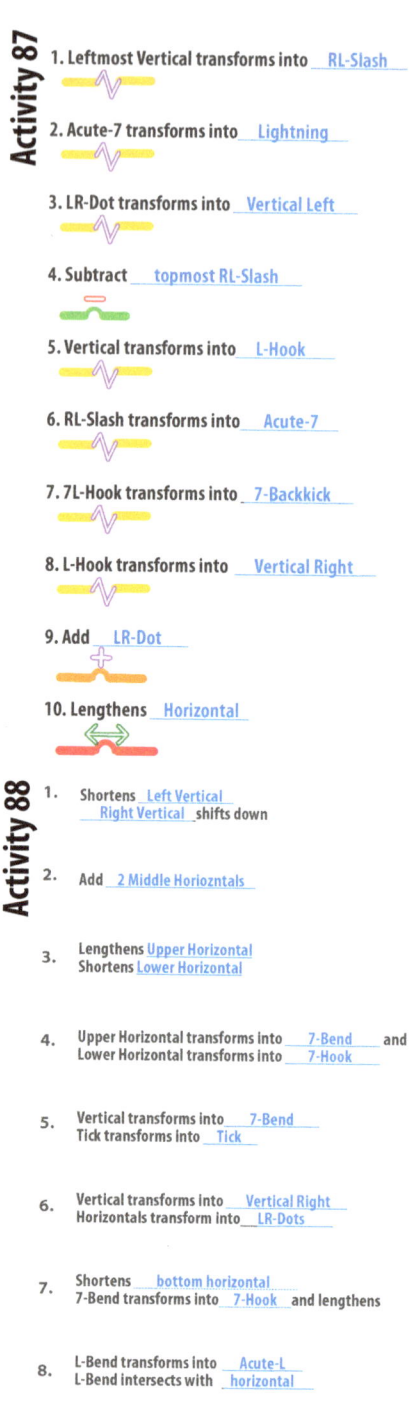

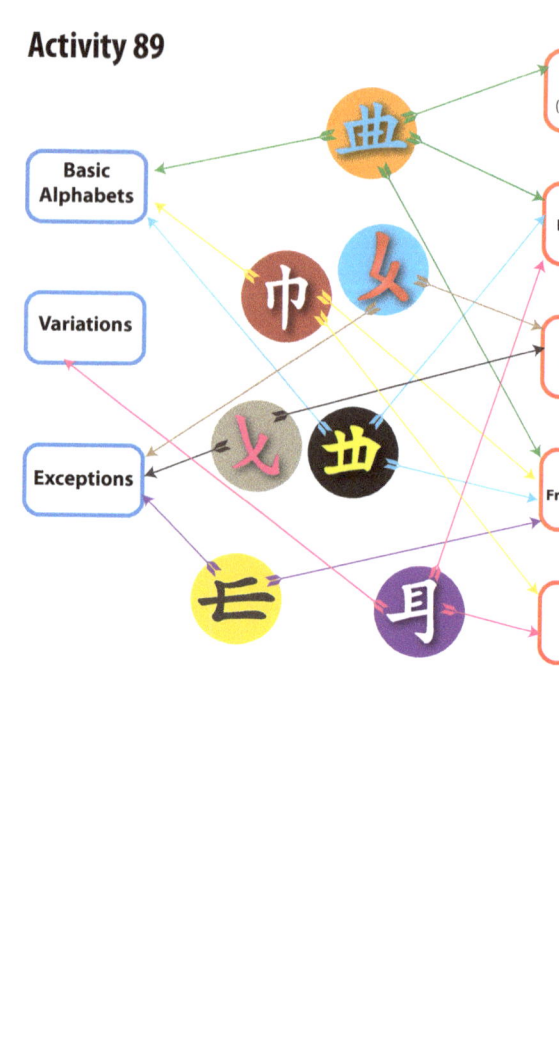

Strokes Flash Cards
Revision on LCWW1

1. Vertical

2. Vertical Left

3. Vertical Right

4. Horizontal

5. Horizontal Hook

6. RL-Slash

7. LR-Slash

Fold

Fold

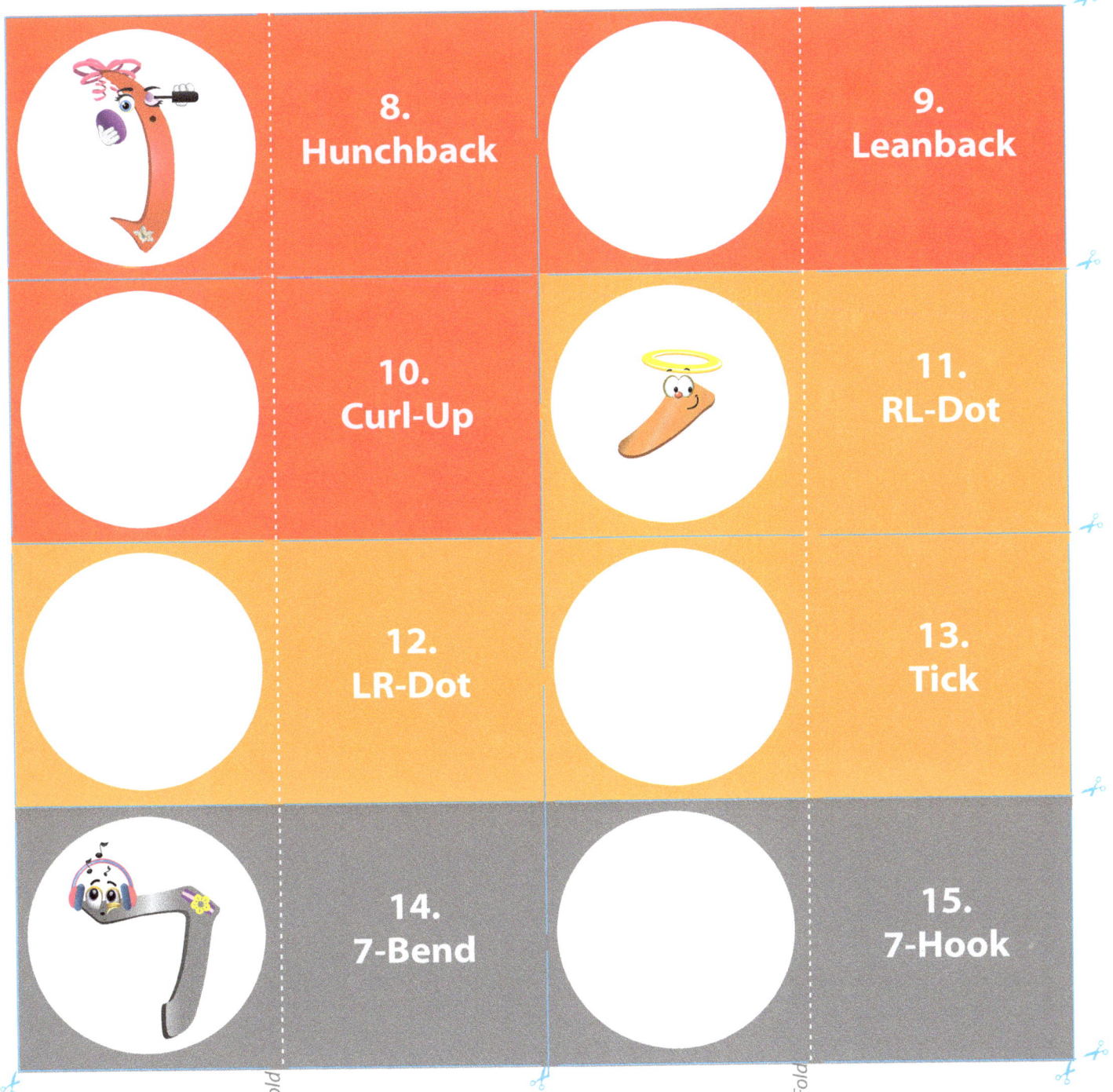

8. Hunchback

9. Leanback

10. Curl-Up

11. RL-Dot

12. LR-Dot

13. Tick

14. 7-Bend

15. 7-Hook

16.
7-Leanback

17.
Acute-7

18.
7-Back-kick

19.
7-Slash

20.
L-Bend

21.
Round-L

22.
L-Hook

23.
Boomerang

Fold

Fold

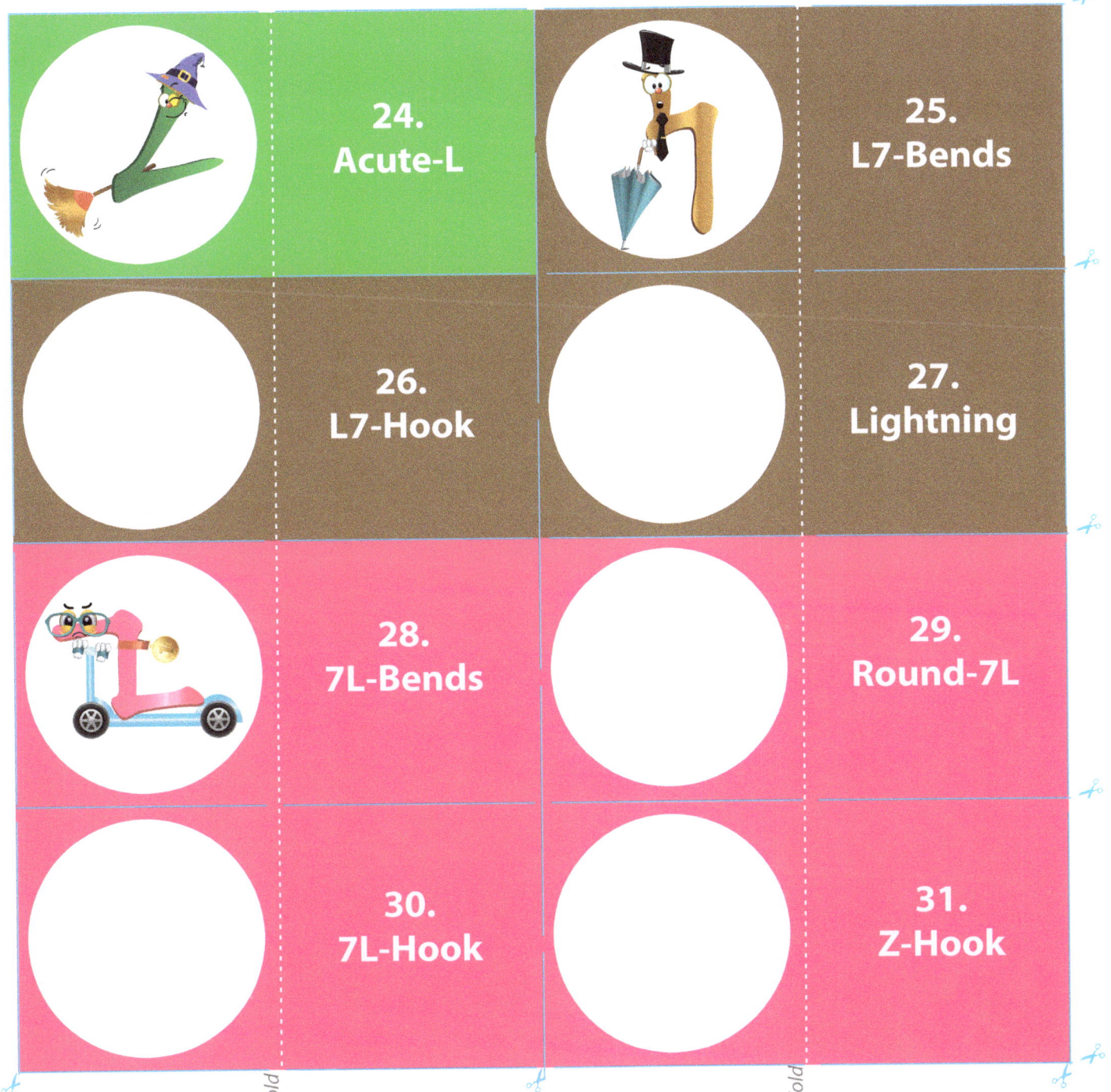

24. Acute-L

25. L7-Bends

26. L7-Hook

27. Lightning

28. 7L-Bends

29. Round-7L

30. 7L-Hook

31. Z-Hook

Fold

Fold

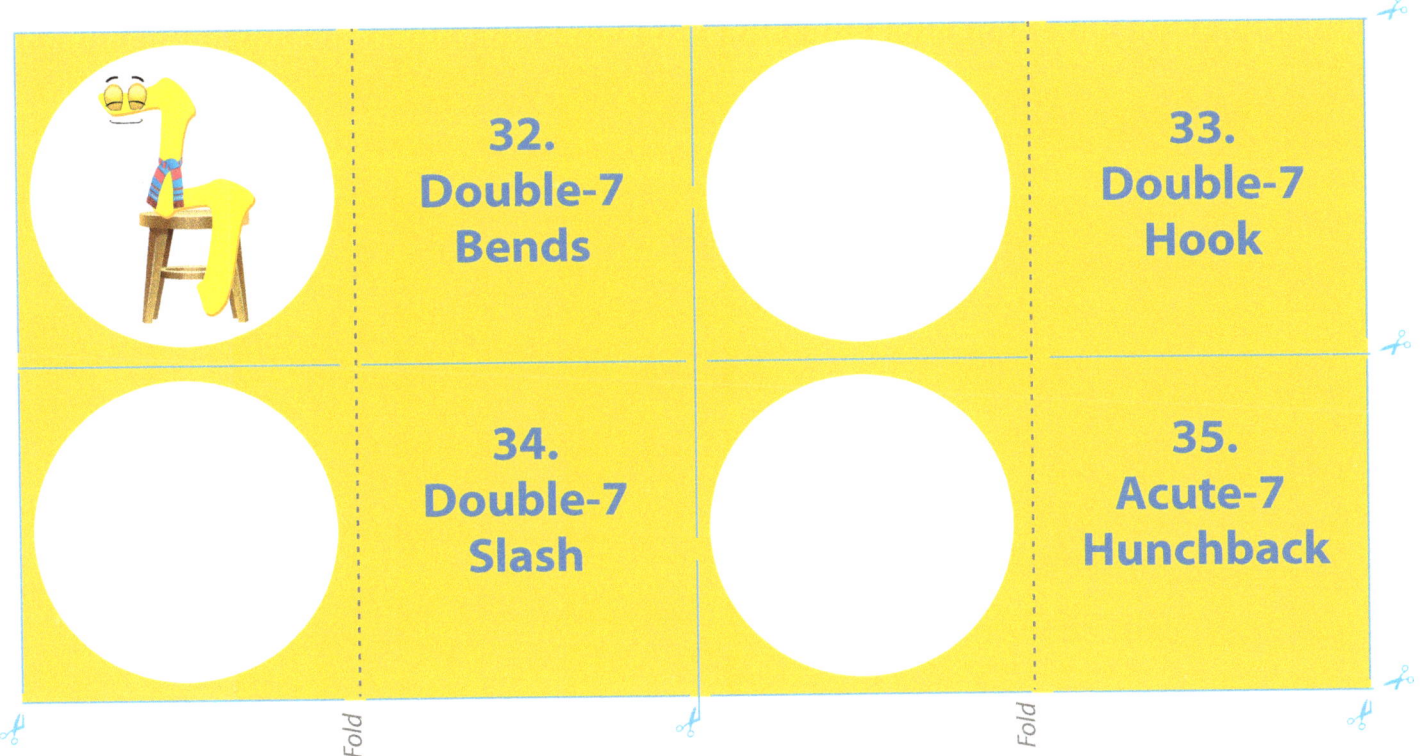

32.
Double-7
Bends

33.
Double-7
Hook

34.
Double-7
Slash

35.
Acute-7
Hunchback

Fold

Fold